Vital Statistics
on Congress, 1982

Vital Statistics on Congress, 1982

Norman J. Ornstein, Thomas E. Mann,
Michael J. Malbin, John F. Bibby

Foreword by Richard F. Fenno, Jr.

American Enterprise Institute for Public Policy Research
Washington and London

Norman J. Ornstein is professor of political science at the Catholic University of America and visiting scholar at the American Enterprise Institute.

Thomas E. Mann is executive director of the American Political Science Association and adjunct scholar at the American Enterprise Institute.

Michael J. Malbin is resident scholar at the American Enterprise Institute and contributing editor of the *National Journal*.

John F. Bibby is professor of political science at the University of Wisconsin, Milwaukee, and adjunct scholar at the American Enterprise Institute.

Library of Congress Cataloging in Publication Data
Main entry under title:

Vital statistics on Congress, 1982.

    (AEI studies ; 359)
    Updated ed. of: Vital statistics on Congress, 1980 /
John F. Bibby, Thomas E. Mann, Norman J. Ornstein.
c1980.
    1. United States. Congress—Statistics.
I. Ornstein, Norman J. II. Bibby, John F. Vital
statistics on Congress, 1980. III. Series.
JK1041.V57 1982   328.73'00212   82-16362

ISBN 0-8447-3496-9
ISBN 0-8447-3493-4 (pbk.)

AEI Studies 359

Printed in the United States of America

Contents

2 ELECTIONS   32

3 CAMPAIGN FINANCE   56

4   COMMITTEES   94

5   CONGRESSIONAL STAFF AND OPERATING EXPENSES   105

6   ACTIVITY   126

7   BUDGETING   *Allen Schick*   142

8   ROLL CALL VOTING   159

APPENDIX: DATA ON INDIVIDUAL MEMBERS OF THE NINETY-SIXTH
AND NINETY-SEVENTH CONGRESSES   179

Foreword

"Congress is the best known and the least understood of our national political institutions." That statement will probably win you a consensus. "Congress is the most fascinating of our national political institutions." That statement will probably get you an argument. But it will quickly flush out those legions of Congress watchers who derive much of their education or their enjoyment or their exasperation from following the activities of the legislative branch. Congress watchers come in many varieties, from political science students who are required to pay attention to Congress to political junkies who cannot imagine life without it. In between are a host of people who do a lot of thinking about Congress, people whose professional lives are tied to the institution—teachers, journalists, staffers, politicians, consultants, lobbyists, and legislators themselves. It is for all such people that this book has been written.

Congress may never rival the weather or baseball as a staple of casual conversation in America. Maybe that is just as well. Those who like to talk about Congress certainly lack the statistical base provided by the Weather Bureau and the *Sporting News*. As one senator commented in a recent interview, "People have asked me how to make the Senate more interesting. I tell them that you need to keep the kinds of statistics that they keep about baseball, the ones I devoured as a boy." No doubt widespread interest precedes the development of statistics in such matters. But the collection and presentation of statistics surely enlivens whatever interest already exists and probably expands it. Further, the existence of more and better statistics probably raises the level of conversation and improves the sense of perspective on the subject. Such, at least, is the hope of the authors of *Vital Statistics on Congress, 1982.*

As every Congress watcher knows, our national legislature is a decentralized and fragmented institution. It should come as no surprise, therefore, to find that the development of statistics about Congress has been an equally decentralized and fragmented enterprise. What, we might ask, do Michael Barone, Charles Brownson,

Joseph Cantor, Albert Cover, Louis Fisher, Harrison Fox, Benjamin Guthrie, Susan Hammond, Robert Keith, Mildred Lehmann, Judy Schneider, and Daniel Strickland have in common? They are all collectors of congressional statistics; they have all contributed, indirectly, to this volume. So, too, have some anonymous researchers at the Congressional Research Service, *Congressional Quarterly*, the Congressional Budget Office, the Federal Election Commission, and Common Cause. And so have the authors of this book. The American Enterprise Institute does not have the data-gathering resources of the Weather Bureau or the *Sporting News*. But it does have a group of first-rate congressional scholars who have pieced together and created, from dozens of disparate sources, a stimulating compilation of statistics to help the rest of us talk and think about Congress.

Vital Statistics on Congress, 1982 is an updated and greatly expanded version of an earlier (1980) volume. Admirers of the original book will find new data-packed chapters on campaign financing and the budget process. They will also find a lengthy appendix with information on each legislator. But the book is not about individuals. It is resolutely a book about Congress as an institution. Its statistics are about overall congressional performance, about groups of legislators, categories of legislators, and their behavior. It is about the House and the Senate taken together and taken separately. It is about elections and parties, about staffs and committees. Its statistics are aggregate statistics, designed to present an overall institutional perspective.

Thus it is neither a replacement for nor a competitor of *Politics in America* or the *Almanac of American Politics*, both of which detail the careers, the constituencies, and the legislative records of 535 individual legislators, one by one. *Vital Statistics* is a companion volume to them—a necessary one, for it provides an institutional scrutiny to frame their concern for individual legislators. *Vital Statistics* is also a companion volume to the daily newspaper and the nightly news, which focus on the stories of the present and not on relationships with the past. This book emphasizes precisely what various other sources of our information neglect—collectivities more than individuals, patterned activity over time more than discrete happenings in the here and now.

Change is the law of institutional life. Accordingly, the statistics in this volume give us a lengthy time perspective on each subject. The book charts changes in matters from election patterns to the costs of running Congress. And it marks, in its eight interpretive introductions, milestones along the way, in areas from committee performance to partisan voting patterns. At the same time, many kinds of comparisons can be made at a single time. This is especially true of comparisons between the House and the Senate but also of those between parties, among committees, and, in the appendix, among individual members. Whether statistics are examined over time or in cross sections, they are available both for instant use and for prolonged reflection.

Many people watch Congress intently because they consider it the most sensitive barometer of our national yet locally derived politics. There is plenty of statistical evidence here for that view: the steady increase in party defection in voting for the House, the steady increase in the costs of political campaigns, the slow rise to national power of women and blacks, the steady growth of expertise in government, the emerging difficulty of controlling the federal budget. Many of these data confirm for us what we already know; but they give us a better basis for knowing. They will be immediately useful as raw material for the conversation of Congress watchers.

There are plenty of puzzles here, too. Why, after a steady increase of various forms of congressional activity, should so many indicators of such activity have started to decline? Why, in recent years, should incumbent senators be so much less successful in winning reelection than House members? Why should there have occurred such a marked increase in the number of amendments, proposed and passed, to appropriations measures in the House? Why, if party-line voting is decreasing among the electorate, should it not be decreasing similarly inside Congress?

There are backward-looking puzzles and forward-looking puzzles here: the statistics may reveal some past event that needs explaining, or they may reveal an event that stimulates speculation about future consequences. We could ask, for example, why it was that corporation political action committees (PACs) changed their campaign contribution strategy between 1978 and 1980. Alternatively, we could ask what effect the growing Republican party advantage in campaign contributions will have on future elections. Why should the defense policy committees of both chambers rank consistently among the most conservative in their makeup while the foreign policy committees of both chambers rank just as consistently among the most liberal? What effect might this difference have on congressional policy making in these closely related policy areas?

If you find yourself puzzling over the most recent changes in some of the patterns here, you may wish to speculate about whether they are more likely to forecast new trends or to be aberrational blips in some well-established trends. The question applies, of course, to the startling changes recorded in 1981. Ronald Reagan had the best record in Congress of the presidents since Lyndon Johnson in 1965. Republican support for him in the Senate was greater than for any other president since Eisenhower in 1955. Every Senate committee but one (Finance) became more conservative in its makeup than it had been at any time in more than twenty years. And conservative coalition victories in the House as well as the Senate were at levels unrecorded since the 1950s. What is happening here? One might want to look backward as well as forward to find answers. And, of course, one might want to move around within the book from aggregate voting statistics inside Congress to aggregate electoral statistics outside Congress.

Looking forward, Congress watchers might wish to record their own evidence and fuel their own speculation by finding and adding the relevant numbers to those tables and figures of special interest to them—beginning in 1982. Thus they can create their own statistics to use as evidence, or as food for thought, between now and the next edition of *Vital Statistics*. By that time it may be widely conceded that Congress is the best known, the best understood, and the most fascinating of our national political institutions. Probably not. Among the readers of *Vital Statistics*, however, the debate over these questions will be better informed. There might even be a few freshly recruited Congress watchers to participate in it.

RICHARD F. FENNO, JR.
University of Rochester
Visiting Scholar, AEI

Acknowledgments

As anyone who has ever compiled a table knows, the amount of work that went into researching, calculating, checking, and rechecking the tables, charts, and graphs in this book is immense. Much of the burden was shouldered by Nina Kerstiens and Jim Barnes, with a good deal of help by Charles Coughlin, Doug Moe, and Tom Skladony. To them we owe special thanks and recognition for their work. Allen Schick, a key member of AEI's Congress Project, contributed the new chapter 7, on budgeting, to provide an invaluable and ingenious additional mine of data for readers of this book. Richard F. Fenno, AEI visiting scholar in 1981–1982, contributed both a foreword and innumerable insights, not to mention moral support. Useful suggestions for improvements of the first edition came from Herbert Asher, David Brady, Charles Bullock, Roger Davidson, Barbara Hinckley, Charles O. Jones, Garrison Nelson, Bruce Oppenheimer, and Raymond Wolfinger. William Schneider contributed valuable data on elections by congressional district. Lynn Balthaser and Randa Murphy did much of the typing and efficiently performed many other duties that kept this book on schedule.

1
Members of Congress

This chapter includes data on the regional distribution, partisanship, and seniority of members of Congress. Table 1–1 examines congressional apportionment within eight regions from 1910 (when the U.S. House of Representatives reached its permanent size of 435) through 1980. Between 1910 and 1980 the South (especially Florida and Texas) and the West (California) gained a significant number of seats. The 1980 census also brought a major gain to the Rocky Mountain states (see figure 1–1). Since 1960 the most notable losses have come in the Mid-Atlantic, the Midwest, and the Plains regions, led by New York (down from a high of forty-five seats in the 1940s to thirty-four in the 1980s) and Pennsylvania (down from thirty-three to twenty-three seats in the same period). In the 1940s New York had by far the largest congressional delegation, followed by Pennsylvania, Illinois, Ohio, and California. In the 1980s California will have much the largest delegation, followed by New York and then Texas.

Shifts in the number of House seats within the various regions have been accompanied by changes in the ratio of Democrats to Republicans within these regions (see tables 1–2 and 1–3 and figure 1–2). In the 1920s, for example, the Democrats completely dominated the South and had a substantial edge in the Border states, while the Republicans were dominant in the other six regions, particularly New England, the Midwest, and the Plains states. By the mid-1930s, the Democrats dominated every region except New England and the Plains (which together had only 63 of the 435 seats). Although Democratic strength in several of these regions fell during the 1940s and 1950s, the Republicans have not come close to achieving in any region the dominance they enjoyed in the 1920s. Party strength within the regions, however, has changed considerably in recent decades. In 1960 House Democrats dominated the South and the Border regions, exhibited strength in the Rocky Mountain area, and were competitive in the formerly Republican New England and Pacific Coast regions. Only in the sparsely populated Plains states did the Republicans have a marked advantage; they also maintained a sizable majority in the Midwest.

1

By 1980 the regional map of party strength had changed again. The Democratic proportion of Southern and Border state seats had fallen from the 90 percent to the 65 percent range, reflecting the increased competitiveness of the parties in these areas. Similarly, Democratic party strength in the Rocky Mountain states fell from 73.3 percent of the seats in 1960 to 36.8 percent after the 1980 election, indicating a marked Republican resurgence. Democrats, however, have increased their strength in the five other regions (which have nearly two-thirds of all the seats in the House), even with their losses in 1980. In 1960 they had a minority or roughly the same number of seats as Republicans had in these regions; now they have majorities in four of them. Indeed, in the post-1980 House, Democrats had numerical majorities in all regions save the small Rocky Mountain and Plains areas. Republicans, however, are gaining in areas—notably the South and the Rocky Mountains—where population, and therefore the number of seats, is increasing. But it will take more than regional population shifts to produce a Republican majority in the House in the foreseeable future.

As table 1–3 demonstrates, the changes in state apportionments and party strength across regions have important implications for the regional composition of the political parties within Congress. In the 1920s the Democratic party in the House was dominated by the Deep South. Most Republican members of the House were from the East and the Midwest. By the 1940s representatives from the South no longer constituted a majority of the Democratic party but a sizable plurality (a majority if one includes Border states), while Republican strength remained concentrated in the East and the Midwest.

By 1981, both parties had changed substantially in regional character. House Democrats still include more members from the South than from any other region, but the proportion is now only 28.5 percent. There is now the smallest number of Democrats from the South in modern times. The Democrats now include increased shares from the Mid-Atlantic, the Midwest, and the Pacific Coast regions. Republicans show an increased proportion of members from the South (up to 20.1 percent of Republican House members from 1.2 percent in 1948), with some decline in the proportion of Republicans from the New England, the Mid-Atlantic, the Midwest, and the Plains regions. It is clear from this table that there has been a transformation in the past several decades of the South and several other regions that has changed the nature of both parties in Congress.

Tables 1–4 and 1–5 reveal similar trends in the Senate. Since the 1980 election, Senate Democrats are much less strong than their House counterparts in the South and weaker too in the New England,

Mid-Atlantic, and Rocky Mountain regions. In spite of the heavy 1980 losses, Senate Democrats continue to maintain greater strength than House Democrats in the Midwest. The reverse, of course, is true for House and Senate Republicans. A comparison of table 1–5 with table 1–3 shows that, although broad party trends over time are similar for the House and the Senate, the different bases of elections for the two bodies lead to significant differences in the regional makeup of the House and Senate Democratic and Republican parties. Both Senate parties (though especially the Republicans) show considerably more Plains and Rocky Mountain influence than their House counterparts do because these two regions, though sparsely populated, elect twenty-eight senators. The same pattern prevails for New England. Conversely, the House Democratic and Republican parties have greater proportions of members from the Mid-Atlantic and the Midwest regions than the Senate parties do. Note especially that only 7.5 percent of the Republican members of the post-1980 Senate were from the Midwest and 7.5 percent from the Mid-Atlantic regions—compared with 21.7 percent and 19.6 percent, respectively, for the House Republican party. These regional differences within parties and across chambers have very interesting implications for House-versus-Senate responses to future Sunbelt-Frostbelt or other regional tensions that may flare over energy or economics.

Tables 1–6 and 1–7 show the experience of members of the House and Senate since 1953. Throughout the 1960s there was a steady increase in the proportion of very senior House members—"careerists"—and an intermittent, but real, decline in the proportion of very junior legislators (see table 1–6). The beginning of the Ninety-second Congress (1971) was the peak of both these trends—the twenty-year club had reached 20 percent of the House membership, while the proportion that had served six years or less had fallen to 34 percent. It was the peak as well in mean terms served.

These trends were reversed, dramatically, during the 1970s. In the Ninety-seventh Congress (1981–1982), junior members made up 47 percent of the House and the careerists only 11 percent. A 1.7-to-1 ratio of juniors to seniors in 1971 had changed to a 4.3-to-1 ratio in only a decade. The postwar record number of retirements was the major factor in this decline of seniority in the House. Clearly these changes contributed mightily to the reforms enacted in the House during the same period.

Table 1–7 shows years of service in the Senate over the same time span. In contrast to the House, a high proportion of the members of the Senate of the 1950s were in their first term. Senior senators with three terms or more composed only 6 percent to 10 percent

3

of the Senate; senators with at least two terms of service accounted for only 15 percent of the chamber. This pattern began to change as the Eighty-sixth Congress convened, after the 1958 elections. The number of senators in their third term swelled from seven to fifteen, with the addition of a group of conservative Southern Democrats and Midwestern Republicans who had first come to the Senate at the end of World War II. These same people expanded the ranks of the most senior group six years later, in 1965, from nine to eighteen. These dates are particularly interesting because they reflect two elections— 1958 and 1964—that are usually noted for the influx of large numbers of new liberal, non-Southern Democrats into the Senate. Indeed, the conjunction of the two patterns no doubt contributed to the changes in the distribution of power in the Senate that took place in the 1960s and 1970s.

At the low end of the seniority scale, other patterns prevail. The number of first-term senators, which averaged about forty in the 1950s and early 1960s, dropped markedly in the mid-1960s to an average of about thirty and reached a low point of twenty-seven in 1971. The number of freshmen climbed again in the 1970s and, paralleling the House, hit a post–World War II high of forty-eight in 1979, then jumped to a remarkable fifty-five after the 1980 election. At the same time, a renewed volatility at the polls and accelerated retirements have thinned the ranks in the middle and upper ranges of seniority. After more than a decade of reform, the large number of junior senators in the current Senate enjoy more power and initiative than did the comparable number of junior senators in the mid-1950s. This is still true in the Republican Ninety-seventh Senate and continues to be reflected by such indicators as subcommittee chairmanships (see chapter 4).

Tables 1–8 through 1–13 list prior occupations of members of Congress, by body and party, from the Eighty-third through the Ninety-seventh Congresses. Overall, it is clear that lawyers, businessmen, and bankers continue to dominate both houses of Congress, though in proportions somewhat different from those in earlier times: 45 percent of the Ninety-seventh House and 59 percent of the Ninety-seventh Senate are lawyers; 31 percent of the House and 28 percent of the Senate had been engaged in business or banking. Although these numbers are high, they do not compare to, say, the Ninetieth House, when 57 percent of the members were lawyers and 37 percent had been in business or banking. The number of lawyers in the Senate has also dropped, from sixty-eight in the Ninetieth Congress to fifty-nine now, while the number of senators who had been in business or banking has risen a bit over the same time. Among other significant occupations, the House and Senate have seen the number of farmers decline since the 1950s and 1960s, from an average of 11 or 12 percent in the House to 6 percent and from 18 or 20 percent in the Senate to 9 percent. The number of journalists has also declined somewhat in both houses. In the House of Representatives, the number of educators has increased, from 10 percent or so in the 1950s to nearly 15 percent in the early 1980s. In the same period in the Senate, the number of educators has declined.

There are party differences, though not startling ones, in occupation. More House Republicans than House Democrats come from the world of business and banking, by roughly 40 percent to 25 percent in the Ninety-seventh Congress. Interestingly, these differences do not prevail in the Senate. More Democrats than Republicans in the House are lawyers and educators. Democratic senators also include a higher proportion of lawyers than Republican senators do. In contrast, Republicans in both houses have more members from farming backgrounds.

Tables 1–14 and 1–15 give the religious affiliations of members of both houses of Congress. Note the increase, since the 1960s, in the number of Catholics and Jews and the decline in the number of Methodists and Presbyterians.

Tables 1–16 and 1–17 show the number of blacks and women, respectively, in Congress. Of particular interest are the party shift, from the nineteenth century to the mid-twentieth, in black members, and their steep increase in the Ninety-first and Ninety-second Congresses, and the increase in the Ninety-seventh Congress of Republican women.

TABLE 1–1

Apportionment of Congressional Seats by Region, 1910–1980
(435 seats)

Region and State	1910	1930	1940	1950	1960	1970	1980
South	104	102	105	106	106	108	116
Alabama	10	9	9	9	8	7	7
Arkansas	7	7	7	6	4	4	4
Florida	4	5	6	8	12	15	19
Georgia	12	10	10	10	10	10	10
Louisiana	8	8	8	8	8	8	8
Mississippi	8	7	7	6	5	5	5
North Carolina	10	11	12	12	11	11	11
South Carolina	7	6	6	6	6	6	6
Tennessee	10	9	10	9	9	8	9
Texas	18	21	21	22	23	24	27
Virginia	10	9	9	10	10	10	10
Border	47	43	42	38	36	35	34
Kentucky	11	9	9	8	7	7	7
Maryland	6	6	6	7	8	8	8
Missouri	16	13	13	11	10	10	9
Oklahoma	8	9	8	6	6	6	6
West Virginia	6	6	6	6	5	4	4
New England	32	29	28	28	25	25	24
Connecticut	5	6	6	6	6	6	6
Maine	4	3	3	3	2	2	2
Massachusetts	16	15	14	14	12	12	11
New Hampshire	2	2	2	2	2	2	2
Rhode Island	3	2	2	2	2	2	2
Vermont	2	1	1	1	1	1	1
Mid-Atlantic	92	94	93	88	84	80	72
Delaware	1	1	1	1	1	1	1
New Jersey	12	14	14	14	15	15	14
New York	43	45	45	43	41	39	34
Pennsylvania	36	34	33	30	27	25	23
Midwest	86	90	87	87	88	86	80
Illinois	27	27	26	25	24	24	22
Indiana	13	12	11	11	11	11	10
Michigan	13	17	17	18	19	19	18
Ohio	22	24	23	23	24	23	21
Wisconsin	11	10	10	10	10	9	9

TABLE 1–1 (continued)

Region and State	1910	1930	1940	1950	1960	1970	1980
Plains	41	34	31	31	27	25	24
Iowa	11	9	8	8	7	6	6
Kansas	8	7	6	6	5	5	5
Minnesota	10	9	9	9	8	8	8
Nebraska	6	5	4	4	3	3	3
North Dakota	3	2	2	2	2	1	1
South Dakota	3	2	2	2	2	2	1
Rocky Mountain	14	14	16	16	17	19	24
Arizona	1	1	2	2	3	4	5
Colorado	4	4	4	4	4	5	6
Idaho	2	2	2	2	2	2	2
Montana	2	2	2	2	2	2	2
Nevada	1	1	1	1	1	1	2
New Mexico	1[a]	1	2	2	2	2	3
Utah	2	2	2	2	2	2	3
Wyoming	1	1	1	1	1	1	1
Pacific Coast	19	29	33	43	52	57	61
Alaska	—	—	—	1	1	1	1
California	11	20	23	30	38	43	45
Hawaii	—	—	—	1	2	2	2
Oregon	3	3	4	4	4	4	5
Washington	5	6	6	7	7	7	8

a. New Mexico became a state in 1912; in 1910 it had a nonvoting delegate in Congress.

Sources: The 1910-1970 figures are taken from Congressional Quarterly, *Guide to U.S. Elections*, p. 531. Data for 1980 are from the Census Bureau.

FIGURE 1-1

APPORTIONMENT OF CONGRESSIONAL SEATS BY REGION, 1910 AND 1980

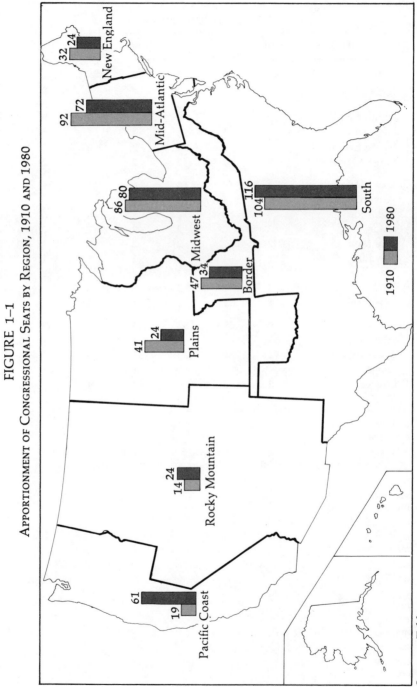

SOURCE: Table 1-1.

TABLE 1–2

DEMOCRATIC PARTY STRENGTH IN THE HOUSE BY REGION, 1924–1980

Region	1924	1936	1948	1960	1972	1978	1980
South							
Percent	97.1	98.0	98.1	94.2	68.2	71.3	64.5
Seats	104	101	105	104	107	108	107
Border							
Percent	58.7	95.2	88.1	84.2	77.1	77.1	67.6
Seats	46	42	42	38	35	35	34
New England							
Percent	12.5	44.8	39.3	50.0	64.0	72.0	64.0
Seats	32	29	28	28	25	25	25
Mid-Atlantic							
Percent	26.7	68.0	48.9	49.4	53.8	63.8	53.8
Seats	90[a]	94	92[b]	87	80	80	80
Midwest							
Percent	16.9	78.3	43.7	40.7	38.4	55.3	51.2
Seats	83[c]	83[d]	87	86	86	85	84
Plains							
Percent	15.4	44.8	16.1	19.4	33.3	40.0	36.0
Seats	39[e]	29[f]	31	31	24	25	25
Rocky Mountain							
Percent	28.6	93.3	75.0	73.3	42.1	47.4	36.8
Seats	14	15	16	15	19	19	19
Pacific Coast							
Percent	19.0	80.0	37.1	51.2	57.9	66.1	56.1
Seats	21	30[g]	35	43	57	56	57

NOTE: Numbers refer to the Congress that followed the election. Number of seats is total for all parties in the region (exceptions noted below). Does not include vacant seats.

a. Excludes one seat held by a Socialist from New York.

b. Excludes one seat occupied by a representative from New York who was a member of the American Labor party.

c. Excludes one seat held by a Socialist from Wisconsin.

d. Excludes seven seats held by Progressives from Wisconsin.

e. Excludes two seats occupied by representatives from Minnesota who were members of the Farmer Labor Party.

f. Excludes five seats occupied by representatives from Minnesota who were members of the Farmer Labor party.

g. Excludes one seat held by a Progressive from California.

SOURCES: 1925, 1937, 1949, 1961, 1973, 1979, and 1981 *Congressional Directory*, compiled under the direction of the U.S. Congress, Joint Committee on Printing.

TABLE 1–3
REGIONAL DISTRIBUTION OF DEMOCRATIC AND REPUBLICAN SEATS IN THE HOUSE, 1924–1980

Region	1924		1936		1948		1960		1972		1978		1980	
	D	R	D	R	D	R	D	R	D	R	D	R	D	R
South														
Percent	54.9	1.2	29.8	2.2	39.2	1.2	37.5	3.5	30.3	17.7	27.9	19.7	28.5	20.1
Seats	101	3	99	2	103	2	98	6	73	34	77	31	69	38
Border														
Percent	14.7	7.8	12.0	2.2	14.1	2.9	12.3	3.5	11.2	4.2	9.8	5.1	9.5	5.8
Seats	27	19	40	2	37	5	32	6	27	8	27	8	23	11
New England														
Percent	2.2	11.4	3.9	17.6	4.2	9.9	5.4	8.2	6.6	4.7	6.5	4.5	6.6	4.8
Seats	4	28	13	16	11	17	14	14	16	9	18	7	16	9
Mid-Atlantic														
Percent	13.0	26.9	19.3	33.0	17.1	27.5	16.5	25.7	17.8	19.3	18.5	18.5	17.8	19.6
Seats	24	66	64	30	45	47	43	44	43	37	51	29	43	37

Midwest														
Percent	7.6	28.2	19.6	19.8	14.4	28.7	13.4	29.8	13.7	27.6	17.0	24.2	17.8	21.7
Seats	14	69	65	18	38	49	35	51	33	53	47	38	43	41
Plains														
Percent	3.3	13.5	4.0	17.6	1.9	15.2	2.3	14.6	3.3	8.3	3.6	9.6	3.7	8.5
Seats	6	33	13	16	5	26	6	25	8	16	10	15	9	16
Rocky Mountain														
Percent	2.2	4.1	4.2	1.1	4.6	2.3	4.2	2.3	3.3	5.7	3.3	6.4	2.9	6.3
Seats	4	10	14	1	12	4	11	4	8	11	9	10	7	12
Pacific Coast														
Percent	2.2	6.9	7.2	6.6	4.6	12.3	8.4	12.3	13.7	12.5	13.4	12.1	13.2	13.2
Seats	4	17	24	6	12	21	22	21	33	24	37	19	32	25
Total														
Percent	100.0	100.0	100.0	100.0	100.0	100.0	100.0	100.0	100.0	100.0	100.0	100.0	100.0	100.0
Seats	184	245	332	91	263	171[a]	261	171	241	192	276	157	242	189

NOTE: D indicates Democrats; R indicates Republicans. Third-party members and vacant seats have been excluded. Percentages may not add to totals because of rounding.

a. There was one independent elected in 1948.

SOURCES: 1925, 1937, 1949, 1961, 1973, 1979, and 1981 *Congressional Directory*.

TABLE 1–4

Democratic Party Strength in the Senate by Region, 1924–1980

Region	1924	1936	1948	1960	1972	1978	1980
South							
Percent	100.0	100.0	100.0	100.0	68.2	72.7	54.4
Seats	22	22	22	22	22	22	22
Border							
Percent	50.0	100.0	80.0	60.0	50.0	70.0	70.0
Seats	10	10	10	10	10	10	10
New England							
Percent	8.3	50.0	25.0	41.7	58.3	58.3	50.0
Seats	12	12	12	12	12	12	12
Mid-Atlantic							
Percent	37.5	75.0	37.5	25.0	37.5	50.0	50.0
Seats	8	8	8	8	8	8	8
Midwest							
Percent	10.0	88.9	20.0	70.0	60.0	80.0	60.0
Seats	10	9[a]	10	10	10	10	10
Plains							
Percent	0.0	66.7	16.7	25.0	58.3	41.7	25.0
Seats	11[b]	9[c]	12	12	12	12	12
Rocky Mountain							
Percent	50.0	93.8	75.0	75.0	43.8	37.5	31.3
Seats	16	16	16	16	16	16	16
Pacific Coast							
Percent	16.7	50.0	33.3	80.0	60.0	60.0	40.0
Seats	6	6	6	10	10	10	10

Note: Number of seats is total for all parties in the region (exceptions noted below).

a. Excludes one Progressive from Wisconsin.

b. Excludes one senator from Minnesota who was a member of the Farmer Labor party.

c. Excludes two senators from Minnesota and one senator from Nebraska who were members of the Farmer Labor party.

Sources: 1925, 1937, 1949, 1961, 1973, 1979, and 1981 *Congressional Directory.*

FIGURE 1–2
Democratic Party Strength in Congress by Region, 1924–1980
(percentage of Democratic seats in regional delegation)

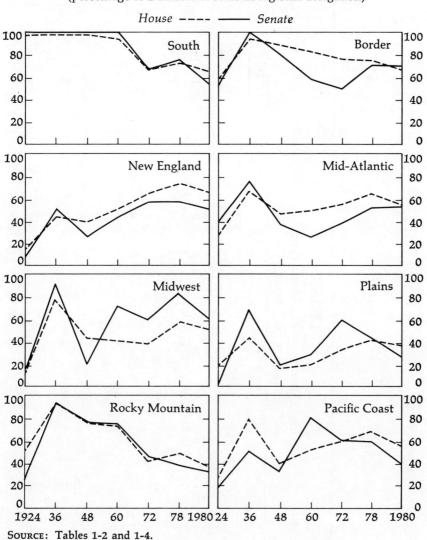

Source: Tables 1-2 and 1-4.

TABLE 1-5

REGIONAL DISTRIBUTION OF DEMOCRATIC AND REPUBLICAN SEATS IN THE SENATE, 1924–1980

Region	1924 D	1924 R	1936 D	1936 R	1948 D	1948 R	1960 D	1960 R	1972 D	1972 R	1978 D	1978 R	1980 D	1980 R
South														
Percent	53.7	0.0	28.9	0.0	40.7	0.0	33.8	0.0	26.3	16.3	27.1	14.6	25.5	18.9
Seats	22	0	22	0	22	0	22	0	15	7	16	6	12	10
Border														
Percent	12.2	9.3	13.2	0.0	14.8	4.8	9.2	11.4	8.8	11.6	11.9	7.3	14.9	5.7
Seats	5	5	10	0	8	2	6	4	5	5	7	3	7	3
New England														
Percent	2.4	20.4	7.9	37.5	5.6	21.4	7.7	20.0	12.3	11.6	11.9	12.2	12.8	11.3
Seats	1	11	6	6	3	9	5	7	7	5	7	5	6	6
Mid-Atlantic														
Percent	7.3	9.3	7.9	12.5	5.6	11.9	3.1	17.1	3.5	13.9	6.8	9.8	8.5	7.5
Seats	3	5	6	2	3	5	2	6	2	6	4	4	4	4

Midwest														
Percent	2.4	16.7	10.5	6.3	3.7	19.0	10.8	8.6	10.5	9.3	13.6	4.9	12.8	7.5
Seats	1	9	8	1	2	8	7	3	6	4	8	2	6	4
Plains														
Percent	0.0	20.4	7.9	18.8	3.7	23.8	4.6	25.7	12.3	11.6	8.5	17.1	6.4	17.0
Seats	0	11	6	3	2	10	3	9	7	5	5	7	3	9
Rocky Mountain														
Percent	19.5	14.8	19.7	6.3	22.2	9.5	18.5	11.4	15.8	16.3	10.2	24.4	10.6	20.8
Seats	8	8	15	1	12	4	12	4	9	7	6	10	5	11
Pacific Coast														
Percent	2.4	9.3	3.9	18.8	3.7	9.5	12.3	5.7	10.5	9.3	10.2	9.8	8.5	11.3
Seats	1	5	3	3	2	4	8	2	6	4	6	4	4	6
Total														
Percent	100.0	100.0	100.0	100.0	100.0	100.0	100.0	100.0	100.0	100.0	100.0	100.0	100.0	100.0
Seats	41	54	76	16	54	42	65	35	57	43	59	41	47	53

NOTE: D indicates Democrats; R indicates Republicans. Third-party members who did not caucus with either major party have been excluded. Percentages may not add to totals because of rounding.

SOURCES: 1925, 1937, 1949, 1961, 1973, 1979, and 1981 *Congressional Directory*.

TABLE 1–6
Terms of Service in the House, 1953–1981

| Congress | Percentage of Representatives Serving | | | | | | | | Mean Term (years) | Median Term (years) |
	1 term	2 terms	3 terms	1–3 terms	4–6 terms	7–9 terms	10+ terms	Total		
83d (1953)										
Percent	18	14	12	44	29	16	10	100	4.9	4
Seats	78	62	53	193	127	70	42	432		
84th (1955)										
Percent	11	17	13	42	26	19	12	100	5.2	4
Seats	50	74	58	182	115	84	54	435		
85th (1957)										
Percent	9	11	16	36	31	17	16	100	5.5	5
Seats	40	46	69	155	133	74	71	433		
86th (1959)										
Percent	18	10	10	38	30	17	15	100	5.6	4
Seats	79	43	43	165	131	74	66	436		
87th (1961)										
Percent	13	15	8	36	29	18	17	100	5.8	5
Seats	55	65	35	155	126	77	74	432		
88th (1963)										
Percent	15	13	13	41	24	19	17	100	5.7	5
Seats	66	55	55	176	104	81	74	435		
89th (1965)										
Percent	19	14	11	44	22	18	17	100	5.5	4
Seats	83	60	47	190	94	78	72	434		
90th (1967)										
Percent	14	15	12	41	25	16	17	100	5.6	4
Seats	60	65	54	179	110	70	75	434		
91st (1969)										
Percent	8	15	14	37	31	15	18	100	5.7	5
Seats	36	65	58	159	132	64	76	431		
92d (1971)										
Percent	11	10	13	34	29	16	20	100	6.0	5
Seats	48	45	57	150	127	69	87	433		
93d (1973)										
Percent	16	11	10	37	30	16	18	100	5.7	5
Seats	67	49	41	157	131	67	78	433		

16

TABLE 1–6 (continued)

	Percentage of Representatives Serving									Me-
	1	2	3	1–3	4–6	7–9	10+		*Mean*	*dian*
Congress	term	terms	terms	terms	terms	terms	terms	*Total*	*Term*	*Term*
94th (1975)										
Percent	20	14	10	44	24	19	14	100	5.4	4
Seats	86	61	42	189	102	81	61	433		
95th (1977)										
Percent	15	21	12	48	21	17	14	100	4.6	4
Seats	64	92	54	210	90	73	60	433		
96th (1979)										
Percent	18	14	17	49	22	16	13	100	5.0	4
Seats	77	61	76	214	96	70	55	435		
97th (1981)										
Percent	17	17	13	47	28	14	11	100	4.9	4
Seats	73	75	57	205	120	60	50	435		

NOTE: Percentages may not add to totals because of rounding.
SOURCES: 1953-1981 *Congressional Directory.*

TABLE 1–7

YEARS OF SERVICE IN THE SENATE, 1953–1981

	Number of Senators Serving					*Mean*	*Median*
	6 years	7–12	13–18	19 years		*Years*	*Years*
Congress	or less	years	years	or more	*Total*	*Service*	*Service*
83d (1953)	38	43	9	6	96	8.5	7
84th (1955)	43	38	9	6	96	8.4	7
85th (1957)	36	44	7	9	96	9.6	9
86th (1959)	41	32	15	10	98	9.4	8
87th (1961)	42	32	17	9	100	9.7	8.5
88th (1963)	44	27	20	9	100	9.9	7
89th (1965)	29	40	13	18	100	11.1	9
90th (1967)	28	37	17	18	100	11.6	9
91st (1969)	31	37	15	17	100	11.2	11
92d (1971)	27	40	18	15	100	11.5	10.5
93d (1973)	40	23	19	18	100	11.2	9
94th (1975)	35	27	22	15	99	11.5	9
95th (1977)	43	26	16	15	100	10.6	9
96th (1979)	48	26	10	16	100	9.6	7
97th (1981)	55	19	12	14	100	8.5	5

SOURCES: 1953-1981 *Congressional Directory.*

TABLE 1–8

Prior Occupations of Members of the House of Representatives, Eighty-third through Ninety-seventh Congresses, 1953–1981

Occupation	83d 1953	84th 1955	85th 1957	86th 1959	87th 1961	88th 1963	89th 1965	90th 1967	91st 1969	92d 1971	93d 1973	94th 1975	95th 1977	96th 1979	97th 1981
Agriculture	53	51	48	45	48	45	44	39	34	36	38	13	16	19	28
Business or banking	131	127	129	130	134	134	156	161	159	145	155	140	118	127	134
Engineering	5	5	3	3	3	3	9	6	6	3	2	3	2	2	5
Medicine	6	5	6	4	6	3	3	3	5	6	5	5	2	6	6
Science	—	—	—	—	—	—	—	—	1	1	2	2	2	2	0
Education	46	47	46	41	39	36	68	57	59	61	59	64	70	57	59
Labor leader	—	—	—	—	—	3	3	2	3	3	3	3	6	4	5
Law	247	245	234	242	244	250	247	246	242	236	221	221	222	205	194
Law enforcement	—	—	—	—	—	—	—	—	2	1	2	2	7	5	5
Clergyman	—	—	—	—	—	3	3	3	2	2	4	5	6	6	3
Journalism	36	33	31	35	36	33	43	39	39	30	23	24	27	11	21
Veteran	246	261	258	261	270	291	310	320	320	316	317	307	—	—	—

NOTE: Dashes indicate years and occupations for which Congressional Quarterly did not compile data. Congressional Quarterly stopped tabulating the number of veterans after the Ninety-fourth Congress.

SOURCE: *Congressional Quarterly Almanac*, annual volumes.

TABLE 1-9

PRIOR OCCUPATIONS OF DEMOCRATIC MEMBERS OF THE HOUSE OF REPRESENTATIVES, EIGHTY-THIRD THROUGH NINETY-SEVENTH CONGRESSES, 1953–1981

Occupation	83d 1953	84th 1955	85th 1957	86th 1959	87th 1961	88th 1963	89th 1965	90th 1967	91st 1969	92d 1971	93d 1973	94th 1975	95th 1977	96th 1979	97th 1981
Agriculture	21	22	22	28	23	21	26	17	14	19	14	13	6	10	11
Business or banking	55	59	57	71	64	67	98	82	76	70	72	84	69	71	58
Engineering	3	3	2	2	2	2	6	4	3	2	1	1	0	0	2
Medicine	2	2	2	2	2	1	1	1	2	4	3	3	1	1	2
Science	—	—	—	—	—	—	—	—	0	1	2	2	2	2	0
Education	18	26	26	30	24	24	54	43	40	39	41	51	56	44	39
Labor leader	—	—	—	—	—	3	3	2	3	3	3	3	6	3	4
Law	130	136	137	168	159	158	171	150	150	150	137	158	154	135	114
Law enforcement	—	—	—	—	—	—	—	—	1	1	1	2	7	4	4
Clergyman	—	—	—	—	—	1	2	1	1	1	2	4	4	4	2
Journalism	18	16	14	21	22	18	27	22	22	17	16	19	15	6	9
Veteran	118	131	133	175	161	175	210	183	181	185	175	198	—	—	—
Total number of Democratic members	213	232	234	283	262	258	295	248	243	255	242	291	292	277	243

NOTE: Dashes indicate years and occupations for which Congressional Quarterly did not compile data. Congressional Quarterly stopped tabulating the number of veterans after the Ninety-fourth Congress.

SOURCE: *Congressional Quarterly Almanac*, annual volumes.

TABLE 1-10

PRIOR OCCUPATIONS OF REPUBLICAN MEMBERS OF THE HOUSE OF REPRESENTATIVES, EIGHTY-THIRD THROUGH NINETY-SEVENTH CONGRESSES, 1953–1981

Occupation	83d 1953	84th 1955	85th 1957	86th 1959	87th 1961	88th 1963	89th 1965	90th 1967	91st 1969	92d 1971	93d 1973	94th 1975	95th 1977	96th 1979	97th 1981
Agriculture	32	29	26	17	25	24	18	22	20	17	24	18	10	9	17
Business or banking	76	68	72	59	70	67	58	79	83	75	83	56	49	56	76
Engineering	2	2	1	1	1	1	3	2	3	1	1	2	2	2	3
Medicine	4	3	4	2	4	2	2	2	3	2	2	2	1	5	4
Science	—	—	—	—	—	—	—	—	1	0	0	0	0	0	0
Education	28	21	20	11	15	12	14	14	19	22	18	13	14	13	20
Labor leader	—	—	—	—	—	0	0	0	0	0	0	0	0	1	1
Law	117	109	97	74	85	92	76	96	92	86	84	63	68	70	80
Law enforcement	—	—	—	—	—	—	—	—	1	0	1	0	0	1	1
Clergyman	—	—	—	—	—	2	1	2	1	1	2	1	2	2	1
Journalism	18	17	17	14	14	15	16	17	17	13	7	5	12	5	12
Veteran	128	130	125	86	109	116	100	137	139	131	142	109	—	—	—
Total number of Democratic members	221	203	201	153	175	176	140	187	192	180	192	144	143	158	192

NOTE: Dashes indicate years and occupations for which Congressional Quarterly did not compile data. Congressional Quarterly stopped tabulating the number of veterans after the Ninety-fourth Congress.

SOURCE: *Congressional Quarterly Almanac*, annual volumes.

TABLE 1–11

PRIOR OCCUPATIONS OF MEMBERS OF THE SENATE, EIGHTY-THIRD THROUGH NINETY-SEVENTH CONGRESSES, 1953–1981

Occupation	83d 1953	84th 1955	85th 1957	86th 1959	87th 1961	88th 1963	89th 1965	90th 1967	91st 1969	92d 1971	93d 1973	94th 1975	95th 1977	96th 1979	97th 1981
Agriculture	22	21	20	17	18	16	18	18	16	13	11	10	9	6	9
Business or banking	28	28	28	28	31	23	25	23	25	27	22	22	24	29	28
Engineering	5	2	2	2	2	2	2	2	2	2	2	2	0	0	2
Medicine	1	2	2	1	1	1	1	1	0	1	1	1	1	1	1
Science	—	—	—	—	—	—	—	—	1	0	0	0	1	2	1
Education	17	17	17	16	14	15	16	15	14	11	10	8	13	7	10
Labor leader	—	—	—	—	—	1	1	0	0	0	0	0	0	0	0
Law	59	60	59	61	63	66	67	68	68	65	68	67	68	65	59
Law enforcement	—	—	—	—	—	—	—	—	0	0	0	0	0	0	0
Clergyman	—	—	—	—	—	0	0	0	0	0	0	0	1	1	1
Journalism	10	10	9	13	10	8	10	10	8	7	5	5	6	2	7
Veteran	63	62	65	61	62	62	63	65	69	73	73	73	—	—	—

NOTE: Dashes indicate years and occupations for which Congressional Quarterly did not compile data. Congressional Quarterly stopped tabulating the number of veterans after the Ninety-fourth Congress.

SOURCE: *Congressional Quarterly Almanac*, annual volumes.

TABLE 1-12

PRIOR OCCUPATIONS OF DEMOCRATIC MEMBERS OF THE SENATE, EIGHTY-THIRD THROUGH NINETY-SEVENTH CONGRESSES, 1953–1981

Occupation	83d 1953	84th 1955	85th 1957	86th 1959	87th 1961	88th 1963	89th 1965	90th 1967	91st 1969	92d 1971	93d 1973	94th 1975	95th 1977	96th 1979	97th 1981
Agriculture	8	7	7	7	8	9	10	9	7	5	4	5	3	2	2
Business or banking	11	10	10	14	17	12	14	12	12	15	12	12	14	15	13
Engineering	2	0	0	2	2	2	2	2	2	2	2	2	0	0	1
Medicine	1	2	2	1	1	1	1	1	0	1	1	1	1	1	1
Science	—	—	—	—	—	—	—	—	0	0	0	0	0	1	0
Education	11	11	11	13	11	12	12	10	9	6	7	6	8	4	5
Labor leader	—	—	—	—	—	1	1	0	0	0	0	0	0	0	0
Law	34	27	35	43	44	46	48	48	42	41	42	45	46	43	33
Law enforcement	—	—	—	—	—	—	—	—	0	0	0	0	0	0	0
Clergyman	—	—	—	—	—	0	0	0	0	0	0	0	0	0	0
Journalism	5	6	5	10	7	7	7	7	5	5	4	4	4	2	4
Veteran	31	32	33	40	39	41	44	43	41	41	42	45	—	—	—
Total number of Democratic members	46	48	49	64	64	67	68	64	58	54	56	60	61	58	46

NOTE: Dashes indicate years and occupations for which Congressional Quarterly did not compile data. Congressional Quarterly stopped tabulating the number of veterans after the Ninety-fourth Congress.
SOURCE: *Congressional Quarterly Almanac*, annual volumes.

TABLE 1-13

PRIOR OCCUPATIONS OF REPUBLICAN MEMBERS OF THE SENATE, EIGHTY-THIRD THROUGH NINETY-SEVENTH CONGRESSES, 1953–1981

Occupation	83d 1953	84th 1955	85th 1957	86th 1959	87th 1961	88th 1963	89th 1965	90th 1967	91st 1969	92d 1971	93d 1973	94th 1975	95th 1977	96th 1979	97th 1981
Agriculture	14	14	13	10	10	7	8	9	9	8	7	5	6	4	7
Business or banking	17	18	18	14	14	11	11	11	13	12	10	10	10	14	15
Engineering	3	2	2	0	0	0	0	0	0	0	0	0	0	0	1
Medicine	0	0	0	0	0	0	0	0	0	0	0	0	0	0	0
Science	—	—	—	—	—	—	—	—	1	0	0	0	1	1	1
Education	6	6	6	3	3	3	4	5	5	5	3	2	5	3	5
Labor leader	—	—	—	—	—	0	0	0	0	0	0	0	0	0	0
Law	25	33	24	18	19	20	19	20	26	24	26	22	22	22	26
Law enforcement	—	—	—	—	—	—	—	0	0	0	0	0	0	0	0
Clergyman	—	—	—	—	—	0	0	0	0	0	0	0	1	1	1
Journalism	5	4	4	3	3	1	3	3	3	2	1	1	2	0	3
Veteran	32	30	32	21	23	21	19	22	28	32	31	28	—	—	—
Total number of Democratic members	48	47	47	34	36	33	32	36	42	44	42	37	38	41	53

NOTE: Dashes indicate years and occupations for which Congressional Quarterly did not compile data. Congressional Quarterly stopped tabulating the number of veterans after the Ninety-fourth Congress.

SOURCE: *Congressional Quarterly Almanac*, annual volumes.

TABLE 1–14

Religious Affiliations of Members of the House of Representatives, Eighty-eighth through Ninety-seventh Congresses, 1963–1981

	88th (1963)			89th (1965)			90th (1967)			91st (1969)		
	D	R	Total	D	R	Total	D	R	Total	D	R	Total
Catholic	72	15	87	81	13	94	73	22	95	72	24	96
Jewish	8	1	9	14	1	15	14	2	16	15	2	17
Protestant												
Baptist	38	10	48	33	9	42	30	12	42	30	13	43
Episcopal	23	22	45	29	25	54	25	25	50	22	27	49
Methodist	48	30	78	46	23	69	37	32	69	34	32	66
Presbyterian	28	40	68	30	26	56	27	37	64	26	38	64
All other	41	58	99	62	43	105	43	54	97	44	56	100
Total	258	176	434	295	140	435	249	184	433	243	192	435

NOTE: D indicates Democrats; R indicates Republicans.
SOURCE: *Congressional Quarterly Almanac*, annual volumes.

TABLE 1–15

Religious Affiliations of Members of the Senate, Eighty-eighth through Ninety-seventh Congresses, 1963–1981

	88th (1963)			89th (1965)			90th (1967)			91st (1969)		
	D	R	Total	D	R	Total	D	R	Total	D	R	Total
Catholic	10	1	11	12	2	14	11	2	13	10	3	13
Jewish	1	1	2	1	1	2	1	1	2	1	1	2
Protestant												
Baptist	10	2	12	9	3	12	7	4	11	6	3	9
Episcopal	7	8	15	8	7	15	8	7	15	5	10	15
Methodist	15	8	23	15	7	22	15	8	23	14	8	22
Presbyterian	7	4	11	8	3	11	8	4	12	8	5	13
All other	17	9	26	15	9	24	14	10	24	14	12	26
Total	67	33	100	68	32	100	64	36	100	58	42	100

NOTE: D indicates Democrats; R indicates Republicans.
SOURCE: *Congressional Quarterly Almanac*, annual volumes.

TABLE 1–14 (continued)

92d (1971)			93d (1973)			94th (1975)			95th (1977)			96th (1979)			97th (1981)		
D	R	Total	D	R	Total	D	R	Total	D	R	Total	D	R	Total	D	R	Total
77	24	101	69	30	99	88	22	110	95	24	119	93	23	116	81	38	119
10	2	12	10	2	12	17	3	20	20	3	23	18	5	23	21	6	27
32	10	42	33	12	45	37	10	47	36	10	46	33	10	43	28	13	41
27	22	49	25	25	50	29	21	50	26	22	48	29	22	51	25	27	52
33	32	65	30	33	63	40	23	63	36	24	60	32	26	58	26	30	56
26	41	67	25	35	60	25	25	50	23	22	45	25	27	52	18	28	46
49	49	98	50	55	105	55	40	95	56	38	94	47	45	92	44	50	94
254	180	434	242	192	434	291	144	435	292	143	435	277	158	435	243	192	435

TABLE 1–15 (continued)

92d (1971)			93d (1973)			94th (1975)			95th (1977)			96th (1979)			97th (1981)		
D	R	Total	D	R	Total	D	R	Total	D	R	Total	D	R	Total	D	R	Total
9	3	12	10	4	14	11	4	15	10	3	13	9	4	13	9	8	17
1	1	2	1	1	2	2	1	3	4	1	5	5	2	7	3	3	6
5	3	8	5	3	8	6	3	9	6	3	9	6	5	11	3	6	9
4	13	17	6	11	17	6	9	15	6	11	17	5	12	17	5	15	20
13	7	20	13	5	18	11	5	16	13	7	20	13	6	19	9	9	18
10	6	16	8	6	14	10	7	17	9	5	14	10	2	12	8	2	10
13	12	25	15	12	27	15	9	24	14	8	22	11	10	21	10	10	20
55	45	100	58	42	100	61	38	99	62	38	100	59	41	100	47	53	100

TABLE 1–16

BLACKS IN CONGRESS, FORTY-FIRST THROUGH NINETY-SEVENTH
CONGRESSES, 1869–1981

Congress	House D	House R	Senate D	Senate R	Congress	House D	House R	Senate D	Senate R
41st (1869)	—	2	—	1	76th (1939)	1	—	—	—
42d (1871)	—	5	—	—	77th (1941)	1	—	—	—
43d (1873)	—	7	—	—	78th (1943)	1	—	—	—
44th (1875)	—	7	—	1	79th (1945)	1	—	—	—
45th (1877)	—	3	—	1	80th (1947)	1	—	—	—
46th (1879)	—	—	—	1	81st (1949)	1	—	—	—
47th (1881)	—	2	—	—	82d (1951)	1	—	—	—
48th (1883)	—	2	—	—	83d (1953)	1	—	—	—
49th (1885)	—	2	—	—	84th (1955)	2	—	—	—
50th (1887)	—	—	—	—	85th (1957)	3	—	—	—
51st (1889)	—	3	—	—	86th (1959)	3	—	—	—
52d (1891)	—	1	—	—	87th (1961)	11	7	1	1
53d (1893)	—	1	—	—	88th (1963)	4	—	—	—
54th (1895)	—	1	—	—	89th (1965)	5	—	—	—
55th (1897)	—	1	—	—	90th (1967)	5	—	—	1
56th (1899) [a]	—	1	—	—	91st (1969)	9	—	—	1
					92d (1971)	13	—	—	1
71st (1929)	—	1	—	—	93d (1973)	16	—	—	1
72d (1931)	—	1	—	—	94th (1975)	16	—	—	1
73d (1933)	—	1	—	—	95th (1977)	15	—	—	1
74th (1935)	1	—	—	—	96th (1979)	15	—	—	—
75th (1937)	1	—	—	—	97th (1981)	17	—	—	—

NOTE: Does not include Walter E. Fauntroy, a nonvoting delegate who represents Washington, D.C.

a. After the Fifty-sixth Congress, there were no black members in either the House or Senate until the Seventy-first Congress.

SOURCES: U.S. Congress, *Black Americans in Congress, 1870-1977*, House Document 95-258, November 3, 1977; and *Congressional Quarterly Almanac*, annual volumes.

TABLE 1–17
Women in Congress, Sixty-fifth through Ninety-seventh Congresses, 1917–1981

Congress	House D	House R	Senate D	Senate R	Congress	House D	House R	Senate D	Senate R
65th (1917)	—	1	—	—	82d (1951)	4	6	—	1
66th (1919)	—	—	—	—	83d (1953)	5	7	—	3
67th (1921)	—	2	—	1	84th (1953)	10	7	—	1
68th (1923)	—	1	—	—	85th (1957)	9	6	—	1
69th (1925)	1	2	—	—	86th (1959)	9	8	—	1
70th (1927)	2	3	—	—	87th (1961)	11	7	1	1
71st (1929)	4	5	—	—	88th (1963)	6	6	1	1
72d (1931)	4	3	1	—	89th (1965)	7	4	1	1
73d (1933)	4	3	1	—	90th (1967)	5	5	—	1
74th (1935)	4	2	2	—	91st (1969)	6	4	—	1
75th (1937)	4	1	2	—	92d (1971)	10	3	—	1
76th (1939)	4	4	1	—	93d (1973)	14	2	1	—
77th (1941)	4	5	1	—	94th (1975)	14	5	—	—
78th (1943)	2	6	1	—	95th (1977)	13	5	—	—
79th (1945)	6	5	—	—	96th (1979)	11	5	1	1
80th (1947)	3	4	—	1	97th (1981)	10	9	—	2
81st (1949)	5	4	—	1					

Note: Includes only women who were sworn in as members and served more than one day.

Sources: U.S. Congress, *Women in Congress*, House Report 94-1732, September 29, 1976; and *Congressional Quarterly Almanac*, annual volumes.

TABLE 1-18

Political Divisions of the Senate and House, Thirty-fourth through Ninety-seventh Congresses, 1855–1983

Congress	Years	Senate					House of Representatives				
		Number of senators	Demo-crats	Repub-licans	Other parties	Vacant	Number of repre-sentatives	Demo-crats	Repub-licans	Other parties	Vacant
34th	1855–1857	62	42	15	5	—	234	83	108	43	—
35th	1857–1859	64	39	20	5	—	237	131	92	14	—
36th	1859–1861	66	38	26	2	—	237	101	113	23	—
37th	1861–1863	50	11	31	7	1	178	42	106	28	2
38th	1863–1865	51	12	39	—	—	183	80	103	—	—
39th	1865–1867	52	10	42	—	—	191	46	145	—	—
40th	1867–1869	53	11	42	—	—	193	49	143	—	1
41st	1869–1871	74	11	61	—	2	243	73	170	—	—
42d	1871–1873	74	17	57	—	—	243	104	139	—	—
43d	1873–1875	74	19	54	—	1	293	88	203	—	2
44th	1875–1877	76	29	46	—	1	293	181	107	3	2
45th	1877–1879	76	36	39	1	—	293	156	137	—	—
46th	1879–1881	76	43	33	—	—	293	150	128	14	1
47th	1881–1883	76	37	37	2	—	293	130	152	11	—
48th	1883–1885	76	36	40	—	—	325	200	119	6	—
49th	1885–1887	76	34	41	—	1	325	182	140	2	1
50th	1887–1889	76	37	39	—	—	325	170	151	4	—
51st	1889–1891	84	37	47	—	—	330	156	173	1	—

52d	1891–1893	88	39	47	2	—	333	231	88	14	—
53d	1893–1895	88	44	38	3	3	356	220	126	10	—
54th	1895–1897	88	39	44	5	—	357	104	246	7	—
55th	1897–1899	90	34	46	10	—	357	134	206	16	1
56th	1899–1901	90	26	53	11	2	357	163	185	9	—
57th	1901–1903	90	29	56	3	—	357	153	198	5	1
58th	1903–1905	90	32	58	—	—	386	178	207	—	1
59th	1905–1907	90	32	58	—	2	386	136	250	—	—
60th	1907–1909	92	29	61	—	1	386	164	222	—	—
61st	1909–1911	92	32	59	—	1	391	172	219	1	—
62d	1911–1913	92	42	49	1	—	391	228	162	18	—
63d	1913–1915	96	51	44	1	—	435	290	127	8	3
64th	1915–1917	96	56	39	1	—	435	231	193	9	—
65th	1917–1919	96	53	42	1	—	435	210[a]	216	7	2
66th	1919–1921	96	47	48	—	—	435	191	237	1	—
67th	1921–1923	96	37	59	2	—	435	132	300	3	—
68th	1923–1925	96	43	51	1	1	435	207	225	5	—
69th	1925–1927	96	40	54	1	—	435	183	247	3	4
70th	1927–1929	96	47	48	1	—	435	195	237	1	—
71st	1929–1931	96	39	56	1	—	435	163	267	1	—
72d	1931–1933	96	47	48	1	—	435	216[b]	218	5	—
73d	1933–1935	96	59	36	1	—	435	313	117	10	—
74th	1935–1937	96	69	25	2	—	435	322	103	13	—
75th	1937–1939	96	75	17	4	—	435	333	89	4	—
76th	1939–1941	96	69	23	4	—	435	262	169	6	—
77th	1941–1943	96	66	28	2	—	435	267	162	6	—

(Table continues)

TABLE 1-18 (continued)

Congress	Years	Senate					House of Representatives				
		Number of senators	Demo-crats	Repub-licans	Other parties	Vacant	Number of repre-sentatives	Demo-crats	Repub-licans	Other parties	Vacant
78th	1943–1945	96	57	38	1	—	435	222	209	4	—
79th	1945–1947	96	57	38	1	—	435	243	190	2	—
80th	1947–1949	96	45	51	—	—	435	188	246	1	—
81st	1949–1951	96	54	42	—	—	435	263	171	1	—
82d	1951–1953	96	48	47	1	—	435	234	199	2	—
83d	1953–1955	96	46	48	2	—	435	213	221	1	—
84th	1955–1957	96	48	47	1	—	435	232	203	—	—
85th	1957–1959	96	49	47	—	—	435	234	201	—	—
86th	1959–1961	98	64	34	—	—	436[c]	283	153	—	—

87th	1961–1963	100	64	36	—	—	437[d]	262	175	—	—
88th	1963–1965	100	67	33	—	—	435	258	176	—	1
89th	1965–1967	100	68	32	—	—	435	295	140	—	—
90th	1967–1969	100	64	36	—	—	435	248	187	—	—
91st	1969–1971	100	58	42	—	—	435	243	192	—	—
92d	1971–1973	100	54	44	2	—	435	255	180	—	—
93d	1973–1975	100	56	42	2	—	435	242	192	1	—
94th	1975–1977	100	61	37	2	—	435	291	144	—	—
95th	1977–1979	100	61	38	1	—	435	292	143	—	—
96th	1979–1981	100	58	41	1	—	435	277	158	—	—
97th	1981–1983	100	46	53	1	—	435	243	192	—	—

NOTE: All figures reflect immediate result of elections.

a. Democrats organized House with help of other parties.

b. Democrats organized House because of Republican deaths.

c. Proclamation declaring Alaska a state issued January 3, 1959.

d. Proclamation declaring Hawaii a state issued August 21, 1959.

SOURCE: *Statistics of the Presidential and Congressional Elections of November 4, 1980.* Compiled from official sources by Thomas E. Ladd, under direction of Edmund L. Henshaw, Jr., clerk of the House of Representatives (Washington, D.C., 1981).

2
Elections

For the members of the House and Senate, there are no more vital statistics than those on congressional elections. Whatever their personal goals within Congress, winning reelection is the necessary first step for members. Yet, as the dramatic change in party control of the Senate in the 1980 election made clear, individual electoral success is not enough—the fate of one's party colleagues is extraordinarily important in shaping the internal character of Congress and therefore the ability of individual members to accomplish their legislative and political goals.

The data in table 2–1 remind us that the important decisions in the electoral arena are being made by a smaller and smaller percentage of citizens. Just over one-third of the eligible electorate participated in the 1978 House elections, the lowest proportion since World War II. This gradual downward trend continued in the 1980 presidential and congressional elections. While voter turnout has declined in recent years, however, the number of people engaged in more demanding forms of political participation—contributing money to campaigns, writing letters to congressmen—has increased.[1]

Table 2–2 relates the party's popular vote to the percentage of seats in the House of Representatives actually won over the past two decades. The long-term Democratic control of the Congress is evident in this table, although Democratic support appears slightly less robust when one concentrates on the national popular vote for the parties rather than on the seats won. In the mid-1960s and again in 1980, the Republicans came within striking distance of the Democrats in national popular vote; yet they never won more than 44 percent of the seats in those years. This form of malapportionment, in which the majority party enjoys seat margins much more favorable than its vote margins—shown clearly by the figures in the last column of table 2–2—is common to electoral systems with single-member dis-

1. Richard A. Brody, "The Puzzle of Political Participation in America," in Anthony King, ed., *The New American Political System* (Washington, D.C.: American Enterprise Institute, 1978), pp. 287-324.

tricts. A gain of a certain percentage in a party's popular vote usually allows it to pick up two or three times that percentage in seats. Republican successes in the 1980 House elections, however, cut the Democratic majority party seat bonus to half what it was in 1978 and 1980. Poised once again to end the long-term Democratic control of the House, the Republicans in 1982 face the bleak prospect of a traditional loss of seats by the president's party.

Net seats picked up by each party as a result of House and Senate general and special elections are shown in table 2–3. The election of 1958 was especially important to Senate Democrats in maintaining their majority during the subsequent two decades, a majority that ended abruptly with the surprising pickup of twelve seats by the Republicans in the 1980 elections. House Democrats, however, saw their strength wax and wane in pairs of elections until the Watergate year of 1974, which gave them a margin sufficient to protect their majority in the face of Republican gains in 1978 and 1980. Despite the widespread belief about parliamentary by-elections, special elections in the United States send no clear message about how the national tides will run in the next general election.

Table 2–4 presents the number of seats lost or gained by the president's party in midterm elections, data which have long fascinated analysts of American politics. In every midterm election except one since the Civil War, the party of the president has lost ground in the House of Representatives. The exception was 1934, which signaled the last major realignment in our party system. Although the number of seats changing party hands has varied widely over time, during the past thirty years the president's party has not once sustained a loss as deep as fifty seats. In fact, in the last four midterm elections occurring in the first term of a president, the average loss was only twelve seats.

The midterm pattern of Senate elections is different from that of the House, chiefly because only a third of the Senate is up for reelection at a time. In the thirty midterm elections since the Civil War, the president's party gained seats in ten.

As table 2–5 and figure 2–1 demonstrate, although more seats change party control than the net shifts in table 2–3 suggest, the stabilizing impact of party in House elections remains impressive: in no election since 1954 have more than 13 percent of the 435 seats changed party hands. By contrast, as many as one-third of the Senate seats up for election in any one year have changed party control (see table 2–6 and figure 2–2). In addition, in spite of the impressive advantages of incumbency, parties pick up most of their gains not in open seats but in races contested by incumbents. Finally, one is struck again by the importance of particular elections for long-term party control. In 1958 for the Senate and in 1974 for the House, the Democrats posted impressive gains that were maintained in the subsequent elections. The jury is still out on the durability of the Republican gains in 1980.

Tables 2–7 and 2–8 chronicle the fate of House and Senate incumbents. In the House, incumbents who seek reelection usually succeed, a result that has been strikingly constant over the years of the modern Congress. Renomination poses no serious problem for most incumbents, although each year a handful are defeated in primaries. And even landslides in the general election ordinarily lead to the defeat of only 10 percent of the incumbents seeking reelection. A substantial increase in retirements in the 1970s was largely responsible for the relatively high turnover during that period.

Senate incumbents have usually fared less well than their House counterparts, the level of competition in statewide races being generally higher. Both renomination and reelection have proved to be more difficult hurdles for senators than for representatives. Moreover, if the last three elections are any guide to the future, senators may soon have no better than a fifty-fifty chance of winning reelection. Retirements have also increased in the Senate, although they contribute to a smaller proportion of the overall turnover in the Senate than in the House. Table 2–9 provides a party breakdown of those House and Senate retirements.

In terms of the margin of victory rather than the rate of reelection, some change has occurred in the electoral standing of House and Senate incumbents. The proportion of House incumbents who have won reelection with at least 60 percent of the major party vote has increased from about three-fifths in the 1950s and early 1960s to three-fourths in the 1970s (table 2–10). Various scholars, led by David Mayhew, have investigated the sources of this phenomenon of "vanishing" marginal seats; their explanations have ranged from a decline in the quality of challengers to an increasing public relations orientation of new-style congressmen. The resources provided incumbents for communicating with their constituents have increased substantially during this period (see chapter 5).

Table 2–11 demonstrates that a similar though more subtle change is evident in Senate elections. The overall figures obscure divergent regional shifts: while in recent years the South has lost safe seats, in the rest of the country the proportion of senators who have won reelection by a wide margin has increased from less than one-fifth to more than one-third. Of course, the contrast with the House remains. Most Senate races fall in the marginal range, and there is ample opportunity to defeat incumbents.

Yet incumbents consider themselves less electorally secure than these particular measures of marginality merit. Viewed from the perspective of congressional careers, elections pose more of a challenge to incumbents than one might think. Table 2–12 reveals that a majority of senators and representatives serving in the Ninety-seventh Congress have received less than 55 percent of the vote, and three-fourths of them less than 60 percent, in at least one election. Moreover, when the conditions of initial election to the Congress are examined (table 2–13), it is apparent that many representatives and a majority of senators have themselves either defeated incumbents or replaced retiring incumbents of the other party.

Tables 2–14 and 2–15 point to the substantial divergence between presidential and congressional voting. Since 1956, when the Democrats in the House and Senate withstood Eisenhower's sweeping victory in the presidential election, more than one-fourth of all congressional districts have supported a presidential candidate of one party and a House candidate of the other (table 2–14). The proportion of districts with split results reached a peak in 1972, when George McGovern received 37.5 percent of the presidential vote while his party's candidates won 51.7 percent of the congressional vote and maintained a solid majority of seats in the House. The strong party-based election of 1980 in no way departed from that pattern.

A president's ability to claim long coattails depends upon both the size of his victory margin and the number of seats his party gains in the Congress. Presidents Kennedy and Carter lost on both counts: the Republicans actually gained twenty-two House seats in 1960 and held their ground in 1976 while both victorious Democratic presidents ran ahead of Democratic representatives in only twenty-two districts (table 2–15). In 1972 Richard Nixon ran ahead of a majority of the Republicans elected to the House, but this was small consolation in view of his failure to pull a sizable bloc of new Republicans into the House. In contrast, Lyndon Johnson could claim credit for dramatically increasing his party's margin in the Congress. His reward was the Great Society legislation of 1965 and 1966. In 1980 Ronald Reagan's presidential victory was accompanied by impressive Republican gains in the House, but well short of the number needed to take control. Moreover, Reagan ran behind most of his party colleagues in the House. The more important manifestation of a Reagan tide was thought to be in the Senate, where a total of 50,000 votes accounted for seven Republican victories and, as a consequence, majority status.

The past two decades have witnessed a substantial increase in the impact of local forces in congressional elections. Although the United States has never had a uniform swing across constituencies as Britain has, the figures in table 2–16 illustrate how difficult it is to make national interpretations of the results of U.S. congressional elections. Election returns at the district level increasingly diverge from the national returns. These figures suggest an electoral base for the increasingly individualized behavior in the House of Representatives. The range in the swing across districts has increased markedly since the 1950s, and the variance—which measures the extent to which changes in local returns differ from the change in national returns—has tripled. This localization of political forces in House elections continued in 1980.

Finally, table 2–17 presents data that confirm the basis in individual voting behavior for many of the electoral patterns reported in this chapter. The decline in the proportion of party-line voters in House elections is consistent with the view that voting is increasingly candidate centered. In this respect elections for the House, the Senate, and the presidency are becoming more alike.

TABLE 2–1

TURNOUT IN PRESIDENTIAL AND HOUSE ELECTIONS, 1930–1980
(percentage of voting age population)

Year	Presidential Elections	House Elections
1930	—	33.7
1932	52.4	49.7
1934	—	41.4
1936	56.9	53.5
1938	—	44.0
1940	58.9	55.4
1942	—	32.5
1944	56.0	52.7
1946	—	37.1
1948	51.1	48.1
1950	—	41.1
1952	61.6	57.6
1954	—	41.7
1956	59.3	55.9
1958	—	43.0
1960	62.6	58.5
1962	—	45.4
1964	61.9	57.8
1966	—	45.4
1968	60.9	55.1
1970	—	43.5
1972	55.4	50.9
1974	—	36.1
1976	54.4	49.5
1978	—	35.1
1980	53.4	48.1

SOURCES: U.S. Bureau of the Census, *Statistical Abstract of the United States,* 1930-1976, Washington, D.C.; *Congressional Quarterly Weekly Report,* vol. 37 (March 31, 1979), p. 571, and vol. 39 (April 25, 1981), p. 716.

TABLE 2-2

National Popular Vote and Seats Won by Party in House Elections, 1946–1980

Year	Democratic Candidates		Republican Candidates		Change from Last Election[a]		Difference between Democratic Percentage of Seats and Votes Won
	Percentage of all votes	Percentage of seats won	Percentage of all votes	Percentage of seats won	Percentage of major-party votes	Percentage of seats won	
1946	44.3	43.3	53.5	56.7	6.4R	12.8R	−1.0
1948	51.6	60.6	45.4	39.4	7.9D	17.3D	+9.0
1950	48.9	54.0	48.9	46.0	3.2R	6.6R	+5.1
1952	49.2	49.1	49.3	50.9	0.1R	4.9R	−0.1
1954	52.1	53.3	47.0	46.7	2.6D	4.2D	+1.2
1956	50.7	53.8	48.7	46.2	1.5R	0.5D	+3.1

1958	55.5	64.9	43.6	35.1	5.0D	11.1D	+9.4
1960	54.4	60.0	44.8	40.0	1.2R	4.9R	+5.6
1962	52.1	59.4	47.1	40.6	2.3R	0.6R	+7.3
1964	56.9	67.8	42.4	32.2	4.8D	8.4D	+10.9
1966	50.5	57.0	48.0	43.0	6.0R	10.8R	+6.5
1968	50.0	55.9	48.2	44.1	0.3R	1.1R	+5.9
1970	53.0	58.6	44.5	41.4	3.4D	2.7D	+5.6
1972	51.7	55.8	46.4	44.2	1.7R	2.8R	+4.1
1974	57.1	66.9	40.5	33.1	5.8D	11.1D	+9.8
1976	56.2	67.1	42.1	32.9	1.3R	0.2D	+10.9
1978	53.4	63.7	44.7	36.3	2.8R	3.4R	+10.3
1980	50.4	55.9	48.0	44.1	3.2R	7.8R	+5.5

a. Data show percentage-point increase over previous election in votes or seats won by Republicans (R) or Democrats (D).

SOURCES: *Congressional Quarterly Weekly Report*, vol. 35 (June 11, 1977), p. 1141, vol. 37 (March 31, 1979), p. 571, and vol. 39 (April 25, 1981), p. 713; and *Statistics of the Congressional Election of November 7, 1978*, compiled from official sources by Benjamin J. Guthrie, under direction of Edmund L. Henshaw, Jr., clerk of the House of Representatives (Washington, D.C., 1979), p. 45.

TABLE 2–3

NET PARTY SHIFT IN SEATS IN HOUSE AND SENATE, GENERAL AND SPECIAL ELECTIONS, 1946–1980

Year	General Elections[a]		Special Elections[b]	
	House	Senate	House	Senate
1946	56R	13R	1R (8)	3R (8)
1948	75D	9D	0 (4)	0 (3)
1950	28R	5R	0 (10)	2R (6)
1952	22R	1R	2R (10)	2R (4)
1954	19D	2D	2D (8)	0 (9)
1956	2D	1D	0 (3)	2R (3)
1958	49D	15D	0 (10)	1D (4)
1960	22R	2R	1R (8)	1D (3)
1962	1R	3D	0 (12)	0 (6)
1964	37D	1D	2R (12)	0 (2)
1966	47R	4R	1D (10)	1R (3)
1968	5R	6R	1R (6)	0 (0)
1970	12D	2R	2D (14)	0 (2)
1972	12R	2D	0 (10)	0 (2)
1974	49D	4D	4D (10)	0 (0)
1976	1D	0	0 (7)	1D (1)
1978	15R	3R	4R (6)	1R (2)
1980	34R	12R	1R (7)	0 (0)

NOTE: D indicates Democrats; R indicates Republicans.

a. The general election figure for each year is the difference between the number of seats won by the party gaining seats in that election and the number of seats won by that party in the preceding general election.

b. The special election figure for each pair of elections is the net shift in seats held by the major parties as a result of special elections held between the two general elections. The number of special elections is given in parentheses.

SOURCES: *Statistics of the Congressional Election of November 7, 1978*, p. 45; Congressional Quarterly, *Congressional Quarterly Almanac*, vols. 2-36; and Congressional Quarterly, *Guide to U.S. Elections*, 1975.

TABLE 2–4
Losses by President's Party in Midterm Elections, 1862–1978

Year	Party Holding Presidency	President's Party Gain/Loss of Seats in House	President's Party Gain/Loss of Seats in Senate
1862	R	−3	8
1866	R	−2	0
1870	R	−31	−4
1874	R	−96	−8
1878	R	−9	−6
1882	R	−33	3
1886	D	−12	3
1890	R	−85	0
1894	D	−116	−5
1898	R	−21	7
1902	R	9[a]	2
1906	R	−28	3
1910	R	−57	−10
1914	D	−59	5
1918	D	−19	−6
1922	R	−75	−8
1926	R	−10	−6
1930	R	−49	−8
1934	D	9	10
1938	D	−71	−6
1942	D	−55	−9
1946	D	−55	−12
1950	D	−29	−6
1954	R	−18	−1
1958	R	−48	−13
1962	D	−4	3
1966	D	−47	−4
1970	R	−12	2
1974	R	−48	−5
1978	D	−15	−3

NOTE: Each entry is the difference between the number of seats won by the president's party in that midterm election and the number of seats won by that party in the preceding general election. Because of changes in the overall number of seats in the Senate and House, in the number of seats won by third parties, and in the number of vacancies, a Republican loss is not always matched precisely by a Democratic gain, or vice versa.

a. Although the Republicans gained nine seats in the 1902 elections, they actually lost ground to the Democrats, who gained twenty-five seats after the increase in the overall number of representatives after the 1900 census.

SOURCE: Statistics of the Congressional Election of November 7, 1978, pp. 44-45. Reprinted from Thomas Mann and Norman Ornstein, "The 1982 Election: What Will It Mean?" Public Opinion (June/July 1981), p. 49.

TABLE 2-5
House Seats That Changed Party, 1954–1980

Year	Total Changes	Incumbent Defeated		Open Seat	
		D→R	R→D	D→R	R→D
1954	26	3	18	2	3
1956	20	7	7	2	4
1958	50	1	35	0	14
1960	37	23	2	6	6
1962	19	9	5	2	3
1964	57	5	39	5	8
1966	47	39	1	4	3
1968	11	5	0	2	4
1970	25	2	9	6	8
1972	23	6	3	9	5
1974	55	4	36	2	13
1976	22	7	5	3	7
1978	33	14	5	8	6
1980	41	27	3	10	1

NOTE: This table reflects shift in party control of seats from immediately before to immediately after the November elections. It does not include party gains resulting from the creation of new districts and does not account for situations in which two districts were reduced to one, thus forcing incumbents to run against each other. D indicates Democrat; R indicates Republican.

SOURCE: *Congressional Quarterly Almanac*, vols. 10-36.

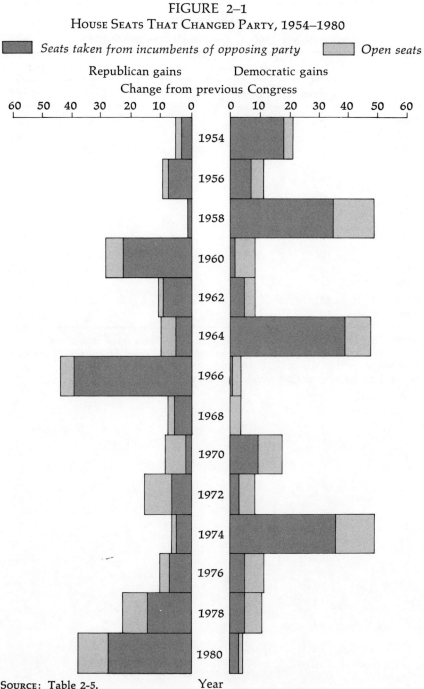

FIGURE 2–1
House Seats That Changed Party, 1954–1980

■ *Seats taken from incumbents of opposing party*   □ *Open seats*

Republican gains   Democratic gains

Change from previous Congress

60 50 40 30 20 10   0   0 10 20 30 40 50 60

1954

1956

1958

1960

1962

1964

1966

1968

1970

1972

1974

1976

1978

1980

Source: Table 2-5.   Year

TABLE 2-6

SENATE SEATS THAT CHANGED PARTY, 1954–1980

Year	Total Changes	Incumbent Defeated		Open Seat	
		D→R	R→D	D→R	R→D
1954	8	2	4	1	1
1956	8	1	3	3	1
1958	13	0	11	0	2
1960	2	1	0	1	0
1962	8	2	3	0	3
1964	4	1	3	0	0
1966	3	1	0	2	0
1968	9	4	0	3	2
1970	6	3	2	1	0
1972	10	1	4	3	2
1974	6	0	2	1	3
1976	14	5	4	2	3
1978	13	5	2	3	3
1980	12	9	0	3	0

NOTE: This table reflects shift in party control of seats from immediately before to immediately after the November election. D indicates Democrat; R indicates Republican.

SOURCE: *Congressional Quarterly Almanac,* vols. 10-36.

FIGURE 2–2
Senate Seats That Changed Party, 1954–1980

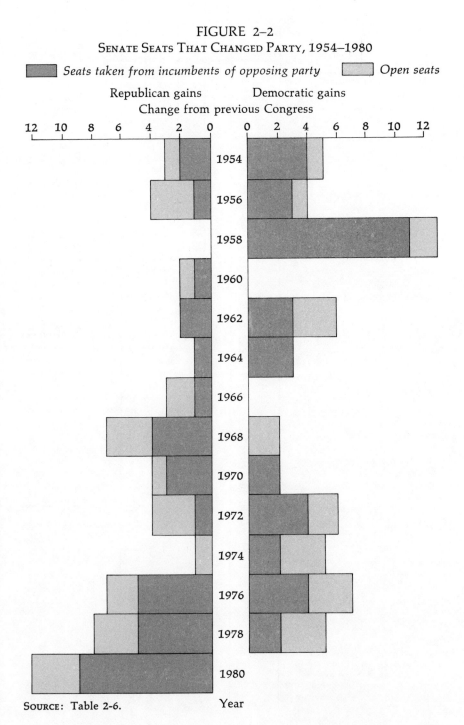

Source: Table 2-6.

45

TABLE 2-7

House Incumbents Reelected, Defeated, or Retired, 1946–1980

Year	Retired[a]	Sought Reelection			Reelected		
		Total	Defeated in primaries	Defeated in general election	Total	Percentage of those seeking reelection	Percentage of House membership
1946	32	398	18	52	328	82.4	75.4
1948	29	400	15	68	317	79.3	72.9
1950	29	400	6	32	362	90.5	83.2
1952	42	389	9	26	354	91.0	81.4
1954	24	407	6	22	379	93.1	87.1
1956	21	411	6	16	389	94.6	89.4

1958	33	396	3	37	356	89.9	81.8
1960	26	405	5	25	375	92.6	86.2
1962	24	402	12	22	368	91.5	84.6
1964	33	397	8	45	344	86.6	79.1
1966	22	411	8	41	362	88.1	83.2
1968	23	409	4	9	396	96.8	91.0
1970	29	401	10	12	379	94.5	87.1
1972	40	390	12	13	365	93.6	83.9
1974	43	391	8	40	343	87.7	78.9
1976	47	384	3	13	368	95.8	84.6
1978	49	382	5	19	358	93.7	82.3
1980	34	398	6	31	361	90.7	83.0

a. Does not include persons who died or resigned from office before the election.

Source: *Congressional Quarterly Weekly Report*, vol. 38 (January 12, 1980), p. 81, vol. 38 (April 5, 1980), p. 908, and vol. 38 (November 8, 1980), pp. 3320-21.

TABLE 2–8

SENATE INCUMBENTS REELECTED, DEFEATED, OR RETIRED, 1946–1980

Year	Retired[a]	Sought Reelection				
		Total	Defeated in primaries	Defeated in general election	Total relected	Reelected as percentage of those seeking reelection
1946	9	30	6	7	17	56.7
1948	8	25	2	8	15	60.0
1950	4	32	5	5	22	68.8
1952	4	31	2	9	20	64.5
1954	6	32	2	6	24	75.0
1956	6	29	0	4	25	86.2
1958	6	28	0	10	18	64.3
1960	5	29	0	1	28	96.6
1962	4	35	1	5	29	82.9
1964	2	33	1	4	28	84.8
1966	3	32	3	1	28	87.5
1968	6	28	4	4	20	71.4
1970	4	31	1	6	24	77.4
1972	6	27	2	5	20	74.1
1974	7	27	2	2	23	85.2
1976	8	25	0	9	16	64.0
1978	10	25	3	7	15	60.0
1980	5	29	4	9	16	55.2

a. Does not include persons who died or resigned from office before the election.
SOURCE: *Congressional Quarterly Weekly Report*, vol. 38 (January 12, 1980), p. 81, vol. 38 (April 5, 1980), p. 908, and vol. 38 (November 8, 1980), p. 3302.

TABLE 2–9

HOUSE AND SENATE RETIREMENTS BY PARTY, 1930–1980

Year	House		Senate	
	D	R	D	R
1930	8	15	2	5
1932	16	23	1	1
1934	29	9	3	1
1936	29	3	4	2
1938	21	5	3	1
1940	16	6	1	2
1942	20	12	0	0
1944	17	5	3	2
1946	17	15	4	3
1948	17	12	3	4
1950	12	17	3	1
1952	25	17	2	1
1954	11	13	1	1
1956	7	13	4	1
1958	6	27	0	6
1960	11	15	3	1
1962	10	14	2	2
1964	17	16	1	1
1966	14	8	1	2
1968	12	10	3	3
1970	11	19	3	1
1972	20	20	3	3
1974	23	21	3	4
1976	31	16	4	4
1978	31	18	5	5
1980	21	13	2	3

NOTE: These figures include members who did not run again for the office they held and members who sought other offices; they do not include members who died or resigned from office before the end of the Congress.

SOURCES: 1930-1978, Mildred L. Lehmann, "Members of Congress Who Choose Not to Run for Reelection to the Seats They Occupy, 1930-1978," Congressional Research Service, May 18, 1978; 1908, *Congressional Quarterly Weekly Report*, vol. 38 (November 8, 1980), pp. 3302, 3320-21.

TABLE 2–10

House Elections Won by 60 Percent, 1956–1980

Year	Number of Incumbents Running in General Election	Percentage of Incumbents Reelected with at Least 60 Percent of the Major Party Vote
1956	403	59.1
1958	390	63.1
1960	400	58.9
1962	376	63.6
1964	388	58.5
1966	401	67.7
1968	397	72.2
1970	389	77.3
1972	373	77.8
1974	383	66.4
1976	381	71.9
1978	377	78.0
1980	392	72.9

Source: Albert D. Cover and David R. Mayhew, "Congressional Dynamics and the Decline of Competitive Congressional Elections," in Lawrence C. Dodd and Bruce I. Oppenheimer, eds., *Congress Reconsidered*, 2d ed. (Washington, D.C.: Congressional Quarterly Press, 1981); and *Congressional Quarterly Weekly Report*, vol. 39 (April 25, 1981), pp. 717-25.

TABLE 2–11

SENATE ELECTIONS WON BY 60 PERCENT, 1944–1980

Election Period	Number of Incumbents Running in General Election	Percentage of Incumbents Reelected with at Least 60 Percent of the Major Party Vote[a]		
		South	North	Total U.S.
1944–48	61	100.0	22.9	39.3
1950–54	76	100.0	18.3	35.5
1956–60	84	95.5	24.2	42.9
1962–66	86	70.0	36.4	44.2
1968–72	74	71.4	38.3	44.6
1974–78	70	57.1	37.5	41.4
1980	25	40.0[b]	40.0	40.0

a. For the purposes of this table, senators appointed to the Senate are not considered incumbents in the elections just after appointment.

b. Includes Russell Long (D-La.), who, by winning 59.8 percent of the vote in his state's all-party primary, avoided a general election contest.

SOURCES: Albert D. Cover and David R. Mayhew, "Congressional Dynamics"; and *Congressional Quaterly Weekly Report*, vol. 39 (April 25, 1981), pp. 717-25.

TABLE 2–12

HISTORY OF MARGINAL RACES AMONG MEMBERS OF THE NINETY-SEVENTH CONGRESS, 1981

Chamber	Members Who Ever Won a Congressional Election by 60 Percent or Less		Members Who Ever Won a Congressional Election by 55 Percent or Less	
	Number	Percentage	Number	Percentage
House	312	71.7	226	52.0
Senate	87	87.0	63	63.0

SOURCES: Congressional Quarterly, *Guide to U.S. Elections*; and *Congressional Quarterly Weekly Report*, vol. 38 (November 8, 1980).

TABLE 2-13

CONDITIONS OF ENTRY TO THE CONGRESS AMONG MEMBERS OF THE NINETY-SEVENTH CONGRESS, 1981

Condition	House				Senate		
	Democrats	Republicans	Total	%	Democrats	Republicans	Total
Defeated incumbent							
In primary	25	6	31	7.1	7	1	8
In general election	50	61	111	25.5	14	24	38
Succeeded retiring incumbent							
Of same party	108	78	186	42.8	12	11	23
Of other party	31	25	56	12.9	9	9	18
Succeeded deceased incumbent							
Of same party	13	7	20	4.6	2	3	5
Of other party	1	5	6	1.4	1	0	1
Defeated candidate in general election who had earlier defeated incumbent in primary	1	3	4	0.9	2	5	7
New districts	14	7	21	4.8	0	0	0
Total	243	192	435	100.0	47	53	100

SOURCES: Compiled from information taken from *Congressional Quarterly Almanac*, vols. 11-36; and the *1981 Congressional Directory*, 97th Congress, 1st Session, compiled under the direction of the U.S. Congress, Joint Committee on Printing.

TABLE 2–14

TICKET SPLITTING BETWEEN PRESIDENTIAL AND HOUSE CANDIDATES,
1900–1980

Year	Districts[a]	Districts with Split Results[b]	
		Number	Percentage
1900	295	10	3.4
1904	310	5	1.6
1908	314	21	6.7
1912	333	84	25.2
1916	333	35	10.5
1920	344	11	3.2
1924	356	42	11.8
1928	359	68	18.9
1932	355	50	14.1
1936	361	51	14.1
1940	362	53	14.6
1944	367	41	11.2
1948	422	90	21.3
1952	435	84	19.3
1956	435	130	29.9
1960	437	114	26.1
1964	435	145	33.3
1968	435	139	32.0
1972	435	192	44.1
1976	435	124	28.5
1980	435	143	32.8

a. Before 1952, complete data are not available on every congressional district.

b. Congressional districts carried by a presidential candidate of one party and a House candidate of another party.

SOURCES: *Congressional Quarterly Weekly Report*, vol. 36 (April 1978), p. 9; Walter Dean Burnham, *Critical Elections* (New York: Norton, 1970), p. 109; and Michael Barone and Grant Ujifusa, *The Almanac of American Politics 1982* (Washington: Barone and Co., 1981).

TABLE 2–15

PRESIDENTIAL VOTE IN CONGRESSIONAL DISTRICTS, 1960–1980

Year	Number of Districts Carried by President[a]	President ran ahead	President ran behind
		President's Vote Compared with Vote for His Party's Successful House Candidates	
1960	204	22	243
1964	375	134[b]	158[b]
1972	377	104	88
1976	220	22	270
1980	309	38[c]	150[c]

a. Refers to the winning presidential candidate in each election.

b. Does not include districts where the percentage of the total district vote won by House members equaled the percentage of the total district vote won by the president.

c. Computed on the basis of the actual presidential vote with John Anderson and others included. If recomputed on the basis of Reagan's percentage of the major party vote, the president ran ahead in fifty-nine districts.

SOURCES: Compiled from information in the *Congressional Quarterly Weekly Report*, vol. 36 (April 22, 1978), p. 972; *1967 Congressional Quarterly Almanac*; and Barone and Ujifusa, *Almanac of American Politics 1982*.

TABLE 2–16

SHIFTS IN PARTY VOTING WITHIN CONGRESSIONAL DISTRICTS, 1956–1980

Period	Change in Democratic Percentage Nationally	Greatest loss	Greatest gain	Variance[a]
		Change in Democratic Percentage within Congressional Districts		
1956–58	5.0	−9.5	27.3	30.3
1958–60	−1.2	−22.1	14.4	31.4
1972–74	5.8	−18.8	36.2	92.2
1974–76	−1.3	−30.7	31.6	81.0
1976–78	−2.8	−37.6	39.6	106.1
1978–80	−3.2	−27.8	37.0	85.0

a. Variance, the square of the standard deviation, measures the extent to which the changes in local returns differ from the change in national returns.

SOURCES: Information for 1956-1976 taken from Thomas E. Mann, *Unsafe at Any Margin* (Washington, D.C.: American Enterprise Institute, 1978); for 1978, computed from official election returns; for 1980, computed by Larry Bartels of the University of California, Berkeley.

TABLE 2-17

PARTY-LINE VOTERS, DEFECTORS, AND PURE INDEPENDENTS IN
PRESIDENTIAL, SENATE, AND HOUSE ELECTIONS, 1956–1980
(as a percentage of all voters)

	Presidential Elections			Senate Elections			House Elections		
Year	Party-line voters[a]	Defectors[b]	Pure independents	Party-line voters[a]	Defectors[b]	Pure independents	Party-line voters[a]	Defectors[b]	Pure independents
1956	76	15	9	79	12	9	82	9	9
1958				85	9	15	84	11	5
1960	79	13	8	77	15	8	80	12	8
1962				n.a.	n.a.	n.a.	83	12	6
1964	79	15	5	78	16	6	79	15	5
1966				n.a.	n.a.	n.a.	76	16	8
1968	69	23	9	74	19	7	74	19	7
1970				78	12	10	76	16	8
1972	67	25	8	69	22	9	75	17	8
1974				73	19	8	74	18	8
1976	74	15	11	70	19	11	72	19	9
1978				71	20	9	69	22	9
1980	70	22	8	71	21	8	69	23	8

NOTE: n.a. = not available. Percentages may not add to 100 because of rounding.
a. Party identifiers who vote for the candidate of their party.
b. Party identifiers who vote for the candidate of the other party.
SOURCES: Tabulated from SRC/CPS *National Election Studies, 1956-1980*, by Thomas E. Mann and Raymond E. Wolfinger, "Candidates and Parties in Congressional Elections," *American Political Science Review* (September 1980); and Gary C. Jacobson, *The Politics of Congressional Elections* (Boston: Little, Brown, 1982).

3

Campaign Finance

If election data are a senator's or a representative's own most vital statistics, campaign finance data may be the best way for an outsider to see how congressional elections have been changing in recent years. Campaign costs have been going up much more quickly than the consumer price index since 1974. Over the same years, there have also been structural changes in campaign funding: candidates have raised more money from political action committees, party participation has become more centralized, and ideological groups have increased their independent expenditures. Assessments of these changes depend somewhat, of course, on one's perspective. Some people are shocked by the cost of campaigning and worry that the growing role of political action committees means interest groups have too much influence in the legislative process. Others dispute the direct connection between campaign contributions and legislation and see the growth in expenditures as a healthy sign of increased political communication that partially offsets the advantages of incumbency. (For incumbents' office allowances, see chapter 5, tables 5–12 and 5–13.) Whatever one's perspective, these data surely will provide fuel for some fruitful debate.

The increase in campaign costs during the 1974–1980 period is underscored when compared with the consumer price index (CPI). With 1967 as the base year for the CPI (100.0), consumer prices went up from 147.7 in 1974 to 246.8 in 1980, an increase of 67 percent (see chapter 5, table 5–9). Over that same period, total expenditures for major party general election candidates increased in House races by 163 percent (table 3–1) and in Senate races by 150 percent (table 3–2). The amount it cost to defeat an incumbent increased over the same period by a whopping 242 percent in the House (table 3–3 and figure 3–2) and by 101 percent in the Senate (table 3–4). In fact, it took almost as much money to defeat a House incumbent in 1980 as it once took to run a respectable campaign for the Senate in many states—about $350,000. The largest two-year increase came between 1976 and 1978, when House expenditures increased 44 percent (table 3–1), Senate expenditures increased 70 percent (table 3–2), and the CPI went up only 15 percent. In the most expensive House races, there were only 10 House candidates who spent $200,000 or more in 1974, 31 in 1976, 128 in 1978, and 205 in 1980 (figure 3–1).

Although campaign costs went up, not all candidates fared equally well with their fund rasing. Challengers facing safe House and Senate incumbents (those who won with 60 percent or more) had a particularly hard time, and the gap between incumbents and challengers in those races has been widening almost every year (tables 3–3 and 3–4). In fact, if one includes some assumed figures for low-budget nonfilers, the money raised by challengers to safe incumbents in 1980 just about equaled 1978 levels, in nominal dollars, despite a 26 percent rate of inflation (table 3–3, notes b and c). Once one eliminates these lopsided races, however, the much-vaunted fund-raising advantage of incumbents all but disappears.

Structural shifts in the sources of funds have been just as important as the increase in campaign spending. Small contributors still make up the bread and butter of campaign finance, particularly when one includes small contributions channeled through intermediary organizations. Three kinds of intermediary organizations have become increasingly important in recent years: political parties, political action committees (PACs) that contribute directly to candidates, and PACs that make independent expenditures. Independent expenditures are treated in more detail below.

The national committees of the two major political parties modestly increased the proportional importance of their direct contributions to and expenditures on behalf of congressional candidates in the 1974–1980 period (table 3–5). These overall figures, however, hide some significant party differences. Democratic party committee contributions, or "441a(d)" expenditures, accounted for only 2 percent of the $61.4 million (including party expenditures) raised by 1980 Democratic general election candidates for the House, but Republican committees accounted for 9 percent of the $64.6 million raised by Republican candidates. (For a definition and description of 441a[d] party expenditures, see table 3–5, note a.) The data are even more dramatic for the Senate: Democratic committees contributed or spent only 4 percent of the $42.0 million raised by Democratic general election candidates for the Senate, but Republican committees accounted for 15 percent of their candidates' $41.2 million. Moreover, a full discussion of the role of the national party committees would have to include the many millions of "soft" dollars spent by the Republican party on national advertising, candidate training, polls, state and local party registration, getting out the vote, and more.[1]

PAC money cumulatively outweighed even the Republican party's contributions and expenditures in 1980 House and Senate races. When one realizes the myriad contradictory influences that these PAC funds represented, however, one is tempted to conclude that even for the House, the party may well have been the single most important factor in the Republican campaign finance picture. Given the present state of Democratic party fund raising, Democratic candidates cannot expect to receive a similar level of assistance from their party for at least several more years. Table 3–6 details political party financial activity from 1976 through 1980 (see also figure 3–3).

Political action committee contributions continued to increase in 1980, both absolutely and as a proportion of total campaign funds. PACs accounted for 22 percent of all House funds and 15 percent of all Senate funds in 1976, the first year the campaign laws simplified PAC formation and prohibited individual contributions of more than $1,000. By 1980 the figures were 28 percent for the House and 19 percent for the Senate (table 3–5). The number of PACs, particularly corporate PACs, has been growing steadily (table 3–7, figure 3–4), as has their financial activity (table 3–8). Labor PACs grew significantly between 1978 and 1980 (tables 3–9 and 3–10), but their rate of growth was dwarfed by both corporate and nonconnected PACs. (The Federal Election Commission's "nonconnected" grouping includes most of the ideological and single-issue PACs.) Labor and corporate contributions grew in proportion to their expenditures. A comparison of contributions (table 3–10) with expenditures (table 3–9) for nonconnected groups, however, makes their independent spending strategy and direct-mail fund-raising costs stand out clearly.

Tables 3–11 through 3–15 detail PAC contributions to candidates, by type of PAC and candidates' status as incumbents, challengers, or contestants for open seats. The last four of these tables also give the percentage of candidates in each category. These percentages can be used as a base line for comparisons, because they

---

1. For more on the Republican party's role, see Thomas E. Mann and Norman J. Ornstein, "The Republican Surge in Congress," in Austin Ranney, ed., *The American Elections of 1980* (Washington, D.C.: American Enterprise Institute, 1981), pp. 263-302; Xandra Kayden, "The Nationalizing of the Party System," in Michael J. Malbin, ed., *Parties, Interest Groups, and Campaign Finance Laws* (Washington, D.C.: American Enterprise Institute, 1980), pp. 257-82; and David Adamany, "Political Parties in the 1980 Election," in Michael J. Malbin, *Parties, Interest Groups, and Money in the 1980 Elections* (Washington, D.C.: American Enterprise Institute, forthcoming).

show how funds would be distributed if they were contributed randomly. Deviations from random distribution can then be used as a basis for making inferences about the political strategy of a giver (or a group of givers). Compare, for example, the contributions given to Republican challengers by corporations in two different elections. In 1977–1978 House and Senate races (tables 3–12 and 3–13) and in 1979–1980 House races (table 3–14), corporate committees were cautious, giving Republican challengers only about as much as one might expect from a random distribution. The picture was different in 1979–1980 Senate races, however, as corporate PACs gave heavily to unseat Democratic incumbents (table 3–14). Labor committees, in contrast, were much more worried about protecting Senate incumbents in 1979–1980 than they were in the 1977–1978 Senate races.

Tables 3–16 and 3–17 list the largest PACs for 1972–1980 by amount of contribution and by adjusted expenditures. The lists are interesting both because of the change in composition over time (note the declining importance of dairy money) and because of the ever-increasing amounts needed to make the top ten.

Tables 3–18 through 3–21 deal with independent expenditures. According to the Supreme Court's 1976 decision in *Buckley* v. *Valeo*, the First Amendment prohibits Congress from infringing a person's right to spend unlimited amounts of money on behalf of or in opposition to a candidate, as long as the expenditures are truly independent. (For a full definition of "independent," see note to table 3–18.) The decision produced little before the 1979–1980 election cycle. Less than $400,000 was spent independently on House and Senate races in 1976 and barely $300,000 in 1978. (Another $1.6 million was spent on the 1976 presidential campaign.) The picture changed dramatically in 1979–1980, with the $1 million negative advertising campaign run by the National Conservative Political Action Committee (NCPAC) against six incumbent Democratic senators. NCPAC's spending accounted for more than 60 percent of all independent expenditures in 1980 Senate races. The amount of money spent independently on Senate races in 1980 was about ten times the amount spent in 1978. Even without NCPAC, spending would have more than tripled in the Senate and more than quadrupled in the House between 1978 and 1980. These figures can be expected to increase again in 1982, as NCPAC is joined by negative advertising groups on the other side of the political spectrum. In the 1980 presidential race, independent expenditures topped $13.7 million, more than eight times the level of 1976.

The tables on independent expenditures show the levels of negative and positive independent spending by office and party (table 3–18), the candidates most affected (table 3–19), and the biggest independent spenders (tables 3–20 and 3–21). As the last tables show clearly, there are still plenty of ways in the postreform campaign world for fat cats to spend political money, if they know how to do it.

TABLE 3–1

HOUSE CAMPAIGN EXPENDITURES, 1974–1980
(dollars)

	1974	1976	1978	1980
All candidates				
Total expenditures	44,051,125	60,046,006	86,736,548	115,960,213
Mean expenditure	54,384	73,316	108,829	157,128
	(N = 810)	(N = 819)	(N = 797)	(N = 738)[a]
Mean, Democrats	53,993	74,563	110,114	147,463
	(N = 434)	(N = 429)	(N = 416)	(N = 387)
Mean, Republicans	54,835	71,945	107,426	167,784
	(N = 376)	(N = 390)	(N = 381)	(N = 351)
Incumbents				
Mean, all incumbents	56,539	79,398	111,557	165,502
	(N = 382)	(N = 382)	(N = 377)	(N = 391)
Mean, Democrats	38,743	73,322	103,559	159,382
	(N = 218)	(N = 254)	(N = 249)	(N = 245)
Mean, Republicans	80,339	91,456	127,115	175,771[b]
	(N = 163)	(N = 128)	(N = 128)	(N = 146)
Challengers				
Mean, all challengers	40,015	50,795	72,373	128,293[a]
	(N = 323)	(N = 335)	(N = 309)	(N = 264)
Mean, Democrats	59,266	46,330	71,597	99,428[a]
	(N = 162)	(N = 122)	(N = 109)	(N = 99)
Mean, Republicans	20,644	53,352	73,153	145,613[a]
	(N = 161)	(N = 213)	(N = 200)	(N = 165)
Open seats				
Mean, all open seat candidates	90,426	124,506	201,049	209,393
	(N = 106)	(N = 102)	(N = 111)	(N = 83)
Mean, Democrats	99,743	145,497	211,872	190,145
	(N = 54)	(N = 53)	(N = 58)	(N = 43)
Mean, Republicans	80,751	101,802	189,205	230,085
	(N = 52)	(N = 49)	(N = 53)	(N = 40)

NOTE: Includes primary and general election expenditures for general election candidates only.

a. At least eighty-four major party candidates were on the ballot in 1980 general elections but were not included in the Federal Election Commission's final report on 1979-1980 financial activity, probably because of the 1979 amendments to the Federal Election Campaign Act, which exempted low-budget campaigns (under $5,000) from reporting requirements. Because of these nonfilers, the data for 1980 are not strictly comparable to those for previous years, particularly the data for challengers. The eighty-four major party nonfilers included four running for open seats, two incumbents, and seventy-eight challengers (forty-six Republicans and thirty-two Democrats). If we assume arbitrarily that each of the seventy-eight spent $5,000, the mean for all challengers would drop from $128,293 to $100,174, for Republican challengers from $145,613 to $114,958, and for Democratic challengers from $99,428 to $76,361.

b. If one excludes Representative Robert Dornan's $1.9 million expenditure in California's twenty-seventh district, this figure would be $163,555.

SOURCES: For 1974: Common Cause, *1974 Congressional Campaign Finances,* vol. 2, Washington, D.C., 1976. For 1976: Federal Election Commission, *Disclosure Series No. 9* (House of Representatives Campaigns), September 1977. For 1978: Federal Election Commission, *Reports on Financial Activity, 1977-78,* Interim Report no. 5 (U.S. Senate and House Campaigns), June 1979. For 1980: Federal Election Commission, *Reports on Financial Activity, 1979-80,* Final Report (U.S. Senate and House Campaigns), January 1982.

FIGURE 3–1
HOUSE CANDIDATES WITH NET EXPENDITURES GREATER Than $200,000, 1974–1980

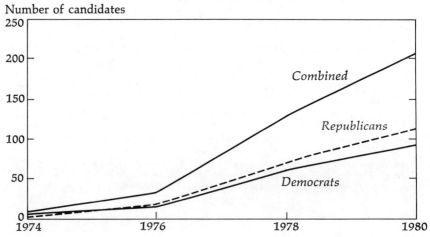

SOURCES: For 1974-1978; John F. Bibby, Thomas E. Mann, and Norman Ornstein, *Vital Statistics on Congress, 1980* (Washington, D.C.: American Enterprise Institute, 1980), pp. 26, 31, 35. For 1980: Federal Election Commission, *Report on Financial Activity, 1979-80,* Final Report (U.S. Senate and House Compaigns).

TABLE 3–2
Senate Campaign Expenditures, 1974–1980
(dollars)

	1974	1976	1978	1980
All candidates				
Total expenditures	28,436,308	38,108,745	64,694,516	70,982,667
Mean expenditure	437,482	595,449	951,390	1,075,495
	(n = 65)	(n = 64)[a]	(n = 68)	(n = 66)
Mean, Democrats	487,775	569,902	762,831	1,140,390
	(n = 34)	(n = 33)	(n = 35)	(n = 33)
Mean, Republicans	382,343	616,635	1,151,377	1,010,599
	(n = 31)	(n = 30)	(n = 33)	(n = 33)
Incumbents				
Mean, all incumbents	555,714	623,809[a]	1,341,942[b]	1,265,644
	(n = 25)	(n = 25)	(n = 22)	(n = 24)
Mean, Democrats	525,766	503,111	618,211	1,310,594
	(n = 15)	(n = 17)	(n = 11)	(n = 18)
Mean, Republicans	600,636	891,342	2,065,674[b]	1,130,791
	(n = 10)	(n = 7)	(n = 11)	(n = 6)
Challengers				
Mean, all challengers	332,579	452,275	697,766	842,547
	(n = 22)	(n = 23)	(n = 21)	(n = 24)
Mean, Democrats	390,297	645,441	830,282	557,006
	(n = 10)	(n = 8)	(n = 11)	(n = 6)
Mean, Republicans	284,480	349,253	551,999	937,727
	(n = 12)	(n = 15)	(n = 10)	(n = 18)
Open seats				
Mean, all open seat candidates	401,484	756,951	820,787	1,132,560
	(n = 18)	(n = 16)	(n = 25)	(n = 18)
Mean, Democrats	532,691	636,295	828,127	1,188,902
	(n = 9)	(n = 8)	(n = 13)	(n = 9)
Mean, Republicans	270,277	877,606	812,836	1,076,217
	(n = 9)	(n = 8)	(n = 12)	(n = 9)

Note: Includes primary and general election expenditures for general election candidates only.

a. Includes one incumbent independent, Senator Harry F. Byrd of Virginia, $802,928.

b. These figures include the $7.5 million Helms reelection campaign in North Carolina. Without it the Republican mean would be $1,526,145, and the mean for all incumbents would be $1,050,560.

Sources: For 1974: Common Cause, *1974 Congressional Campaign Finances*, vol. 1, Washington, D.C., 1976. For 1976: Federal Election Commission, *Disclosure Series No. 6* (Senatorial Campaigns), April 1977. For 1978: Federal Election Commission, *Reports on Financial Activity, 1977-78*, Interim Report no. 5 (U.S. Senate and House Campaigns). For 1980: Federal Election Commission, *Reports on Financial Activity, 1979-80*, Final Report (U.S. Senate and House Campaigns).

TABLE 3–3

Mean House Expenditures by Election Outcome, 1974–1980
(dollars)

	1974	1976	1978	1980
Incumbent won with 60% or more[a]				
Democratic incumbent	35,146	56,937	85,478	118,323
	(N = 194)	(N = 185)	(N = 184)	(N = 165)
Republican challenger	12,481	24,865	30,404	53,065[b]
	(N = 137)	(N = 144)	(N = 135)	(N = 88)
Republican incumbent	60,593	77,855	107,046	137,093
	(N = 57)	(N = 87)	(N = 103)	(N = 117)
Democratic challenger	25,891	26,606	36,035	48,557[c]
	(N = 56)	(N = 81)	(N = 84)	(N = 69)
Difference between incumbents and challengers[d]	32,023	42,968	68,917	104,600[e]
	(N = 192)	(N = 226)	(N = 219)	(N = 155)
Incumbent won with less than 60%				
Democratic incumbent	68,513	119,440	145,065	221,983
	(N = 20)	(N = 62)	(N = 51)	(N = 51)
Republican challenger	66,405	109,079	144,348	199,784
	(N = 20)	(N = 62)	(N = 51)	(N = 51)
Republican incumbent	83,632	104,465	204,674	336,046[f]
	(N = 70)	(N = 36)	(N = 20)	(N = 26)
Democratic challenger	63,134	77,075	187,291	195,288
	(N = 70)	(N = 36)	(N = 20)	(N = 26)
Difference between incumbents and challengers[d]	16,747	16,616	5,412	62,231[g]
	(N = 90)	(N = 98)	(N = 71)	(N = 77)
Incumbent was defeated				
Democratic incumbent	64,191	97,874	189,994	285,636
	(N = 4)	(N = 7)	(N = 14)	(N = 28)
Republican challenger	71,404	144,883	226,028	341,498
	(N = 4)	(N = 7)	(N = 14)	(N = 27)
Republican incumbent	105,203	234,435	230,323	295,169
	(N = 36)	(N = 5)	(N = 5)	(N = 3)
Democratic challenger	103,661	144,491	192,038	353,855
	(N = 36)	(N = 5)	(N = 5)	(N = 4)

TABLE 3–3 (continued)

	1974	1976	1978	1980
Difference between incumbents and challengers[d]	1,185 (N = 40)	10,055[h] (N = 12)	−16,476 (N = 19)	−74,032 (N = 31)

a. Percentage of vote received by two leading candidates.

b. For reasons explained in table 3-2, note a, figures do not include a significant number of major party nonfilers. If one assumes arbitrarily that each of the forty-six nonfiling Republican challengers spent $5,000, this figure drops to $36,661.

c. Assuming each of the thirty-two nonfiling Democratic challengers spent $5,000 (see note b) would reduce this figure to $34,757.

d. Includes only races contested in general election, both candidates filing.

e. Making the assumptions indicated in notes b and c, with an equivalent assumption for two Democratic incumbent nonfilers, changes this number to $98,953 for 234 races.

f. This figure includes Representative Robert Dornan's $1.9 million expenditure in California's twenty-seventh district. Without Dornan the mean would be $272,000.

g. Eliminating the Dornan race (note f) would reduce this figure to $36,943.

h. If the 1976 race in Texas's twenty-second district between Republican Ron Paul and Democrat Bob Gummage is omitted, this figure becomes −16,704.

SOURCES: For 1974: Common Cause, *1974 Congressional Campaign Finances*, vol. 2. For 1976: Federal Election Commission, *Disclosure Series No. 9* (House of Representatives Campaigns), September 1977. For 1978: Federal Election Commission, *Report on Financial Activity, 1977-78*, Interim Report no. 5 (U.S. Senate and House Campaigns). For 1980: Federal Election Commission, *Report on Financial Activity, 1979-80*, Final Report (U.S. Senate and House Campaigns).

FIGURE 3–2
MEAN EXPENDITURES OF HOUSE CHALLENGERS WHO BEAT INCUMBENTS,
1974–1980

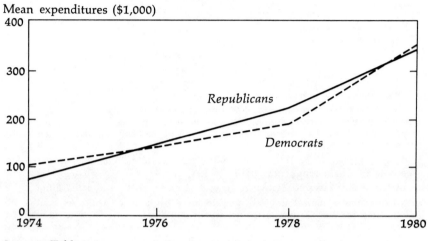

SOURCE: Table 3-3.

TABLE 3–4

Mean Senate Expenditures by Election Outcome, 1974–1980
(dollars)

	1974	1976	1978	1980
Incumbent won with 60% or more[a]				
Democratic incumbent	447,234 (N = 11)	340,362 (N = 11)	559,046 (N = 4)	1,031,371 (N = 5)
Republican challenger	222,955 (N = 8)	171,997 (N = 9)	56,233 (N = 3)	332,404 (N = 5)
Republican incumbent	—	—	318,739 (N = 3)	1,075,038 (N = 4)
Democratic challenger	—	—	38,458 (N = 3)	265,821 (N = 4)
Difference between incumbents and challengers[b]	299,321 (N = 8)	220,202 (N = 9)	341,749 (N = 6)	747,967 (N = 9)
Incumbent won with less than 60%				
Democratic incumbent	741,729 (N = 4)	1,237,910 (N = 1)	586,055 (N = 2)	796,983 (N = 4)
Republican challenger	407,531 (N = 4)	665,058 (N = 1)	332,537 (N = 2)	727,616 (N = 4)
Republican incumbent	497,945 (N = 10)	320,239 (N = 3)	3,133,293[c] (N = 6)	1,242,299 (N = 2)
Democratic challenger	254,374 (N = 10)	282,441 (N = 4)	1,212,929 (N = 6)	1,139,376 (N = 2)
Difference between incumbents and challengers[b]	314,376 (N = 14)	241,346[d] (N = 5)	1,503,653[e] (N = 8)	80,553 (N = 6)
Incumbent was defeated				
Democratic incumbent	—	714,201 (N = 5)	678,406 (N = 5)	1,693,990 (N = 9)
Republican challenger	—	605,153 (N = 5)	937,244 (N = 5)	1,367,400 (N = 9)
Republican incumbent	513,456 (N = 2)	1,319,670 (N = 4)	1,483,203 (N = 2)	—
Democratic challenger	679,614 (N = 2)	1,008,440 (N = 4)	870,079 (N = 2)	—

(Table continues)

67

TABLE 3-4 (continued)

	1974	1976	1978	1980
Difference between incumbents and challengers[b] races)[b]	−166,158 (N = 2)	198,906 (N = 9)	−9,706 (N = 7)	326,591 (N = 9)

a. Percentage of the vote received by two leading candidates.

b. Includes only races contested in general election, both candidates filing.

c. If one excludes the 1978 race between Republican Senator Jesse Helms of North Carolina and his challenger, John Ingram, this figure becomes $2,267,758.

d. 1976 Senate incumbents who won with less than 60 percent included one independent, Senator Harry F. Byrd of Virginia, who spent $802,928.

e. If the Helms-Ingram race is excluded, this figure becomes $690,335.

Sources: For 1974: Common Cause, *1974 Congressional Campaign Finances*, vol. 1. For 1976: Federal Election Commission, *Disclosure Series No. 6* (Senatorial Campaigns), April 1977. For 1978: Federal Election Commission, *Reports on Financial Activity, 1977-78*, Interim Report no. 5 (U.S. Senate and House Campaigns). For 1980: Federal Election Commission, *Reports on Financial Activity, 1979-80*, Final Report (U.S. Senate and House Campaigns).

TABLE 3–5

FUNDING SOURCES FOR CANDIDATES IN HOUSE AND SENATE
GENERAL ELECTIONS, BY PARTY, 1974–1980

	Amount Raised by Candidates and Party Expenditures on Behalf of Candidates ($ millions)[a]	Percentage Distribution			
		Non-party PACs	Party (contributions plus 441a[d] expenditures)[a]	Individual contributions, $55 +	Other (individuals to $500, candidate to self, and unrepaid loans)[b]
House					
1974[c]					
All candidates	45.7	17	4	15	64
Democrats	23.9	22	1	16	61
Republicans	21.7	10	7	15	68
1976					
All candidates	66.1	22	8	11	59
Democrats	35.1	27	4	11	58
Republicans	30.5	17	13	11	59
1978[d]					
All candidates	93.6	24	7	12	57
Democrats	48.7	27	3	13	57
Republicans	44.2	22	11	12	55
1980					
All candidates	127.1	28	6	15	51
Democrats	61.4	32	2	17	49
Republicans	64.6	25	9	13	53
Senate					
1974[c]					
All candidates	28.2	11	6	27	56
Democrats	16.2	13	2	27	58
Republicans	11.6	7	13	28	52
1976					
All candidates	39.2	15	4	27	54
Democrats	19.5	19	2	32	47
Republicans	18.8	11	6	22	61

(Table continues)

TABLE 3–5   (continued)

	Amount Raised by Candidates and Party Expenditures on Behalf of Candidates ($ millions)[a]	Percentage Distribution			
		Non-party PACs	Party (contributions plus 441a[d] expenditures)[a]	Individual contributions, $500 +	Other (individuals to $500, candidate to self, and unrepaid loans)[b]
1978[d]					
All candidates	68.9	13	6	21	60
Democrats	27.8	14	3	27	56
Republicans	40.6	12	8	17	63
1980					
All candidates	83.5	19	9	24	48
Democrats	42.0	18	4	27	51
Republicans	41.2	21	15	21	43

a. Under U.S. Code, Title 2, Sec. 441a(d), national party committees are allowed to spend money on behalf of federal candidates in addition to the money they may contribute directly to the candidates. The limits on 441a(d) expenditures are as follows: (a) for Senate candidates and House candidates in states with only one representative, two cents times the state's voting-age population, or $20,000 in 1975 dollars adjusted for inflation, whichever is greater; (b) for all other House candidates, $10,000 in 1975 dollars adjusted for inflation. In 1978 the $10,000 adjusted for inflation equaled $12,290, in 1980 it was $14,700, and in 1982 it will be $18,400. State parties, including subordinate local committees, were also allowed to spend these amounts on behalf of Senate and House candidates. Court decisions upheld a Republican party practice under which state committees designated national party committees as their agents, and the national party committees spent up to the combined national and state party limits, or four cents times the voting-age population in most Senate races.

Combining state and national party contributions and 441a(d) limits, the maximum amount of help a House candidate could receive from party committees in 1980 was $59,440—more than the average House campaign cost in 1974 (see table 3-1). The figure is derived as follows: $10,000 each ($5,000 in the primary and $5,000 in the general election) from the national party, congressional campaign committee, and state or local party, $14,720 in 441a(d) expenditures by the national or congressional committee, and another $14,720 in expenditures from state or local committees. In 1982, when the 441a(d) limit is $18,440, the total can climb to $66,880 per candidate. Senate candidates may receive a total of $17,500 in contributions from the national committee and senatorial campaign committee, another $10,000 from state or local committees, and 441a(d) expenditures as described above. In 1980 the combined limits ranged from a low of $86,380 to a maximum of $997,548 for California. In 1982 the lowest limit will be $101,260. The limit in California will increase because of inflation and population growth to $1,399,248.

The "amount raised" column includes the sum of what general election candidates raised from January 1 of the odd-numbered year preceding an election through December 31 of the election year plus 441a(d) party expenditures on behalf of those candidates. The 441a(d) expenditures for each year were as follows: 1974, none; 1976, House, $330,353 (Republicans $329,853, Democrats $500), Senate, $118,335 (Republicans $113,976, Democrats $4,359) (in 1976 the FEC reported that the Democratic National Committee spent an additional $222,705 on behalf of congressional candidates; this money is not included in the table because the FEC disclosure series did not indicate how the money was divided between Senate and House candidates); 1978, House, $1,319,971 (Republicans $1,247,079, Democrats $72,892), Senate, $2,953,098 (Republicans $2,723,880, Democrats $229,218); 1980, House, $2,460,094 (Republicans $2,203,748, Democrats $256,346), Senate $6,567,670 (Republicans $5,434,758, Democrats $1,132,912).

b. "Other" includes contributions from individuals of less than $500, contributions from the candidate to himself or herself, unpaid loans, and, for the 1974 Senate races, some funds whose sources were not identified. Because of confusion over unpaid loans, the FEC says that it cannot specify loan amounts or candidate self-financing and that its numbers from 1976 and 1978 are unreliable. This also affects the data for small individual contributions, many of which need not be reported individually, because those figures had been derived by subtracting all other categories from the total.

c. The figures for 1974 are only for candidates who were opposed in the general election.

d. Louisiana instituted a two-step election process in 1978 in which candidates of all parties run against each other in a September primary. If no candidate wins 50 percent or more of the vote at that time, the top two candidates run against each other in November. In these data, candidates in a September Louisiana primary are considered "general election candidates" when the September balloting produces a clear winner with more than half the total vote.

SOURCES: 1974: Gary C. Jacobson, *Money in Congressional Elections* (New Haven: Yale University Press, 1980); and idem, "The Pattern of Campaign Contributions to Candidates for the U.S. House of Representatives, 1972-78," in *An Analysis of the Federal Election Campaign Act, 1972-78: A Report by the Campaign Finance Study Group to the Committee on House Administration, U.S. House of Representatives* (Cambridge, Mass.: Institute of Politics, Harvard University, May 1979), pp. 2-19 and 2-14. For 1976: Federal Election Commission, *Disclosure Series No. 4* (National Party Committees), *No. 6* (Senate Campaigns), and *No. 9* (House Campaigns). For 1978: Federal Election Commission, *Report on Financial Activity, 1977-78*, Interim Report no. 5 (U.S. Senate and House Campaigns). For 1980: Federal Election Commission, *Report on Financial Activity, 1979-80*, Final Report (U.S. Senate and House Campaigns).

TABLE 3–6

Political Party Financial Activity, 1976–1980
(dollars)

	Adjusted Receipts	Adjusted Disbursements	Contributions to Presidential, Senate, and House Candidates	Expenditures on Behalf of Presidential, Senate, and House Candidates
1976				
Democratic				
National committee	13,095,630	12,516,979	22,050	3,055,644
Senatorial	1,017,454	971,562	375,237	4,359
Congressional	937,717	1,011,157	423,200	500
Conventions, other national	3,164,573	3,062,675	0	0
State/local	n.a.	n.a.	n.a.	n.a.
Total Democratic	18,215,374	17,562,373	820,487	3,060,503
Republican				
National committee	29,118,930	26,679,143	1,871,726	1,442,773
Senatorial	1,774,815	2,010,629	445,902	113,976
Congressional	12,207,055	9,243,195	2,071,525	329,853
Conventions, other national	2,605,088	2,143,220	11,343	0
State/local	n.a.	n.a.	n.a.	n.a.
Total Republican	45,705,888	40,076,187	4,400,496	1,886,602
1978				
Democratic				
National committee	11,314,008	11,455,639	64,307	68,822
Senatorial	269,981	893,773	427,000	0
Congressional	2,766,963	2,118,161	537,438	0
Conventions, other national	3,324,519	3,428,481	403,502	0
State/local	8,688,999	8,994,213	433,337	329,765
Total Democratic	26,364,470	26,890,267	1,865,584	398,587
Republican				
National committee	34,221,058	36,016,600	905,244	336,981

TABLE 3–6   (continued)

	Adjusted Receipts	Adjusted Disbursements	Contributions to Presidential, Senate, and House Candidates	Expenditures on Behalf of Presidential, Senate, and House Candidates
Senatorial	10,882,480	11,107,961	456,110	2,599,290
Congressional	14,062,070	15,695,690	1,817,424	839,421
Conventions, other national	4,400,216	2,330,882	598,382	0
State/local	20,960,029	20,728,829	745,191	579,974
Total Republican	84,525,853	85,879,962	4,522,351	4,355,666
		1980		
Democratic				
National committee	15,418,300	15,150,984	41,051	3,942,526
Senatorial	1,653,849	1,618,162	481,500	589,316
Congressional	2,864,088	2,828,184	614,097	34,686
Conventions, other national	8,147,837	6,631,517	132,200	0
State/local	9,103,520	8,754,177	384,358	375,660
Total Democratic	37,187,594	34,983,024	1,653,206	4,942,188
Republican				
National committee	77,838,238	75,821,719	844,455	5,352,269
Senatorial	23,308,963	21,211,482	414,893	5,025,802
Congressional	20,287,961	34,790,731	2,005,663	1,229,110
Conventions, other national	6,031,367	6,080,735	482,159	0
State/local	33,781,069	32,545,199	781,207	837,292
Total Republican	161,247,598	170,449,866	4,528,377	12,444,473

NOTE: n.a. = not available.

SOURCES: For 1976: Federal Election Commission, *Disclosure Series No. 4* (National Party Committee Receipts and Expenditures, Democratic and Republican, 1976 Campaign), November 1977. For 1978: Federal Election Commission, *Reports on Financial Activity, 1977-78* (Party and Non-Party Political Committees), vol. 1, summary tables, Final Report, April 1980. For 1980: Federal Election Commission, *Reports on Financial Activity, 1979-80* (Party and Non-Party Political Committees), vol. 1, summary tables, Final Report, January 1982.

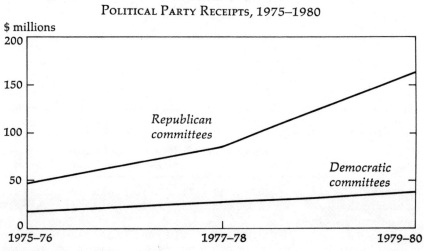

FIGURE 3–3
POLITICAL PARTY RECEIPTS, 1975–1980

SOURCE: Table 3-6.

TABLE 3-7

NUMBER OF REGISTERED POLITICAL ACTION COMMITTEES, 1974–1980

	1974	1975	1976	1977	1978	1979	1980
Corporate	89	139	433	550	784	949	1,204
Labor	201	226	224	234	217	240	297
Trade/member-ship/health[a]	318	357	489	438	451	512	574
Nonconnected	—	—	—	110	165	250	378
Cooperative	—	—	—	8	12	17	42
Corporation without stock	—	—	—	20	24	32	56
Total	608	722	1,146	1,360	1,653	2,000	2,551

NOTE: Data as of December 31 for every year except 1975 (November 24).

a. Includes all noncorporate and nonlabor PACs through December 31, 1976.

SOURCE: U.S. Federal Election Commission, "Election Unit Announces Drop in PAC Growth," press release, July 17, 1981.

FIGURE 3-4

GROWTH OF NONPARTY POLITICAL ACTION COMMITTEES, 1974–1980

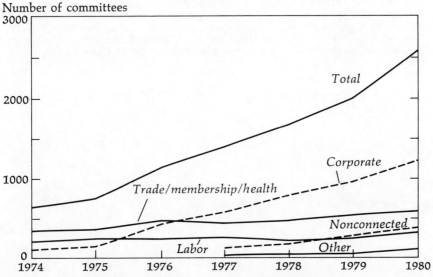

SOURCE: U.S. Federal Election Commission, *FEC Record*, March 1981, p. 2.

TABLE 3–8

FINANCIAL ACTIVITY OF POLITICAL ACTION COMMITTEES, 1972–1980
(dollars)

Election Cycle[a]	Adjusted Receipts[b]	Adjusted Expenditures[b]	Contributions to Congressional Candidates
1972	n.a.	19,168,000	8,500,000[c]
1974	n.a.	25,000,000[d]	12,526,586
1976	54,045,588	52,894,630	22,571,912
1978	79,956,291	77,412,860	35,187,215
1980	137,728,528	131,153,384	58,356,181

NOTE: n.a. = not available. All data are for full election cycle.

a. The periods covered by the election cycles vary. Data for 1972 are limited for the period before April 7, 1972, the effective date for disclosure under the Federal Election Campaign Act of 1971. Until then campaign finance disclosure was governed by the Federal Corrupt Practices Act of 1925, under which much activity went unreported. Data for 1974 cover September 1, 1973, to December 31, 1974. Data for 1976 cover January 1, 1975, to December 31, 1976. Data for 1978 cover January 1, 1977, to December 31, 1978. Data for 1980 cover January 1, 1979, to December 31, 1980.

b. Adjusted receipts and expenditures exclude funds transferred between affiliated committees.

c. Excludes contributions to candidates defeated in primaries.

d. This is a rough estimate and does not correspond to the total in table 3-9.

SOURCES: For 1972-1978: Joseph E. Cantor, *Political Action Committees: Their Evolution and Growth and Their Implications for the Political System*, U.S. Library of Congress, Congressional Research Service, Report No. 81-246 GOV, November 6, 1981, p. 67. For 1980: Federal Election Commission, *Reports on Financial Activity, 1979-80* (Party and Non-Party Political Committees), vol. 1, summary tables, Final Report.

TABLE 3–9

ADJUSTED EXPENDITURES OF POLITICAL ACTION COMMITTEES BY CATEGORY, 1972–1980
(millions of dollars)

Type of PAC	1972	1974[a]	1976	1978	1980
Labor	8.5	11.0	17.5	18.6	25.1
Business-related[b]	8.0	8.1	—	—	—
Corporate	c	c	5.8	15.2	31.4
Trade/membership/health	c	c	d	23.8	32.0
Nonconnected[e]	2.6	0.8	d	17.4	38.6
Other[f]	—	1.1	29.6	2.4	4.0
Total[g]	19.2	20.9	52.9	77.4	131.2

NOTE: Adjusted expenditures exclude transfers of funds between affiliated committees.

a. Data for 1974 do not correspond with those in table 3-8, which reflects an estimated amount, because the data in this table were thought to be low.

b. This category is based on a large assumption that the majority of PACs it encompasses do indeed have a basically probusiness orientation. It is included here for the purpose of listing the data for 1972 and 1974, before the specific breakdowns were devised by the FEC for the corporate and other categories, and it is only roughly comparable to the combined corporate and trade/membership/health data in 1978 and 1980. For 1972 it includes PACs listed by the Citizens Research Foundation as business/professional, dairy, education, health, and rural; for 1974 it includes those PACs grouped by Common Cause under the headings of business/professional, health, and agriculture/dairy. Most of these PACs would today fall into the corporate and trade/membership/health categories used by the FEC, although some would be scattered in the nonconnected, cooperative, and corporation without stock categories.

c. Included in business-related.

d. Included in other.

e. For 1972 and 1974 this represents spending by ideological PACs, as grouped by the Citizens Research Foundation (1972) or Common Cause (1974). After 1976 it corresponds directly to the FEC category by that name (which is dominated by the ideological groups).

f. This is a catchall category, for which only the 1978 and 1980 figures are comparable to each other. For 1974 this represents PACs grouped as "miscellaneous" by Common Cause and includes such groups as the NEA (and affiliates), environmentalists, and some cooperatives. For 1976 it includes all PACs now grouped by the FEC as trade/membership/health, nonconnected, cooperative, and corporation without stock. For 1978 and 1980, it combines the FEC categories of cooperatives and corporations without stock.

g. Figures may not add to totals because of rounding.

SOURCES: For 1972-1978: Cantor, *Political Action Committees*, pp. 83-84. For 1980: Federal Election Commission, *Reports on Financial Activity, 1979-80* (Party and Non-Party Political Committees), vol. 1, summary tables, Final Report.

TABLE 3–10

CONTRIBUTIONS TO CONGRESSIONAL CANDIDATES OF POLITICAL ACTION COMMITTEES BY CATEGORY, 1972–1980
(millions of dollars)

Type of PAC	1972	1974	1976	1978	1980
Labor	3.6	6.3	8.2	10.3	13.9
Business-related[a]	2.7	4.4	10.0	—	—
Corporate	—	—	—	9.8	20.5
Trade/membership/ health	—	—	—	11.3	16.7
Nonconnected[b]	—	0.7	1.5	2.8	5.1
Other[c]	2.2	1.0	2.8	1.0	2.1
Total[d]	8.5	12.5	22.6	35.2	58.4

NOTE: All data are for full election cycle, except for 1972, where primary losers are excluded.

a. This encompasses the Common Cause categories for business, health, and, in 1976, lawyers. This category is included here for the purpose of listing the data for 1972-1976, before the specific breakdowns were devised by the FEC for the corporate and other categories, and it is based on the assumption that the majority of PACs it includes have a basically probusiness orientation. It is only roughly comparable to the combined corporate and trade/membership/health groups in 1978 and 1980, but most of the business-related PACs would fall into those two FEC categories (some would be scattered in the nonconnected, cooperative, and corporation without stock groups).

b. For 1974 and 1976 the nonconnected category, as defined by the FEC, correlates with the ideological group used by Common Cause for those two years. Most of the ideological PACs are today listed in the nonconnected group, but the latter also includes PACs that are not ideological. Thus the data for 1974 and 1976 are not exactly comparable to those for 1978 and 1980, in view of the different standards applied to the nonconnected and the ideological groups. (Ideological PACs in 1972 were lumped into Common Cause's "miscellaneous" group.)

c. This is a catchall category, in which the earlier figures are only roughly comparable to the later ones. For 1972-1976 the data represent Common Cause's "miscellaneous" category, which included such groups as the NEA (and affiliates), environmentalists, and some cooperatives, and its agriculture/dairy category. In 1972 Common Cause included the ideological PACs under "miscellaneous," before their separate listing in 1974; thus 1972 includes more types of PACs than the 1974 and 1976 data do. For 1978-1980 the "other" data equate directly with the FEC's cooperatives and corporations without stock groups. Thus the data for 1972 are not exactly comparable with those for 1974 and 1976, which, in turn, are not highly comparable with those for 1978-1980. The common thread is the inclusion of the major dairy PACs—ADEPT, C-TAPE, and SPACE—in "other" in all five election years.

d. Figures may not add to totals (which are keyed to table 3-8) because of rounding.

SOURCES: For 1972-1978: Cantor, *Political Action Committees*, pp. 87-88. For 1980: Federal Election Commission, *Reports on Financial Activity, 1979-80* (Party and Non-Party Political Committees), vol. 1, summary tables, Final Report.

TABLE 3–11

POLITICAL ACTION COMMITTEE CONTRIBUTIONS, 1978 AND 1980

Committee Type	1978					1980				
	Number making contributions	Total	Contributions ($ millions)			Number making contributions	Total	Contributions ($ millions)		
			Presidential	Senate	House			Presidential	Senate	House
Labor	215	10.3	0.03	2.8	7.4	240	14.2	0.3	4.2	9.7
Corporation	704	9.8	0.01	3.6	6.1	1,101	21.6	1.1	7.7	12.7
Nonconnected	122	2.8	0.001	0.7	2.1	243	5.2	0.1	1.9	3.2
Trade/member-ship/health	400	11.3	0.001	2.8	8.6	490	17.0	0.3	4.6	12.1
Cooperative	11	0.9	0.009	0.2	0.7	31	1.5	0.04	0.4	1.1
Corporation without stock	22	0.1	0	0.03	0.1	50	0.7	0.04	0.2	0.4
Total	1,474	35.2	0.05	10.1	25.0	2,155	60.2	1.8	19.1	39.9

NOTE: Figures may not add to totals because of rounding.

SOURCES: For 1978: Federal Election Commission, *Reports on Financial Activity, 1977-78* (Party and Non-Party Political Committees), vol. 1, summary tables, Final Report. For 1980: Federal Election Commission, *Reports on Financial Activity, 1979-80* (Party and Non-Party Political Committees), vol. 1, summary tables, Final Report.

TABLE 3–12
POLITICAL ACTION COMMITTEE CONTRIBUTIONS TO HOUSE CANDIDATES, BY CANDIDATES' STATUS, 1977–1978

Percentage Distribution

Committee Type	Amount Contributed (dollars)	Incumbent		Challenger		Open seat		Total[a]
		Democrat	Republican	Democrat	Republican	Democrat	Republican	
Distribution of candidates[b]	(N = 797)	31	17	14	25	7	7	100
Labor	7,462,424	60	3	17	0	19	0	100
Corporate	6,158,069	35	28	2	16	7	12	100
Nonconnected	2,064,062	12	13	4	39	6	25	100
Trade/membership/ health	8,571,697	36	27	2	14	9	12	100
Cooperative	674,698	66	16	2	1	9	6	100
Corporation without stock	95,390	48	13	7	4	17	11	100
Total	25,026,340	42	19	7	12	11	10	100

a. Figures may not add to 100 because of rounding.
b. General election candidates only. Contribution figures are for all House candidates, but most went to general election candidates.
SOURCE: Federal Election Commission, *Reports on Financial Activity, 1977-78* (Party and Non-Party Political Committees), vol. 1, summary tables, Final Report, pp. 149-50.

TABLE 3–13

POLITICAL ACTION COMMITTEE CONTRIBUTIONS TO SENATE CANDIDATES, BY CANDIDATES' STATUS, 1977–1978

Percentage Distribution

Committee Type	Amount Contributed (dollars)	Incumbent		Challenger		Open seat		Total[a]
		Democrat	Republican	Democrat	Republican	Democrat	Republican	
Distribution of candidates[b]	(N = 68)	16	16	16	15	19	18	100
Labor	2,831,336	38	9	33	1	20	1	100
Corporate	3,616,388	15	37	6	20	7	15	100
Nonconnected	732,993	10	19	11	37	4	18	100
Trade/membership/ health	2,751,980	19	32	9	17	10	13	100
Cooperative	202,600	22	21	13	10	20	13	100
Corporation without stock	25,578	16	35	7	16	12	15	100
Total	10,160,875	22	26	15	15	11	11	100

a. Figures may not add to 100 because of rounding.
b. General election candidates only. Contribution figures are for all Senate candidates, but most went to general election candidates.

SOURCE: Federal Election Commission, *Reports on Financial Activity, 1977–78* (Party and Non-Party Political Committees), vol. 1, summary tables, Final Report, pp. 147–48.

TABLE 3–14

Political Action Committee Contributions to House Candidates, by Candidates' Status, 1979–1980

Percentage Distribution

Committee Type	Amount Contributed (dollars)	Incumbent		Challenger		Open seat		Total[a]
		Democrat	Republican	Democrat	Republican	Democrat	Republican	
Distribution of candidates[b]	(n = 738)	34	19	13	23	6	5	100
Labor	9,714,307	67	4	16	0	12	0	100
Corporate	12,743,186	35	32	2	19	2	10	100
Nonconnected[c]	3,183,463	19	14	6	39	5	15	99
Trade/membership/health	12,102,781	37	31	3	16	3	9	100
Cooperative	1,068,527	57	26	2	3	4	9	100
Corporation without stock	407,108	46	29	3	11	3	8	100
Total	39,219,372	43	23	6	15	5	8	100

a. Figures may not add to totals because of rounding.

b. General election candidates only. Contribution figures are for all House candidates, but most went to general election candidates.

c. PACs not connected to other organizations also gave 1 percent of their House contributions to challengers who were neither Democrats nor Republicans.

Source: Federal Election Commission, *Reports on Financial Activity, 1977-78* (Party and Non-Party Political Committees), vol. 1, summary tables, Final Report, pp. 107-8.

TABLE 3-15

POLITICAL ACTION COMMITTEE CONTRIBUTIONS TO SENATE CANDIDATES, BY CANDIDATES' STATUS, 1979–1980

Committee Type	Amount Contributed (dollars)	Incumbent		Challenger		Open seat		Total[a]
		Democrat	Republican	Democrat	Republican	Democrat	Republican	
Distribution of candidates[b]	(N = 66)	27	9	9	27	14	14	100
Labor	4,192,159	65	9	16	1	9	1	100
Corporate	7,731,966	28	18	2	42	2	9	100
Nonconnected	1,927,306	23	7	3	52	2	13	100
Trade/membership/health	4,635,748	39	19	3	28	4	7	100
Cooperative	396,437	63	17	2	9	5	5	100
Corporation without stock	253,193	45	18	3	24	5	6	100
Total	19,136,809	39	15	5	30	4	7	100

Percentage Distribution

a. Figures may not add to 100 because of rounding.
b. General election candidates only. Contribution figures are for all Senate candidates, but most went to general election candidates.
SOURCE: Federal Election Commission, *Reports on Financial Activity, 1979–80* (Party and Non-Party Political Committees), vol. 1, summary tables, Final Report, pp. 105-6.

TABLE 3–16

Top Ten Political Action Committee Contributors to Federal Candidates, 1971–1980
(dollars)

Rank	Committee (and Affiliation)	Contributions
	1971–1972	
1	AFL-CIO COPE Political Contributions Committee (AFL-CIO)	824,301
2	UAW Voluntary Community Action Program (United Auto Workers)	599,183
3	American Medical Political Action Committee (American Medical Association)	473,105
4	Business-Industry Political Action Committee (nonconnected)	428,100
5	National Committee for an Effective Congress (nonconnected)	393,888
6	Committee for Thorough Agricultural Political Education (Associated Milk Producers)	301,865
7	United Steelworkers of America Political Action Fund (United Steelworkers of America)	294,935
8	Agricultural and Dairy Educational Political Trust (Mid-America Dairymen, Inc.)	264,150
9	Seafarers Political Activity Donation (Seafarers International Union of North America)	239,234
10	Trust for Special Political Agricultural Community Education (Dairymen, Inc.)	222,900
	1973–1974	
1	AFL-CIO COPE Political Contributions Committee (AFL-CIO)	1,090,696
2	American Medical Political Action Committee (American Medical Association)	861,052
3	UAW Voluntary Community Action Program (United Auto Workers)	835,958
4	Machinists Non-Partisan Political League (International Association of Machinists)	446,680
5	MEBA Political Action Fund (Marine Engineers Beneficial Association)	391,864
6	United Steelworkers of America Political Action Fund (United Steelworkers of America)	357,975
7	Active Ballot Club (Retail Clerks International Association)	276,055

TABLE 3–16 (continued)

Rank	Committee (and Affiliation)	Contributions
8	Business-Industry Political Action Committee (National Association of Manufacturers)	271,000
9	Realtors Political Action Committee (nonconnected)	248,600
10	Laborers' Political League (Laborers Union/AFL-CIO)	237,400

1975–1976

1	American Medical Political Action Committee (American Medical Association)	1,167,365
2	AFL-CIO COPE Political Contributions Committee (AFL-CIO)	935,723
3	UAW Voluntary Community Action Program (United Auto Workers)	894,930
4	Realtors Political Action Committee (National Association of Realtors)	671,525
5	Committee for Thorough Agricultural Political Education (Associated Milk Producers)	635,939
6	NEA Political Action Committee (National Education Association)	611,492
7	Machinists Non-Partisan Political League (International Association of Machinists)	525,100
8	Agricultural and Dairy Educational Political Trust (Mid-America Dairymen, Inc.)	466,035
9	United Steelworkers of America Political Action Fund (United Steelworkers of America)	464,867
10	Transportation Political Education League (United Transportation Union)	450,006

1977–1978

1	American Medical Political Action Committee (American Medical Association)	1,639,795
2	Realtors Political Action Committee (National Association of Realtors)	1,123,378
3	UAW Voluntary Community Action Program (United Auto Workers)	976,245
4	Automobile and Truck Dealers Election Action Committee (National Automobile Dealers Association)	964,175

(Table continues)

TABLE 3–16 (continued)

Rank	Committee (and Affiliation)	Contributions
5	AFL-CIO COPE Political Contributions Committee (AFL-CIO)	884,441
6	United Steelworkers of America Political Action Fund (United Steelworkers of America)	599,930
7	Transportation Political Education League (United Transportation Union)	559,403
8	Machinists Non-Partisan Political League (International Association of Machinists)	525,410
9	American Dental Political Action Committee (American Dental Association)	510,050
10	CWA-COPE Political Contributions Committee (Communication Workers of America)	471,183
	1979–1980	
1	Realtors Political Action Committee (National Association of Realtors)	1,536,573
2	UAW Voluntary Community Action Program (United Auto Workers)	1,422,731
3	American Medical Political Action Committee (American Medical Association)	1,348,985
4	Automobile and Truck Dealers Election Action Committee (National Automobile Dealers Association)	1,035,276
5	Machinists Non-Partisan Political League (International Association of Machinists and Aerospace Workers)	847,708
6	AFL-CIO COPE Political Contributions Committee (AFL-CIO)	776,577
7	Committee for Thorough Agricultural Political Education (Associated Milk Producers)	738,289
8	Seafarers Political Activity Donation (Seafarers International Union of North America)	685,248
9	United Steelworkers of America Political Action Fund (United Steelworkers of America)	681,370
10	National Association of Life Underwriters PAC (National Association of Life Underwriters)	652,112

SOURCES: For 1972-1978: Cantor, *Political Action Committees*, pp. 94-97. For 1980: Federal Election Commission, "FEC Releases Final PAC Report for the 1979-80 Election Cycle," press release, February 21, 1982.

TABLE 3–17

TOP TEN POLITICAL ACTION COMMITTEES RANKED BY ADJUSTED EXPENDITURES, 1975–1980
(dollars)

Rank	Committee (and Affiliation)	Expenditures
	1975–1976	
1	National Conservative Political Action Committee (nonconnected)	2,878,490
2	Committee for the Survival of a Free Congress (nonconnected)	2,249,451
3	Gun Owners of America Campaign Committee (Gun Owners of America)	2,094,821
4	National Committee for an Effective Congress (nonconnected)	1,298,986
5	American Medical Political Action Committee (American Medical Association)	1,297,296
6	Committee for Thorough Agricultural Political Education (Associated Milk Producers)	1,256,019
7	AFL-CIO COPE Political Contributions Committee (AFL-CIO)	1,197,965
8	UAW Voluntary Community Action Program (United Auto Workers)	1,193,188
9	American Conservative Union Political Action Committee (American Conservative Union)	1,116,016
10	Realtors Political Action Committee (National Association of Realtors)	893,656
	1977–1978	
1	Citizens for the Republic (nonconnected, Reagan committee)	4,509,074
2	National Conservative Political Action Committee (nonconnected)	3,030,408
3	Committee for the Survival of a Free Congress (nonconnected)	2,029,122
4	American Medical Political Action Committee (American Medical Association)	1,879,164
5	Realtors Political Action Committee (National Association of Realtors)	1,805,390
6	Gun Owners of America Campaign Committee (Gun Owners of America)	1,548,075

(Table continues)

TABLE 3–17   (continued)

Rank	Committee (and Affiliation)	Expenditures
7	Automobile and Truck Dealers Election Action Committee (National Automobile Dealers Association)	1,541,761
8	AFL-CIO COPE Political Contributions Committee (AFL-CIO)	1,290,404
9	UAW Voluntary Community Action Program (United Auto Workers)	1,158,673
10	National Committee for an Effective Congress (nonconnected)	1,052,142
	1979–1980	
1	National Conservative Political Action Committee (nonconnected)	7,530,060
2	National Congressional Club (nonconnected)	7,212,754
3	Fund for a Conservative Majority (nonconnected)	3,150,496
4	Realtors Political Action Committee (National Association of Realtors)	2,576,077
5	Citizens for the Republic (nonconnected, Reagan committee)	2,384,426
6	UAW Voluntary Community Action Program (United Auto Workers)	2,027,737
7	Americans for an Effective Presidency (nonconnected)	1,874,312
8	American Medical Political Action Committee (American Medical Association)	1,812,021
9	Committee for the Survival of a Free Congress (nonconnected)	1,623,750
10	National Committee for an Effective Congress (nonconnected)	1,420,238

Sources: For 1976-1978: Cantor, *Political Action Committees*, pp. 104-5. For 1980: Federal Election Commission, "FEC Releases Final PAC Report."

TABLE 3-18

INDEPENDENT EXPENDITURES, 1977–1980
(dollars)

Type of Expenditure	1977–1978			1979–1980		
	House	Senate	President	House	Senate	President
For Democrats	28,725 (N = 55)	102,508 (N = 13)	4,442 (N = 2)	190,615 (N = 91)	127,381 (N = 24)	123,058 (N = 2)
Against Democrats	31,034 (N = 7)	36,717 (N = 6)	0	38,023 (N = 32)	1,282,613 (N = 15)	737,796 (N = 3)
For Republicans	70,701 (N = 83)	26,065 (N = 22)	1,726 (N = 1)	410,478 (N = 205)	261,678 (N = 58)	12,537,522 (N = 3)

(Table continues)

TABLE 3-18 (continued)

Type of Expenditure	1977–1978			1979–1980		
	House	Senate	President	House	Senate	President
Against Republicans	5,298 (N = 5)	1,915 (N = 5)	0	45,132 (N = 6)	12,430 (N = 5)	65,040 (N = 2)
Total[a]	143,162 (N = 164)	168,125 (N = 48)	6,168 (N = 3)	684,727 (N = 321)	1,684,102 (N = 89)	13,746,444 (N = 15)

NOTE: N = number of candidates.

An independent expenditure is defined as an expenditure for a person for a communication expressly advocating the election or defeat of a clearly identified candidate that is not made with the cooperation or with the prior consent of or in consultation with or at the request or suggestion of, a candidate or any agent or authorized committee of such candidate (11 C.F.R. 109.1 [a]).

1975–1976: the Federal Election Commission's data on 1975–1976 independent expenditures were not completed or verified. On October 9, 1980, the FEC released the following information about independent expenditures during the 1975–1976 election cycle: $2,033,207 was spent independently for or against 144 candidates; $1,646,540 was spent for or against presidential candidates; $198,787 was spent for or against Senate candidates; $187,880 was spent for or against House candidates.

a. The totals include expenditures made on behalf of, or in opposition to, candidates who were neither Democrats nor Republicans. In 1979–1980, $479 was spent on behalf of one such candidate for the House, $271,978 was spent on behalf of seven presidential candidates (including $199,438 on behalf of John Anderson), and $11,050 was spent in opposition to two presidential candidates. In 1977–1978, $7,404 was spent on behalf of fourteen candidates for the House and $920 on behalf of two Senate candidates. The totals refer to total number of candidates. Because there may have been independent expenditures for and against the same candidates, the total may be less than the sum of the candidates in each column.

SOURCES: For 1975–1978: Federal Election Commission, "FEC Releases Information on Independent Expenditures," press release, October 9, 1980. For 1979–1980: Federal Election Commission, "FEC Study Shows Independent Expenditures Top $16 Million," press release, November 29, 1981.

TABLE 3–19

INDEPENDENT EXPENDITURES, CANDIDATES MOST AFFECTED, 1979–1980
(dollars)

	For	Against	Total
Presidential			
Ronald Reagan (R)	12,246,057	47,868	12,293,925
Edward Kennedy (D)	77,189	491,161	568,350
Jimmy Carter (D)	45,869	245,611	291,480
John B. Connally (R)	288,032	0	288,032
John B. Anderson (I)	199,438	2,635	202,073
Senate			
Frank Church (D-Idaho)	1,945	339,018	340,963
John C. Culver (D-Iowa)	59,584	186,613	246,197
George McGovern (D-S. Dak.)	3,553	222,044	225,597
Alan Cranston (D-Calif.)	2,285	192,039	194,324
Birch Bayh (D-Ind.)	1,027	180,723	181,750
Thomas F. Eagleton (D-Mo.)	22,910	101,794	124,704
House			
Robert W. Edgar (D-Pa.)	39,182	30	39,212
Jack M. Fields (R-Tex.)	38,376	0	38,376
Carey Peck (D-Calif.)	37,734	0	37,734
Harold S. Sawyer (R-Mich.)	14,219	13,912	28,131
Harold Volkmer (D-Mo.)	26,917	0	26,917
Robert F. Drinan (D-Mass.)	0	23,147	23,147
W. J. "Billy" Tauzin (D-La.)	22,535	0	22,535

SOURCE: Federal Election Commission, "FEC Study Shows Independent Expenditures Top $16 Million."

TABLE 3–20

INDEPENDENT EXPENDITURES, BIGGEST SPENDERS IN
CONGRESSIONAL RACES, 1979–1980
(dollars)

Group or Individual	Senate	House	Total
1. National Conservative Political Action Committee (NCPAC)	1,081,683	2,701	1,084,384
2. NRA Political Victory Fund (National Rifle Association)	98,457	115,936	214,393
3. American Medical PAC (AMPAC)	0	172,397	172,397
4. Americans for Life, Inc.	92,468	23,117	115,585
5. League of Conservation Voters	58,746	45,792	104,538
6. Realtors' PAC	0	70,198	70,198
7. Life Amendment PAC (LAPAC)	41,493	11,173	52,666
8. Ruff PAC	49,206	0	49,206
9. Handgun Control, Inc.	0	43,055	43,055
10. Voters for Choice	0	31,820	31,820
11. David B. Melville	29,191	0	29,191
12. Pro Life Action Council	12,721	10,242	22,963
13. Dwight G. Vedder	20,000	0	20,000
14. Texas Medical Association PAC	0	19,220	19,220
15. Positive Action Today	18,642	0	18,642

SOURCE: Federal Election Commission, *Index of Independent Expenditures, 1979-1980.*

TABLE 3–21

INDFPENDENT EXPENDITURES, BIGGEST SPENDERS, ALL RACES, 1979–1980
(dollars)

Political committees

1.	Congressional Club	4,601,069
2.	National Conservative Political Action Committee	3,307,962
3.	Fund for a Conservative Majority	2,062,456
4.	Americans for an Effective Presidency	1,270,208
5.	Americans for Change	711,856
6.	NRA Political Victory Fund	441,891
7.	Christian Voice Moral Government Fund	406,199
8.	1980 Republican Presidential Campaign Committee	314,740
9.	American Medical Political Action Committee	172,397
10.	Gun Owners of America Campaign Committee	119,891

Individuals

1.	Cecil R. Haden	599,333
2.	Stewart Rawlings Mott	110,179
3.	Norman Lear	108,301
4.	Richard M. DeVos	70,575
5.	Jay Van Andel	68,433
6.	Theo N. Law	66,230
7.	David B. Melville	35,159
8.	Henry C. Grover	29,076
9.	Michael Rosen	25,940
10.	Dwight G. Vedder	20,000

SOURCE: Federal Election Commission, "FEC Study Shows Independent Expenditures Top $16 Million."

4

Committees

This chapter provides information on House and Senate committees and chairmanships from 1955 to 1982. Tables 4–1 to 4–3 chart the ebb and flow in the number of committees and subcommittees in the House and Senate. It should be noted that the number of subcommittees in a given Congress is a particularly nebulous figure. During any Congress, subcommittees are added or disappear, and some ad hoc or special units may be listed or omitted from the various directories. At least two sources have been consulted for each Congress before listing the number of subcommittees. Tables 4–1 and 4–2 show an erratic but persistent growth since the 1950s through the Ninety-fourth Congress in the number of House panels, with some stabilization and decline evident by the Ninety-sixth Congress (1979–1980) and continuing into the Ninety-seventh. A very different recent pattern for the Senate is revealed in tables 4–1 and 4–3. As a result of that body's successful committee reorganization in 1977, the number of panels, particularly subcommittees, was cut dramatically— from an overall 205 in 1975–1976 to 130 in 1979–1980. Whereas the House and Senate had an equivalent number of panels in 1975, the House in 1980 had a clear numerical superiority. In the Ninety-seventh Senate—controlled by Republicans—the number of panels rose from its previous base, while the comparable House numbers continued to decline. The gap, however, remained.

Tables 4–4 and 4–5 display the average number of committee assignments of representatives and senators for the same period. House committee and subcommittee assignments have doubled since the 1950s. In 1981–1982 representatives had an average of 6.1 assignments each, up from 5.8 in the previous Congress. Senate assignments were cut back considerably with the 1977 reorganization, from 17.6 on average in 1975 to 10.4 in 1980, then rose again slightly in the Ninety-seventh Congress. Note, however, that even with the dramatic decrease since 1975, senators still average nearly twice as many assignments as their House counterparts.

Tables 4–6 and 4–7 examine chairmanships of committees and subcommittees in Congress. Table 4–6 shows that the proportions of majority party House members with chairmanships of one sort or another have risen steadily in the past two decades, though dropping slightly in the Ninety-seventh House. The rise in the 1950s and 1960s was a direct result of the increase in the number of committees and subcommittees (see table 4–1). Even though the number of panels declined between 1967 and 1971, however, the number and proportion of Democrats chairing them increased. This in turn was a direct result of a 1971 Democratic reform that limited the ability of members to chair more than one subcommittee. The number of members with more than one chairmanship declined accordingly, and for the first time more than half the majority party members held chairmanships of one kind or another. The number holding multiple chairmanships of any sort has been cut even further in 1981.

The Senate has always been a different story on chairmanships (table 4–7). With many fewer members and nearly as many panels as the House, few majority party senators have been denied a gavel of one sort or another since the 1950s; indeed, most majority senators have had at least two chairmanships. The average number of chairmanships rose to 2.9 in the mid-1970s, then declined, with the reorganization, to 2.1 in 1979–1980. Rather than diminishing leadership opportunities for junior senators, however, the reorganization expanded them by limiting the number of chairmanships each senator could hold. In 1979 every Democratic senator save one chaired at least one subcommittee or committee. The stunning arrival of a Republican majority did not change this pattern—every Republican senator except Majority Leader Howard Baker chaired at least one subcommittee in the Ninety-seventh Congress, and the average number of chairmanships was higher than in the Ninety-sixth Democratic Senate. No doubt the influx of sixteen Republican freshmen, making up a full 30 percent of the Senate party, contributed to the continuing decentralization of chairmanships.

Table 4–8 provides insights into the causes and consequences of seniority reforms of the 1970s, in the House of Representatives in particular. In the 1950s and early 1960s, Democrats from the Deep South constituted a near majority of their party (see table 1–2 for a more detailed regional breakdown), but they held an even greater share of committee chairmanships. Their overall strength in numbers, however, discouraged any challenge by non-Southerners who opposed the system's regional unrepresentativeness to the system of selecting chairmen. By the late 1960s, the South's share of the Democratic party in Congress was on the wane, but its hold on chairmanships of committees, especially the most powerful committees, was more tenacious. The declining number of Southern members facilitated a change in the seniority pattern for the selection of chairmen in 1971. After this reform and the dramatic ouster of three Southern chairmen in December 1974, the figures changed markedly. By 1979 Southerners were underrepresented in committee chairmanships, a pattern that continued in the Ninety-seventh Congress.

A similar pattern has occurred in the Senate. Through the departure from the Senate of senior Southerners and their replacement at the top rungs of committee seniority by non-Southern Democrats, a broader and more equal regional distribution of power and subcommittee chairmanships, indicated in table 4–8, was achieved. This meant that few senators felt so shortchanged of power that they would seek to accelerate these trends by a dramatic ouster of chairmen comparable to that in the 1974 House. The South was not disfranchised with the Republican takeover of the Senate in 1981; enough Republicans from the region had accumulated seniority, and enough Southerners had been elected as Republicans, that the Senate numbers for 1981 are not very different from those in the preceding Congress, when the Democrats were in the majority.

Table 4–9 demonstrates the effects of another set of reforms, the 1970 and 1973 rules changes that discouraged the closing of committee meetings in the House and Senate. After the January 1973 change, as the table indicates, closed meetings declined precipitously in number, and they virtually disappeared by 1976. At the same time, the number of informal closed meetings has apparently increased.

TABLE 4–1

NUMBER OF COMMITTEES IN THE HOUSE AND THE SENATE,
EIGHTY-FOURTH THROUGH NINETY-SEVENTH CONGRESSES, 1955–1982

Congress	Senate	House	Total[a]
84th (1955–56)	133	130	242
90th (1967–68)	155	185	315
92d (1971–72)	181	175	333
94th (1975–76)	205	204	385
96th (1979–80)	130	193	314
97th (1981–82)	136	184	310

NOTE: "Committees" includes standing committees, subcommittees of standing committees, select and special committees, subcommittees of select and special committees, joint committees, and subcommittees of joint committees.

a. Total is less than Senate and House combined because joint panels are counted only once.

SOURCES: Compiled from information taken from yearly volumes of Charles B. Brownson, *Congressional Staff Directory* (Washington, D.C.: Congressional Staff Directory); and Congressional Quarterly, *Congressional Quarterly Almanac*.

TABLE 4-2

NUMBER AND TYPE OF HOUSE COMMITTEES,
EIGHTY-FOURTH THROUGH NINETY-SEVENTH CONGRESSES, 1955–1982

Congress	Standing Committees	Subcommittees of Standing Committees	Select and Special Committees	Subcommittees of Select and Special Committees	Joint Committees	Subcommittees of Joint Committees
84th (1955–56)	19	83	2	5	10	11
90th (1967–68)	20	133	1	6	10	15
92d (1971–72)	21	120	3	8	8	15
94th (1975–76)	22	151	3	4	7	17
96th (1979–80)	22	149[a]	5	8	4	5
97th (1981–82)	22	132	3	7	4	6

a. Includes nine budget task forces and the Welfare and Pension Plans Task Force (of the Subcommittee on Labor Management Relations).

SOURCES: Compiled from information taken from yearly volumes of Brownson, *Congressional Staff Directory;* and Congressional Quarterly, *Congressional Quarterly Almanac.*

TABLE 4-3

Number and Type of Senate Committees, Eighty-fourth through Ninety-seventh Congresses, 1955–1982

Congress	Standing Committees	Subcommittees of Standing Committees	Select and Special Committees	Subcommittees of Select and Special Committees	Joint Committees	Subcommittees of Joint Committees
84th (1955–56)	15	88	3	6	10	11
90th (1967–68)	16	99	3	12	10	15
92d (1971–72)	17	123	5	13	8	15
94th (1975–76)	18	140	6	17	7	17
96th (1979–80)	15	91	5	10	4	5
97th (1981–82)	15	94	5	12	4	6

SOURCES: Compiled from information taken from yearly volumes of Brownson, *Congressional Staff Directory; Congressional Quarterly, Congressional Quarterly Almanac;* Walter Oleszek, "Overview of the Senate Committee System," paper prepared for the Commission on the Operation of the Senate, 1977; and the Washington Monitor, *Congressional Yellow Book.*

TABLE 4–4

COMMITTEE ASSIGNMENTS FOR REPRESENTATIVES, EIGHTY-FOURTH THROUGH NINETY-SEVENTH CONGRESSES, 1955–1982

Congress	Mean No. of Standing Committee Assignments	Mean No. of Subcommittees of Standing Committee Assignments	Mean No. of Other Committee Assignments[a]	Total
84th (1955–56)	1.2	1.6	0.2	3.0
92d (1971–72)	1.5	3.2	0.4	5.1
94th (1975–76)	1.8	4.0	0.4	6.2
96th (1979–80)	1.7	3.6	0.5	5.8
97th (1981–82)	1.7	4.0	0.4	6.1

a. "Other" committees include select and special committees, subcommittees of select and special committees, joint committees, and subcommittees of joint committees.

SOURCES: Compiled from information taken from yearly volumes of Brownson, *Congressional Staff Directory;* and Congressional Quarterly, *Congressional Quarterly Almanac.*

TABLE 4–5

COMMITTEE ASSIGNMENTS FOR SENATORS, EIGHTY-FOURTH THROUGH NINETY-SEVENTH CONGRESSES, 1955–1982

Congress	Mean No. of Standing Committee Assignments	Mean No. of Subcommittees of Standing Committee Assignments	Mean No. of Other Assignments[a]	Total
84th (1955–56)	2.2	4.8	0.9	7.9
92d (1971–72)	2.5	9.5	3.3	15.3
94th (1975–76)	2.5	11.0	4.1	17.6
96th (1979–80)	2.3	6.6	1.5	10.4
97th (1981–82)	2.5	6.7	1.5	10.7

a. "Other" committees include select and special committees, subcommittees of select and special committees, joint committees, and subcommittees of joint committees.

SOURCES: Compiled from information taken from yearly volumes of Brownson, *Congressional Staff Directory;* and Congressional Quarterly, *Congressional Quarterly Almanac.*

TABLE 4-6

Majority Party Chairmanships of Committees and Subcommittees in the House, Eighty-fourth through Ninety-seventh Congresses, 1955–1982

Congress	No. of Majority Party Members in House	Party in Majority	No. Chairing Standing Committees and Subcommittees	No. with Two or More Chairmanships	% Chairing Standing Committees and Subcommittees	No. Chairing All Committees and Subcommittees[a]	% Chairing All Committees and Subcommittees[a]
84th (1955–56)	232	D	63	0	27.2	75	32.3
90th (1967–68)	247	D	111	32[b]	44.9	117	47.4
92d (1971–72)	254	D	120	21	47.2	131	51.6
94th (1975–76)	289	D	142	28	49.1	150	51.9
96th (1979–80)	276	D	144	27	52.2	149	54.0
97th (1981–82)	243	D	132	20	49.8	125	51.4

a. Includes standing committees, subcommittees of standing committees, select and special committees, subcommittees of select and special committees, joint committees, and subcommittees of joint committees.

b. Includes nine with three or more chairmanships.

Sources: Compiled from information taken from yearly volumes of Brownson, *Congressional Staff Directory;* and the *Congressional Quarterly, Congressional Quarterly Almanac.*

TABLE 4-7

MAJORITY PARTY CHAIRMANSHIPS OF COMMITTEES AND SUBCOMMITTEES IN THE SENATE, EIGHTY-FOURTH THROUGH NINETY-SEVENTH CONGRESSES, 1955–1982

Congress	No. of Majority Party in Senate	Party in Majority	No. Chairing Standing Committees and Subcommittees	% Chairing Standing Committees and Subcommittees	Average No. of Standing Committees and Subcommittees Chaired by Majority Members	No. Chairing All Committees and Subcommittees[a]	% of Majority Party Chairing All Committees and Subcommittees[a]	Average No. of All Committees and Subcommittees Chaired by Majority Members
84th (1955–56)	48	D	42	87.5	1.8	42	87.5	2.0
90th (1967–68)	64	D	55	85.9	1.8	58	90.6	2.1
92d (1971–72)	55[b]	D	51	92.7	2.6	52	94.5	2.9
94th (1975–76)	62[b]	D	57	91.9	2.4	57	91.9	2.9
96th (1979–80)	59[b]	D	58	98.3	1.8	58	98.3	2.1
97th (1981–82)	53	R	51	96.2	1.9	52	98.1	2.3

a. Includes standing committees, subcommittees of standing committees, select and special committees, joint committees, and subcommittees of joint committees.

b. Includes Harry Byrd, Jr., elected as Independent.

SOURCES: Compiled from information taken from Brownson, 1967, 1971, 1975, 1979, and 1981 *Congressional Staff Directory*; *Congressional Quarterly, 1955 Congressional Quarterly Almanac*.

TABLE 4–8

Southern Chairmanships of House and Senate Standing Committees, 1955–1981

	House				Senate			
Year	Number of Southern chairmen	% of chairmanships held by Southerners	% of three exclusive committees[a] chaired by Southerners	% of majority party from the South	Number of Southern chairmen	% of chairmanships held by Southerners	% of four exclusive committees[a] chaired by Southerners	% of majority party from the South
1955	12	63	67	43	8	53	50	46
1967	10	50	100	35	9	56	100	28
1971	8	38	100	31	9	53	100	30
1975	9	41	33	28	6	33	100	27
1979	5	23	33	28	4	27	50	28
1981[b]	6	27	33	29	3	20	25	19

a. In the House, Ways and Means, Rules, and Appropriations. In the Senate, Appropriations, Finance, Foreign Relations, and Armed Services.

b. In 1981 the Republicans were the majority party in the Senate. For all other years in the table, Democrats were the majority party in both the Senate and the House.

SOURCE: Compiled from information taken from the 1955, 1971, 1975, and 1979 *Congressional Directory*, compiled under the direction of the U.S. Congress, Joint Committee on Printing.

TABLE 4–9
CLOSED COMMITTEE MEETINGS, 1953–1975

Year	Total Meetings	Number Closed	% Closed
1953	2,640[a]	892	34
1954	3,002[a]	1,243	41
1955	2,940[a]	1,055	36
1956	3,120[a]	1,130	36
1957	2,517[a]	854	34
1958	3,472[a]	1,167	34
1959	3,152[a]	940	30
1960	2,424[a]	840	35
1961	3,159[a]	1,109	35
1962	2,929[a]	991	34
1963	3,868[a]	1,463	38
1964	2,393[a]	763	32
1965	3,903	1,537	39
1966	3,869	1,626	42
1967	4,412	1,716	39
1968	3,080	1,328	43
1969	4,029	1,470	36
1970	4,506	1,865	41
1971	4,816	1,731	36
1972	4,073	1,648	40
1973	5,520	887	16
1974	4,731	707	15
1975	6,325	449	7
Total[a]	84,880	27,411	32

NOTE: Subcommittee meetings were included in the totals along with full committee sessions. Open meetings followed by closed meetings were counted twice, once in each category. Joint meetings of separate committees or subcommittees were counted as one meeting for each. The tabulations exclude meetings held when Congress was not in regular session; meetings held outside Washington, D.C.; informal meetings without official status; and meetings of the House Rules Committee to consider sending legislation to the floor. Figures have not been computed after 1975 because virtually all committee meetings have been open.

a. Meetings of the House Appropriations Committee, all reported closed until 1971, were not included in the study until 1965.

SOURCE: Congressional Quarterly, *Guide to Congress*, 2d ed., 1976, p. 370.

5

Congressional Staff and Operating Expenses

Congress is made up of a great deal more than elected senators and representatives. With nearly 31,000 employees in 1981 (table 5–1 and figure 5–1), the legislative branch is larger than the Department of State, Labor, or Housing and Urban Development. In comparison, the second most heavily staffed legislative branch in the world is the Canadian Parliament, which gets by with a staff of fewer than 3,500.[1] Of course, Congress's employees include more than the personal and committee staffs of congressmen and senators. Also included are major research agencies, such as the Congressional Research Service (CRS) of the Library of Congress, and support personnel, such as mail carriers, police officers, barbers, hairdressers, television technicians, computer specialists, printers, carpenters, parking attendants, photographers, and laborers.

The development of this large congressional establishment is a twentieth-century phenomenon. At the turn of the century, representatives had no personal staff, and senators had a total of only thirty-nine personal assistants (table 5–2 and figure 5–1). Committee staffs consisted of a few clerks (table 5–5). By contrast, 11,125 persons served on the personal staffs of representatives and senators in 1981, and over 3,000 people were employed by congressional committees.

The enlargement of Congress's support staff reflects both the expanding role of the government in American society and the changing role of the individual legislator. As government has done more, the congressional workload, in terms of both legislation and constituency service, has increased, and the staffing needs of Congress have expanded accordingly. The most dramatic staff growth has taken place since World War II, the personal staffs of the House and Senate having increased fivefold and sixfold, respectively, since 1947. One

1. Michael J. Malbin, *Unelected Representatives: Congressional Staff and the Future of Representative Government* (New York: Basic Books, 1980, paperback edition 1982), p. 10.

reflection of the increased demands on legislators for constituency services and the members' encouragement of those demands for reelection purposes is the dramatic expansion of congressional staff working in constituency offices. More than one-third of the personal staffs of representatives and one-quarter of those of the senators now work in district or state offices (tables 5–3 and 5–4).

The explosion in congressional staffing is also evident on the standing committees: House committee staffs increased elevenfold and Senate committee staffs more than fourfold between 1947 and 1981 (table 5–5). Committee staffing has grown steadily since the turn of the century, but the most dramatic increases occurred in the 1970s. House committee staffs were two and three-quarters times as large in 1979 as they were in 1970, and Senate committee staffs doubled over the same period. This enlargement of House committee staffs after 1970 is to a significant degree a result of the reform movement that swept the chamber. The sentiment for diluting the powers of committee chairmen extended to their nearly exclusive authority to hire and fire staff. Reforms allowed a much larger number of sub-committee chairmen and ranking members to hire their own staffs. The 1975 surge in committee staffing in the Senate reflects the passage of Senate Resolution 60, which authorized each senator to have a personal legislative assistant for each committee assignment. The modest reductions in Senate committee staffs in 1977 were caused by the committee reorganization that went into effect that year, which among other things shifted people hired under Senate Resolution 60 to personal staff payrolls.

The 1980s have not, so far, been a repeat of the 1970s. Personal staffs have continued to grow in the House, but they have leveled off in the Senate. House committee staffs declined modestly between 1979 and 1981. Senate committee staffs went down by a remarkable 19 percent—mostly after the Republicans gained control in 1981 and promised to reverse the previous decade's trends. Note, however, that more than one-third of these cuts came from one committee, Judiciary (table 5–7). As significant as the cuts may be, they left the Senate with 60 percent more committee staff in 1981 than in 1970.

Tables 5–6 and 5–7 rank the standing committees according to staff size. Each committee except the Senate Judiciary Committee had a significantly larger staff in 1981 than it had in 1960. Most committees employ well over fifty persons, a far cry from the post–World War II era of small, intimate, informal committee staffs. The size of a committee staff does not appear to be related uniformly to the reported power or desirability of an assignment to a particular committee. The powerful Senate Finance Committee, for example, is modestly staffed compared with the less influential Labor and Human Resources or Governmental Affairs committees. Of course, some committees that are generally considered less desirable assignments may well have expanded their staffs to attract new members.

A significant part of the congressional staff works for Congress's four major research agencies (table 5–8). Two of these, the Congressional Budget Office (CBO) and the Office of Technology Assessment (OTA), were created in the mid-1970s, their creation reflecting a basic factor underlying the growth of congressional staff. The expanded role of the government in domestic and international affairs had made Congress increasingly dependent on the executive branch for information. A growing distrust of the executive, festering during the Johnson and Nixon administrations, convinced Congress of the necessity for congressionally controlled sources of information. Congress thus authorized these new agencies and simultaneously expanded the roles of the Congressional Research Service and the General Accounting Office (GAO). The GAO has multiple functions, including audit responsibilities with limited relevance to its role as a congressional agency. The same is true of the Library of Congress. Thus table 5–1 includes a subtotal of GAO and Library of Congress staff, which is an estimate of the number of employees with a direct congressional function.

Although the numbers in these tables describe the growth of congressional staff, they do not reveal the many roles staff members play in the legislative process. The infinite variety of staffing arrangements that exists in members' offices and on committees and the influence exercised by various staff members become apparent only through close examination of individual offices and committees. The role played by staff within individual offices may also change over time with the ebb and flow of political tides. President Reagan's ability to make Congress focus on budget issues in 1981, for example, greatly reduced the number of bills Congress passed that year (see chapter 6). That meant less chance for members to use their staffs as policy entrepreneurs, unless the staffs could come up with programs that did not affect the budget. In short, one should be wary of generalizing too freely about staffing roles and patterns solely on the basis of gross figures.

Returning to those figures, the costs of running Congress have grown along with the staff. Today's Congress is a billion-dollar enterprise. Even though congressional costs may appear puny when compared with those of the executive branch, they have grown at a dramatic pace. In the years between 1946 and 1981, legislative branch appropriations increased 2,279 percent. Over the same period, the consumer price index went up "only" 366 percent (table 5–9). As recently as the mid-1960s, the cost of operating Congress was less than one-fifth what it is today. We may now be seeing some signs of legislative self-control: in the years between 1976, when Congress first approached the billion-dollar threshold, and 1981, legislative branch appropriations went up only 36 percent, while the consumer price index increased by 60 percent.

The figures summarizing legislative branch appropriations include much more than the cost of House and Senate operations. The appropriation also includes the expenses of such agencies as the Library of Congress, the Government Printing Office, the General Accounting Office, the Botanic Garden, and the newly chartered Copyright Royalty Commission. Indeed, these agencies' budgets constitute more than 40 percent of the 1982 legislative branch appropriation (see table 5–10 for a breakdown of the components of the congressional budget).

Table 5–11 traces one of the perquisites of office available to members of Congress—use of the frank to send materials pertaining to the official business of Congress through the U.S. mails. In 1982 the cost of the congressional franking privilege was $75 million, an almost sevenfold increase since 1971. This expanded use of the frank reflects the liberalized provisions of the law, which permit members of Congress to send mail (including newsletters and questionnaires) addressed to "occupant," and the increased value that legislators attach to communications with their constituents.

Tables 5–12 and 5–13 summarize the allowances available to representatives and senators for operating their offices and outline the changes in those allowances since 1970. In the past, expenses for such things as postage, stationery, office furnishings, equipment, and travel were governed by strict individual spending limits. The House in 1978 and the Senate in 1973 consolidated their office expense allowances into one account to give members greater flexibility in using their expense allowances. Because Congress is a labor-intensive enterprise, however, the largest share of the congressional allowance is for staff.

TABLE 5–1

Congressional Staff, 1979 and 1981

	1979	1981
House		
Committee staff[a]	2,027	1,917
Personal staff	7,067	7,487
Leadership staff[b]	162	127
Officers of the House, staff[c]	1,487	1,686
Subtotal, House	10,743	11,217
Senate		
Committee staff[a]	1,410	1,150
Personal staff	3,612	3,638
Leadership staff[b]	170	118
Officers of the Senate, staff[c]	1,351	1,016
Subtotal, Senate	6,543	5,922
Joint committee staffs	138	126
Support agencies		
General Accounting Office	5,303	5,182
(30% of GAO)	(1,591)	(1,555)
Library of Congress	5,390	4,799
(Congressional Research Service)	(847)	(849)
Congressional Budget Office	207	218
Office of Technology Assessment	145	130
Subtotal, support agencies	11,045	10,329
(Subtotal, only CRS in Library, 30% of GAO)	(2,790)	(2,752)
Miscellaneous		
Architect	2,296	1,986
Capitol Police Force	1,167	1,163
Subtotal	3,463	3,149
Total	31,932	30,743
(Total, only CRS in Library and 30% of GAO)	(23,677)	(23,166)

a. Includes select and special committee staffs. Figures therefore do not agree with those in table 5-5.

b. Includes legislative counsels' offices.

c. Doorkeepers, parliamentarians, sergeants-at-arms, clerk of the House, Senate majority and minority secretaries, and postmasters.

Sources: For 1979: *Report of the Clerk of the House*, July 1, 1979, to September 30, 1979; *Report of the Secretary of the Senate*, April 1, 1979, to September 30, 1979; and U.S. Office of Personnel Management, Work Force Analysis and Sta-

(Notes continue)

tistics Branch, *Federal Civilian Workforce Statistics,* monthly release, October 31, 1979, p. 6. For 1981: U.S. Congress, House, Subcommittee on Legislative Branch Appropriations, *Hearings, Legislative Branch Appropriations for 1983,* 97th Congress, 2d session, 1982, pt. 1, pp. 24-28; U.S. Congress, Senate, Committee on Rules and Administration, *Senate Committee Funding,* 97th Congress, 1st session, March 3, 1981, Committee Print No. 2; U.S. Congress, Senate, Committee on Appropriations, *Hearings, Legislative Branch Appropriations, Fiscal Year 1982,* 97th Congress, 1st session, pp. 117, 253, 266; and *Report of the Secretary of the Senate,* October 1, 1981, to March 31, 1982, 97th Congress, 2d session, pp. 1-23.

TABLE 5–2

PERSONAL STAFFS OF MEMBERS OF THE HOUSE AND THE SENATE, 1891–1981

Year	Employees in House	Employees in Senate
1891	n.a.	39
1914	n.a.	72
1930	870	280
1935	870	424
1947	1,440	590
1957	2,441	1,115
1967	4,055	1,749
1972	5,280	2,426
1976	6,939	3,251
1977	6,942	3,554
1978	6,944	3,268
1979	7,067	3,612
1980	7,371	3,746
1981	7,487	3,638

NOTE: n.a. = not available.

SOURCES: For 1891 through 1976: Harrison W. Fox, Jr., and Susan W. Hammond, *Congressional Staffs: The Invisible Force in American Lawmaking* (New York: Free Press, 1977), p. 171. For 1977 and 1978: Judy Schneider, "Congressional Staffing, 1947-78," Congressional Research Service, August 24, 1979, reprinted in U.S. Congress, House, Select Committee on Committees, *Final Report,* April 1, 1980, p. 540. For 1977, 1978, and 1979 House: *Report of the Clerk of the House.* For 1979 Senate: *Report of the Secretary of the Senate.* For 1980: U.S. Congress, House, Subcommittee on Legislative Branch Appropriations, *Hearings, Legislative Branch Appropriations for 1982,* 97th Congress, 1st session, 1981, pt. 1, p. 25; and U.S. Congress, Senate, Committee on Appropriations, *Hearings, Legislative Branch Appropriations, Fiscal Year 1981,* 96th Congress, 2d session, pt. 1, p. 26. For 1981: House, Subcommittee on Legislative Branch Appropriations, *Hearings, Legislative Branch Appropriations for 1983,* pt. 1, pp. 24-28; and Senate, Committee on Appropriations, *Hearings, Legislative Branch Appropriations, Fiscal Year 1982.*

FIGURE 5–1
STAFF OF MEMBERS AND OF COMMITTEES IN CONGRESS, 1891–1981

Number of employees

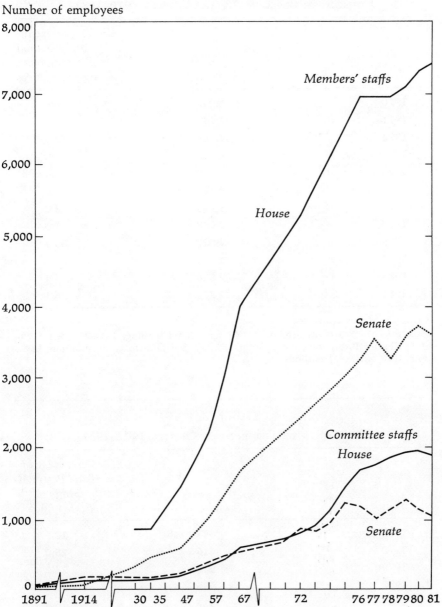

SOURCE: Tables 5-2 and 5-5.

TABLE 5–3
House Staff Based in District Offices, 1970–1981

Year	Employees	Percentage of Total Personal Staffs in District Offices
1970	1,035	n.a.
1971	1,121	n.a.
1972	1,189	22.5
1973	1,347	n.a.
1974	1,519	n.a.
1975	1,732	n.a.
1976	1,943	28.0
1977	2,058	29.6
1978	2,317	33.4
1979	2,445	34.6
1980	2,534	34.4
1981	2,702	36.1

NOTE: n.a. = not available.
SOURCES: For 1970-1978: Schneider, "Congressional Staffing, 1947-78." For 1979-1981: Charles B. Brownson, ed. *Congressional Staff Directory*, Washington, D.C., 1971, 1980, and 1981 editions.

TABLE 5–4
Senate Staff Based in State Offices, 1972–1981

Year	Employees	Percentage of Total Personal Staffs in State Offices
1972	303	12.5
1978	816	25.0
1979	879	24.3
1980	953	25.4
1981	937	25.8

SOURCE: Brownson, *Congressional Staff Directory*, 1972, 1978, 1979, 1980, and 1981 editions.

TABLE 5–5

Staffs of House and Senate Standing Committees, 1891–1981

Year	Employees in House	Employees in Senate
1891	62	41
1914	105	198
1930	112	163
1935	122	172
1947	167	232
1950	246	300
1955	329	386
1960	440	470
1965	571	509
1970	702	635
1971	729	711
1972	817	844
1973	878	873
1974	1,107	948
1975	1,433	1,277
1976	1,680	1,201
1977	1,776	1,028
1978	1,844	1,151
1979	1,909	1,269
1980	1,917	1,191
1981	1,843	1,022

NOTE: Figures for 1947-1981 are for the statutory and investigative staffs of standing committees. They do not include select committee staffs, which varied between 31 and 238 in the House and between 62 and 172 in the Senate during the 1970s. For this reason, the numbers do not agree with those in table 5-1.

SOURCES: For 1891-1935: Fox and Hammond, *Congressional Staffs*, p. 171. For 1947-1978: Schneider, "Congressional Staffing, 1947-78." For 1979-1980 Senate: U.S. Congress, Senate, Committee on Rules and Administration, *Senate Inquiries and Investigations*, 96th Congress, 2d session, Committee Print No. 2, March 5, 1980. For 1981 Senate: Senate, Committee on Rules and Administration, *Senate Committee Funding*. For 1979 House: U.S. Congress, House, Subcommittees on Legislative Branch Appropriations, *Hearings, Legislative Branch Appropriations for 1981*, 96th Congress, 2d session, pt. 2, p. 136. For 1980 House: Office of the Clerk of the House of Representatives. For 1981 House: House, Subcommittee on Legislative Branch Appropriations, *Legislative Branch Appropriations for 1983*, pt. 2, p. 107.

TABLE 5–6
STAFF SIZE OF HOUSE STANDING COMMITTEES, 1947–1981

Committee	1947	1960	1970	1975	1979	1981
House Administration[a]	7	4	25	217	273	252
Energy and Commerce	10	45	42	112	160	151
Appropriations	29	59	71	98	129	127
Education and Labor	10	25	77	114	121	121
Budget	b	b	b	67	86	93
Ways and Means	12	22	24	63	99	91
Banking	4	14	50	85	97	87
Public Works	6	32	40	88	81	86
Foreign Affairs	10	14	21	54	82	84
Government Operations	9	54	60	68	85	84
Merchant Marine and Fisheries	6	9	21	28	91	82
Judiciary	7	27	35	69	80	75
Science and Technology	b	17	26	47	87	74
Post Office and Civil Service	6	9	46	61	66	74
Interior	4	10	14	57	75	70
Agriculture	9	10	17	48	66	62
Small Business	b	b	b	27	46	54
Armed Services	10	15	37	38	48	49
Rules	4	2	7	18	47	43
District of Columbia	7	8	15	43	41	41
Veterans' Affairs	7	18	18	26	34	34
Standards of Official Conduct	b	b	5	5	15	9
Internal Security	10	46	51	27	b	b

NOTE: Committees are ranked in order of their staff size in 1981.

a. After 1972, figures include employees of House Informations Systems, the House of Representatives' central computer facility.

b. Not a standing committee.

SOURCES: For 1947-1975: Schneider, "Congressional Staffing, 1947-78." For 1979: House, Subcommittee on Legislative Branch Appropriations, *Hearings, Legislative Branch Appropriations for 1981*, pt. 2, p. 136. For 1981: House, Subcommittee on Legislative Branch Appropriations, *Hearings, Legislative Branch Appropriations for 1983*, pt. 2, p. 107.

TABLE 5–7
STAFF SIZE OF SENATE STANDING COMMITTEES, 1947–1981

Committee	1947	1960	1970	1975	1979	1981
Governmental Affairs	29	47	55	144	179	153
Judiciary	19	137	190	251	223	134
Labor and Human Resources	9	28	69	150	155	119
Budget	a	a	a	90	91	82
Appropriations	23	31	42	72	80	79
Commerce, Science, and Transportation	8	52	53	111	96	78
Foreign Relations	8	25	31	62	75	59
Environment and Public Works	10	11	34	70	74	56
Energy and Natural Resources (Interior)	7	26	22	53	55	50
Finance	6	6	16	26	67	50
Banking, Housing, and Urban Affairs	9	22	23	55	48	39
Armed Services	10	23	19	30	31	36
Agriculture	3	10	7	22	34	34
Rules and Administration	41	15	13	29	37	31
Veterans' Affairs	a	a	a	32	24	22
Aeronautics and Space Sciences	a	10	12	22	a	a
District of Columbia	4	7	18	33	a	a
Post Office and Civil Service	46	20	31	25	a	a

NOTE: Committees are ranked in the order of their staff size in 1981.

a. Committee not in existence.

SOURCES: For 1947-1975: Schneider, "Congressional Staffing, 1947-78." For 1979: U.S. Congress, Senate, Committee on Rules and Administration, *Senate Committee Funding*, 96th Congress, 2d session, Committee Print No. 2, March 5, 1980; Appropriations staff from secretary of the Senate. For 1981: Senate, Committee on Rules and Administration, *Senate Committee Funding*. This committee print lists the number of positions authorized for each committee; the number actually employed at any one time may be less than the number authorized.

TABLE 5–8

STAFFS OF CONGRESSIONAL SUPPORT AGENCIES, 1946–1981

Year	Library of Congress	Congressional Research Service Only[a]	General Accounting Office[b]	Congressional Budget Office	Office of Technology Assessment
1946			14,219		
1947	1,898	160	10,695		
1950	1,973	161	7,876		
1955	2,459	166	5,776		
1960	2,779	183	5,074		
1965	3,390	231	4,278		
1970	3,848	332	4,704		
1971	3,963	386	4,718		
1972	4,135	479	4,742		
1973	4,375	596	4,908		
1974	4,504	687	5,270		10
1975	4,649	741	4,905	193	54
1976	4,880	806	5,391	203	103
1977	5,075	789	5,315	201	139
1978	5,231	818	5,476	203	164
1979	5,390	847	5,303	207	145
1980	5,047	868	5,196	218	122
1981	4,799	849	5,182	218	130

a. Legislative Reference Service through 1970.

b. Before 1950 the GAO was responsible for auditing all individual federal transactions and keeping a record of them. Legislation in 1950 transferred these responsibilities to the executive branch. The staff reductions through 1965 result from this 1950 change. See Frederich C. Mosher, *The GAO: The Quest for Accountability in American Government* (Boulder, Colo.: Westview Press, 1979), p. 124.

SOURCES: Library of Congress: *Annual Reports of the Librarian of Congress.* GAO (1946-1965): *Annual Reports of the Comptroller General of the United States.* OTA (1974-1976): *Appendixes of the Budget of the United States* for fiscal 1976 (p. 18), 1977 (p. 18), and 1978 (p. 40). CBO (1975): Joel Havemann, *Congress and the Budget* (Bloomington: Indiana University Press, 1978), p. 109. Data are as of October 1975. The CBO's director took office on February 24, 1975. GAO (1970-1978), CBO (1976-1978), and OTA (1977-1978): Schneider, "Congressional Staffing, 1947-78." For 1979: U.S. Office of Personnel Management, *Federal Civilian Workforce Statistics*, monthly release, October 31, 1979. For 1980: House, Subcommittee on Legislative Branch Appropriations, *Hearings, Legislative Branch Appropriations for 1982*, pp. 24-28. For 1981: House, Subcommittee on Legislative Branch Appropriations, *Legislative Branch Appropriations for 1983*, pp. 24-28.

TABLE 5-9

Legislative Branch Appropriations and the Consumer Price Index, 1946–1982

Year	Appropriation (dollars)	Increase (percent)	Consumer Price Index	Increase (percent)
1946	54,065,614	—	58.5	—
1947	61,825,020	14.4	66.9	14.4
1948	62,119,714	0.5	72.1	7.8
1949	62,057,678	− 0.1	71.4	− 1.0
1950	64,313,460	3.6	72.1	1.0
1951	71,888,244	11.8	77.8	7.9
1952	75,673,896	5.3	79.5	2.2
1953	77,670,076	2.6	80.1	0.8
1954	70,925,361	− 8.7	80.5	0.5
1955	86,304,923	21.7	80.2	− 0.4
1956	94,827,986	9.9	81.4	1.5
1957	120,775,798	27.4	84.3	3.6
1958	107,785,560	− 10.8	86.6	2.7
1959	136,153,580	26.3	87.3	0.8
1960	131,055,385	− 3.7	88.7	1.6
1961	140,930,781	7.5	89.6	1.0
1962	136,686,715	− 3.0	90.6	1.1
1963	150,426,185	10.1	91.7	1.2
1964	168,467,869	12.0	92.9	1.3
1965	221,904,318	31.7	94.5	1.7
1966	197,965,307	− 10.8	97.2	2.9
1967	221,715,643	12.0	100.0	2.9
1968	282,003,322	27.2	104.2	4.2
1969	311,542,399	10.5	109.8	5.4
1970	361,024,327	15.9	116.3	5.9
1971	443,104,319	22.7	121.3	4.3
1972	564,107,992	27.3	125.3	3.3
1973	645,127,365	14.4	133.1	6.2
1974	662,180,668	2.6	147.7	11.0
1975	785,618,833	18.6	161.2	9.1
1976[a]	947,185,778	20.6	170.5	5.8

(Table continues)

117

TABLE 5–9 (continued)

Year	Appropriation (dollars)	Increase (percent)	Consumer Price Index	Increase (percent)
1977	963,921,185	1.8	181.5	6.5
1978	1,009,225,350	4.7	195.4	7.7
1979	1,124,766,400	11.4	217.4	11.3
1980	1,199,061,463	6.6	246.8	13.5
1981	1,285,943,826	7.2	272.4	10.4
1982	1,319,455,108	2.6	n.a.	—
1946–81	—	2,278.5	—	365.6

NOTE: n.a. = not available. Appropriations include supplementals, except for 1982; appropriations are for fiscal years, but the consumer price index is for calendar years.

a. From fiscal year 1946 through fiscal year 1976, the fiscal year began on July 1. Beginning with fiscal year 1977, the start of the fiscal year was shifted to October 1. During the transition quarter of July 1-September 30, 1976, the amount appropriated for legislative branch operations was $207,391,365. This amount is not included.

SOURCES: For 1946-1976: U.S. Congress, House, Committee on House Administration, "Studies Dealing with Budgetary, Staffing, and Administrative Activities of the U.S. House of Representatives, 1947-78," 95th Congress, 2d session, November 1978. For 1977-1979: *Congressional Quarterly Almanac*, 1977-1980 editions. For 1980: Senate, Committee on Appropriations, *Hearings, Legislative Branch Appropriations, Fiscal Year 1981*, 96th Congress, 2d session, pt. 1, pp. 10-11; House, Subcommittee on Legislative Branch Appropriations, *Legislative Branch Appropriations for 1981*, pt. 1, pp. 15-23; and U.S. Congress, Public Law 96-304, 96th Congress, July 8, 1980, and Public Law 97-51, 97th Congress, October 1, 1981. For 1981: House, Subcommittee on Legislative Branch Appropriations, *Legislative Branch Appropriations for 1982*, pp. 15-23; Senate, Committee on Appropriations, *Legislative Branch Appropriations, Fiscal Year 1982*, p. 268; U.S. Congress, Senate, Committee on Appropriations, *Comparative Statement of New Budget Authority and Outlays—Fiscal Year 1983*, April 27, 1982, p. 3; and Public Law 97-12, June 5, 1981. For 1982: House, Subcommittee on Legislative Branch Appropriations, *Legislative Branch Appropriations for 1983*, pp. 15-23; and Senate, Committee on Appropriations, *Comparative Statement*, p. 3. For consumer price index (all years): *Economic Report of the President*, February 1982.

TABLE 5–10

LEGISLATIVE BRANCH APPROPRIATIONS BY CATEGORY, 1980–1982
(dollars)

	1980	1981	1982
Senate	216,917,500	227,933,000	214,350,108
House of Representatives	329,126,963	360,980,026	363,794,000
Joint items[a]	60,258,000	61,000,900	84,237,000
Architect of the Capitol	60,964,000	80,062,000	80,980,000
Botanic Garden	1,464,000	1,644,000	2,311,000
Congressional Budget Office	12,386,000	12,767,000	12,386,000
Office of Technology Assessment	11,119,000	11,403,000	12,019,000
Library of Congress	179,517,000	186,445,900	189,827,000
Government Printing Office	121,238,000	122,650,000	129,851,000
General Accounting Office	204,300,000	220,602,000	229,300,000
Cost Accounting Standards Board	1,300,000	—	—
Copyright Royalty Commission	471,000	456,000	400,000

NOTE: Includes supplemental appropriations, except for 1982.
a. Includes such items as joint committees, Capitol Police, and official mail costs.
SOURCES: Same as table 5-9.

TABLE 5–11
OFFICIAL MAILING COSTS, 1971–1982

Year	Appropriations (dollars)	Average Unit Cost of Franked Mail (cents)
1971	11,244,000	8
1972	14,594,000	8
1972 supplement	18,400,000	
1973	21,226,480	8.79
1974	30,500,000	9.9
1975	38,756,015	11.4
1976	46,101,000	13.2
Transition period[a]	11,525,000	
1976 supplement	16,080,000	
1977	46,904,000	13.4
1978	48,926,000	12.7
1979	64,944,000	13.98
1980[b]	50,707,000	13.39
1981	52,033,000	
1982	75,095,000	13.94[c]

NOTE: 1982 figure does not include supplementals. See table 6-6 for number of pieces of franked mail.

a. Reflects change in the fiscal year from July 1 to October 1.

b. Lower figure reflects decrease in bulk mail rates.

c. Estimate.

SOURCES: Same as table 5-9. Source for unit cost of franked mail: U.S. Congress, House, Subcommittee on Legislative Branch Appropriations, *Hearings, Legislative Branch Appropriations for 1980*, 96th Congress, 1st session, p. 1594; and Office of the Clerk of the House.

TABLE 5-12

ALLOWANCES FOR REPRESENTATIVES, 1970-1982

Category	1970	1977	1979	1982
Clerk hire	$149,292[a]	$238,584[b]	$288,156[c]	$352,536[c]
Postage	$700	$211	d	d
Stationery	$3,500	$6,500	d	d
Travel (round trips)	12	33	d	d
Telephone/telegraph	80,000 units[e]	$5,200 for equipment; 15,000 long-distance minutes	d	d
District and state offices rental	$2,400	2,500 sq. ft.[f]	d	d
Furnishings (one-time)	$5,000	$27,000	d	d
Official expenses	$1,200	$7,000[g]	$50,000-130,000[h]	$83,549-256,700[h]
Constituent communications (begun in 1975)	0	$5,000	d	d
Equipment lease	0	$9,000	d	d

a. Each member was entitled to an annual clerk-hire allowance of $149,292 for a staff not to exceed fifteen employees for a member representing a district under 500,000 persons or $157,092 for a staff not to exceed sixteen employees for a member representing a district with 500,000 or more.

b. Each member was entitled to an annual clerk-hire allowance of $215,372 for a staff not to exceed eighteen employees. If a member elected to employ a research assistant, the member's clerk-hire allowance was increased by $23,208 to $238,580.

c. Each member is entitled to an annual clerk-hire allowance of $288,156 for a staff not to exceed twenty-two employees, four of whom must fit into five categories: (1) shared payroll—employees, such as computer experts, who are shared by members; (2) interns—employees hired for an educational experience for not more than 120 days and not paid more than $9,600 on an annual scale ($7,800 in 1979); (3) employees on leave without pay; (4) part-time employees—employees hired for not more than fifteen full days a month and not paid more than $900 per month ($750 in 1979); (5) temporary employees—employees hired for a specific purpose for not more than ninety days.

d. As of January 3, 1978, previous individual allowances for travel, office equipment lease, district office lease, stationery, telecommunications, mass mailings, postage, computer services, and other official expenses were consolidated in a single allowance category—the official expenses allowance. Members may now budget funds for each category as they see fit.

e. Four units equal one telephone minute; one unit equals one telegram word.

f. General Services Administration's applicable rates ranged from $5 to $18 per square foot.

g. On March 2, 1977, an official expenses allowance of $7,000 per session was authorized for official expenses incurred in district and Washington, D.C., offices, to be effective January 3, 1978. From July 1, 1954, to January 3, 1978, an allowance was provided to members for expenses incurred only outside the District of Columbia. The official expenses allowance approved March 2, 1977, provided that funds be available for expenses not only of district offices but also of Washington, D.C., offices. Previously, Washington, D.C., office expenses not met by

(Notes continue)

official individual allowances were paid from such services as unofficial office accounts and members' personal funds. The official expenses allowance approved March 2, 1977, and to have become effective January 3, 1978, however, was superseded by a decision of the Committee on House Administration on November 2, 1977, effective January 3, 1978. The committee's decision provided for two allowances: (1) the official expenses allowance and (2) the clerk-hire allowance. The official expenses allowance, presently in effect, consolidates previous individual allowances for travel, office equipment lease, district office lease, stationery, telecommunications, mass mailings, postage, computer services, and other official expenses.

h. Each member is entitled to a base official expenses allowance of $47,300 ($32,911 in 1979). In addition, there are three variables that determine the total amount allotted for official expenses: (1) transportation costs, (2) telecommunications costs, and (3) cost of office space. The amount allotted for travel is computed as follows: sixty-four multiplied by the rate per mile multiplied by the mileage between the District of Columbia and the farthest point in the member's district, according to the Rand McNally *Standard Highway Mileage Guide*, plus 10 percent.

The amount allotted for telecommunications is computed as follows: 15,000 times the highest long-distance rate per minute from the District of Columbia to the member's district. If the member has elected to use WATS or a similar service in his office, the 15,000-minute multiplier will be reduced by one-half.

The amount allotted for office space costs is computed as follows: 2,500 square feet multiplied by the highest applicable rate per square foot charged to federal agencies in the district for rental of office space. Rates are established by the administrator of general services and range from $7 to $37 per square foot in 1982.

The official expenses allowance may not be used for:

1. expenses relating to the hiring and employment of individuals, including, but not limited to, employment service fees, transportation of interviewees to and from employment interviews, and cost of relocation upon acceptance or termination of employment

2. items purchased from other than the House stationery store that have a useful life greater than current term of the member and that would have a residual value of more than $25 upon the expiration of the current term of the member

3. holiday greeting cards, flowers, and trophies

4. personal advertisements (other than meeting or appearance notices)

5. donations of any type, except flags of the United States flown over the Capitol

6. dues other than to legislative support organizations as approved by the Committee on House Administration

7. educational expenses for courses of study or information or training programs unless the benefit accrues primarily to the House and the skill or knowledge is not commonly available

8. purchases of radio and television time

9. parking for member and employees at district offices, except when included as an integral part of the lease or occupancy agreement for the district office space

In addition, new members do not use their official expenses allowance to cover the expense of attending the presession caucus. Instead, they receive a per diem of $50 plus travel expenses from the House Contingent Fund.

Sources: For 1970: Richard E. Cohen, "Congressional Allowances Are Really Perking Up," *National Journal* (February 4, 1978), p. 182. For 1977 and 1979: Committee on House Administration, "Studies Dealing with Budgetary, Staffing and Administrative Activities of the U.S. House of Representatives, 1946-1978." For 1982: U.S. House of Representatives, *Congressional Handbook*.

TABLE 5–13

ALLOWANCES FOR SENATORS, 1970–1982

Category	1970	1972	1979	1982
Clerk hire	$239,805–401,865[a]	$311,557–558,145[a]	$508,221–1,021,167[a]	$621,054–1,247,879[a]
Legislative assistance	n.a.	n.a.	$157,626[b]	$192,624[b]
Postage	$1,056–1,320	$1,215–1,520	[c]	[c]
Stationery	$3,600[d]	$3,600–5,000[e]	[c]	[c]
Travel (round trips)	12	20–22[f]	[c]	[c]
Telephone	[g]	[g]	[g]	[g]
Telegraph	[h]	[h]	[h]	[h]
District and state office rental	n.a.	n.a.	4,800–8,000 sq. ft.[i]	4,800–8,000 sq. ft.[i]
Furnishings, state offices	n.a.	n.a.	$22,500–30,500[j]	$22,500–30,500[j]
Expenses	$1,600	$1,600	[c]	[c]
Official office expense account	n.a.	n.a.	$33,000–143,000[k]	$33,000–143,000[k]

NOTE: n.a. = not applicable.

a. There is no limit on the number of employees a senator may hire. He must, however, use only the clerk hire or legislative assistance allowance to pay staff salaries. The clerk hire allowance varies according to state population.

b. In addition to clerk hire, each senator has a legislative assistance allowance worth $192,624 in 1982. This allowance is reduced for any committee chairman or ranking minority member of a committee. It is also reduced for any other senator authorized by a committee chairman to recommend or approve any individuals for appointment to the committee staff who will assist that senator "solely and directly" in his duties as a member of the committee. The amount of the reduction would equal the total compensation of all such committee staff, but would not exceed $64,208 (one-third of $192,624) for any one committee.

c. This allowance is one of the allocations of the consolidated office expense allowance. Before January 1, 1973, senators were authorized individually controlled allowances for six expense categories as follows: transportation expenses for the senator and his staff; stationery; mail and delivery service; long-distance telephone calls; telegram charges; and home state expenses, which include home state office expenses—telephone service charges incurred outside Washington, D.C.; subscriptions to newspapers, magazines, periodicals, and clipping or similar services; and home state office rent (repealed effective July 1, 1974).

Effective January 1, 1973, the Supplemental Appropriations Act, 1973, provided for the consolidation of these same allowances to provide flexibility to senators

(Notes continue)

in the management of the same dollars provided for their expense allowances. No limit was imposed on any expense category by this authorization. The allowance was designated as the consolidated office expense allowance. Effective January 1, 1977, the Legislative Branch Appropriation Act redesignated the consolidated office expense allowance as the official office expense account.

d. Before July 1, 1968, senators could be paid the unobligated balance of the stationery allowance at the close of each fiscal year. Effective with fiscal year 1969 and each fiscal year thereafter, the commutation of this allowance was prohibited.

e. This allowance varied according to state population.

f. Effective July 1, 1971, the transportation allowance was changed to a lump-sum amount for each senator, for himself and his employees, in accordance with the following: an amount equal to (a) forty times (for states with a population of less than 10 million), or (b) forty-four times (for states with a population of 10 million or more) the applicable mileage rate times the actual certified one-way mileage of the senator.

g. Prior to 1981 the allowance was authorized not to exceed a fixed number of calls aggregating not more than a fixed number of minutes per month for calls to and from Washington, D.C. Inasmuch as the zone charges for long distance service varied throughout the United States, there was no fixed dollar amount for this item. Since 1981, telephone costs have been allocated to the official office expense account and have no dollar limitation.

h. The allowance formula was a fixed dollar amount plus an amount based on the population of the senator's home state and the Western Union rates from Washington, D.C. Since the Western Union rates varied with distance from Washington, D.C., this allowance was different for each state.

i. Effective July 1, 1974, the Legislative Branch Appropriation Act, 1975, provided a formula for the allowable aggregate square feet of office space in the home state of a senator. There is no limit on the number of offices that may be established by a senator in his home state, but the designated square footage may not be exceeded. The cost of office space in the home state is not chargeable to the official office expense account.

j. An aggregate furniture and furnishings allowance is provided through the General Services Administration for one or more state offices in either federal or privately owned buildings. The $22,500 minimum allowance for office space not greater than 4,800 square feet is increased by $500 for each authorized increase of 200 square feet of space.

k. The expense account may be used for the following expenses (2 U.S.C. 58[a], as amended):

1. official telegrams and long-distance phone calls and related services
2. stationery and other office supplies purchased through the stationery room for official business
3. costs incurred in the mailing or delivery of matters relating to official business
4. official office expenses in home state, other than equipment or furniture (purchase of office equipment beyond stated allocations may be made through 10 percent funds listed under item 9 below)
5. official telephone charges incurred outside Washington, D.C.
6. subscriptions to newspapers, magazines, periodicals, or clipping or similar services
7. travel expenses incurred by a senator or staff member, subject to certain limitations
8. expenses incurred by individuals selected by a senator to serve on panels or other bodies making recommendations for nominees to service academies or federal judgeships

124

9. other official expenses as the senator determines are necessary, including (a) additional office equipment for Washington, D.C., or state offices; (b) actual transportation expenses incurred by the senator and employees for official business in the Washington metropolitan area (this is also allowed to employees assigned to a state office for actual transportation expenses in the general vicinity of the office to which assigned, but is not available for a change of assignment within the state or for commuting between home and office); but not including official office expenses incurred in the senator's state, except additional office equipment.

The total reimbursement expense for the calendar year may not exceed 10 percent of the total official office expense account.

Beginning with fiscal year 1981, each senator was also allowed to transfer funds from the administrative, clerical, and legislative assistance allowances to the official office expense account. The maximum transfer is $15,000 or 25 percent of the official office expense account, whichever is greater.

SOURCES: For 1970: Cohen, "Congressional Allowances Are Really Perking Up," p. 182. For 1972: U.S. Congress, Senate, Committee on Appropriations, *Legislative Branch Appropriations, Fiscal Year 1980.* For 1979 and 1982: U.S. Senate, *Congressional Handbook.*

6

Activity

The tables in this chapter provide a picture of an institution in which the workload increased dramatically in the 1970s, peaking in about 1976 or 1977, and then began to decline, though not to its level in the 1950s. The overall number of bills, votes, hours in session, meetings, and hearings has multiplied over the past two decades (see tables 6–1 and 6–2). On the other hand, through much of the 1970s, paradoxically, the number of bills passed by the House and the Senate and the number of bills enacted into law decreased. More and more activity was combined with fewer and fewer products. In 1980 and 1981 the workload—hearings, meetings, etc.—slowed to mesh more directly with the reduced output. In 1981, however, bills and votes declined even more markedly, leaving a decided gap between activity and output.

Bills Introduced

The number of bills introduced in the House has had several step increases or decreases. From an average of about 10,000 per Congress in the 1940s and early 1950s, the number jumped to 13,169 in the Eighty-fourth Congress (1955–1956). It remained at approximately 14,000 until the Eighty-ninth Congress (1965–1966), when it jumped again, to nearly 20,000. In the 1970s, bills introduced declined steadily, to 15,587 in the Ninety-fifth Congress, in part because of changes in the rules regarding cosponsorship, which reduced the need to introduce multiple numbers of an identical bill. The numbers dropped dramatically in the Ninety-sixth Congress—by 42 percent—and stabilized in the first session of the Ninety-seventh. The Senate has shown no such distinct ebbs and flows, though some decline is evident in the Ninety-third through the Ninety-seventh Congresses.

Bills Passed

An examination of bills passed in both houses shows a definite decline in the 1960s and again in the 1970s, though not in a uniform fashion, followed by a sharp drop, especially in the House, in 1981. Overall, however, bills passed in each house went from a rough average of 2,000 per Congress in the 1950s to 1,500 in the 1960s and to 1,000 in the 1970s. It remains to be seen whether 1981 was an anomalous year

126

in the House or the beginning of an entirely new pattern for the 1980s. Table 6–2 also examines the ratio of bills passed to those introduced (see also figure 6–1). Although the significance of these figures is limited because some bills are introduced by more than one member and some that are passed may originally have been introduced in the other body, the ratios can be used for comparisons over time. In both institutions, there has been a steady and marked decline since 1947 in the proportion of bills passed. A bill introduced now has about one-fifth of the chance of success in the House that it would have had in the Eightieth Congress and about one-fourth the chance of success in the Senate. Note the particularly low figure for the 1981 House.

Recorded Votes

The number of recorded votes remained quite low in the House through the 1940s and 1950s, increased somewhat in the mid-1960s, and jumped dramatically in the 1970s with each Congress from the Ninety-second (1971–1972) through the Ninety-fifth (1977–1978). A rules change in 1971, which permitted recorded teller votes and thereby expanded the opportunities for recorded votes on amendments, has clearly been a major factor in increasing the number of recorded votes in the House. The Senate also showed a marked increase in recorded votes beginning in 1971, even though no comparable procedural reform was introduced there, but the increase in the Senate was not as great as that in the House. In the Ninety-fifth Congress (1977–1978) the House for the first time had more recorded votes than the Senate. It would appear that both procedural reforms and a decentralization of power and initiative in the House and Senate contributed to the trend toward increased numbers of votes.

Table 6–3, which breaks down recorded votes by year, shows a small but relatively steady decline in the votes in the Senate since 1977 (see also figure 6–2). The House rates declined significantly in 1979 and 1980 and dropped sharply in 1981 to levels of a decade earlier. Whether this reflects a temporary aberration or a longer-range return to earlier levels of activity remains to be seen. It is interesting, indeed, that the Senate—in transition from a Democratic to a Republican majority—shows basic continuity in trends begun about 1977 while the House, with no change in party majority in 1981, shows a sharp break from the past.

Time in Session

As tables 6–1 and 6–2 indicate, there has been substantial fluctuation in the numbers of days in session per Congress, with no particular

127

longitudinal pattern. The number of hours per day in session, however, clearly increased over time, especially in the House, through the 1970s. The House went from an average of 4.2 hours per day in the 1950s to 4.4 in the 1960s and to 5.3 in the 1970s, with an average of 5.8 hours per day in 1979–1980. In 1981 the average dropped markedly, to 4.0 hours per day, a level last achieved in 1963–1964.

In the Senate, where floor procedures have always been looser and more informal and filibusters have periodically extended the time in session, there is no comparable increase over time nor any comparable sharp drop. Sessions in the 1970s, however, were consistently long, never falling below 2,000 hours; in the earlier period they demonstrated considerably more fluctuation, only five of the twelve between 1947 and 1970 being over 2,000 hours. Sessions in 1981 fit well within recent trend lines.

Committee and Subcommittee Meetings

The number of committee and subcommittee meetings and hearings rose consistently in the House of Representatives after 1965–1966, the most substantial increases occurring in the late 1970s. The 1979–1980 figures for the House were more than double the average number per Congress in the 1950s and 1960s. The expansion of power and initiative to subcommittees and the wider distribution of chairmanships probably account for much of this change. The figures for 1981 indicate a marked cutback in committee and subcommittee activity, to levels of a decade or more earlier.

In the Senate a rather different pattern has occurred. The number of meetings and hearings jumped substantially in the late 1960s and early 1970s, beginning especially with the famous "Great Society" Eighty-ninth Congress (1965–1966) and reaching a peak a decade later in the Ninety-fourth Congress (1975–1976) of 4,265, some 70 percent higher than in the 1950s. Beginning in 1977, however—after the committee system reorganization that cut back drastically the number of subcommittees and assignments (see chapter 4)—the number of meetings and hearings began to decline, to 3,960 in the Ninety-fifth Congress and to 3,790 in the Ninety-sixth. The activity for the first year of the Ninety-seventh Congress indicates a further decline, though not a precipitous one. The Ninety-seventh Senate, however, may well end up with committee activity levels very close to those of the mid-1960s or earlier, given that committee activity is always higher in the first year of a Congress.

Laws and Other Output

Table 6–4, focusing more directly on congressional output, shows the number of public and private bills enacted into law (that is, passed by both the House and the Senate and signed by the president) and the number of pages of enacted bills (see also figure 6–3). There has been a decline in recent congresses in the number of public bills enacted, combined with a striking increase in the average page length of the statutes since 1975–1976. From the 1950s through the mid-1960s, the average number of pages per statute was approximately 2.5. The average jumped to approximately 5 pages in the mid-1970s, reached a high of 7.0 pages in the Ninety-fourth Congress, and remained high in the Ninety-fifth and Ninety-sixth Congresses. In 1981, the first session of the Ninety-seventh Congress, the conclusion that fewer but much longer laws are being passed was underscored and accentuated. The number of bills passed dropped dramatically, while the average page length soared to 11.9. The enormous length of the omnibus budget reconciliation bill had much to do with the increase in bill length and complexity. The private bills enacted have also declined substantially but, in contrast to public bills, have not changed in average length.

Actions of Congress, in votes and laws, affect the workload, job difficulty, and output of the federal executive as well. Table 6–5 shows the number of pages in the *Federal Register* per year since 1966, along with those of some earlier years for comparison. As the average length of statutes increased in Congress in the 1970s, the number of pages in the *Federal Register*—which among other things displays regulations mandated by these statutes—jumped correspondingly. In 1981, as deregulation proceeded in the Reagan administration and the number of substantive bills declined, the pages of the *Federal Register* dropped by 27 percent—to the level of 1977–1978, at the beginning of the Carter administration.

Table 6–6 shows that the amount of franked mail generated by Congress has increased tremendously since the 1960s, lately averaging nearly 400 million pieces per year, or nearly 800,000 pieces per legislator (see table 5–11 for costs). This reached a record 511 million pieces in the election year of 1980—nearly a million pieces per legislator—then receded to about 400 million in 1981. Note, of course, the regular increases in election years, and the decline in off years.

As table 6–7 shows, figures on incoming mail are not wholly consistent or reliable. Nevertheless, recent trends are interesting— especially the dramatic increase in letters to the House of Representatives, after several years of relative stability, in 1981. No comparable increase occurred in the Senate. One obvious explanation is the heavy focus on President Reagan's economic program and the three pivotal 1981 vote battles in the House. Each resulted in heavy mail, breaking previous records in several instances.

TABLE 6-1

House Workload, Eightieth to Ninety-seventh Congresses, 1947–1981

Congress	Bills Introduced[a]	Average No. of Bills Introduced per Member	Bills Passed	Ratio of Bills Passed to Bills Introduced	Recorded Votes	Time in Session		Hours per Day in Session	Committee, Subcommittee Meetings[b]
						Days	Hours		
80th (1947–48)	7,611	17.5	1,739	0.228	159	254	1,224	4.8	n.a.
81st (1949–50)	10,502	24.1	2,482	0.236	275	345	1,501	4.4	n.a.
82d (1951–52)	9,065	20.8	2,008	0.222	181	274	1,163	4.2	n.a.
83d (1953–54)	10,875	25.0	2,129	0.196	147	240	1,033	4.3	n.a.
84th (1955–56)	13,169	30.3	2,360	0.179	147	230	937	4.1	3,210
85th (1957–58)	14,580	33.5	2,064	0.142	193	276	1,147	4.2	3,750
86th (1959–60)	14,112	32.4	1,636	0.116	180	265	1,039	3.9	3,059
87th (1961–62)	14,328	32.8	1,927	0.134	240	304	1,227	4.0	3,402
88th (1963–64)	14,022	32.2	1,267	0.090	232	334	1,251	3.7	3,596

89th (1965–66)	19,874	45.7	1,565	0.079	394	336	1,547	4.6	4,367
90th (1967–68)	22,060	50.7	1,213	0.055	478	328	1,595	4.9	4,386
91st (1969–70)	21,436	49.3	1,130	0.053	443	350	1,613	4.6	5,066
92d (1971–72)	18,561	42.7	970	0.052	649	298	1,429	4.8	5,114
93d (1973–74)	18,872	43.4	923	0.049	1,078	318	1,487	4.7	5,888
94th (1975–76)	16,982	39.0	968	0.057	1,273	311	1,788	5.7	6,975
95th (1977–78)	15,587	35.8	1,027	0.066	1,540	323	1,898	5.9	6,771
96th (1979–80)	9,103	20.9	929	0.102	1,276	326	1,876	5.8	7,022
97th, 1st session (1981)	5,688	13.1	270	0.047	353	163	653	4.0	3,097

NOTE: n.a. = not available.

a. All bills and joint resolutions introduced.

b. Figures do not include the House Appropriations Committee for the Eighty-fourth to Eighty-eighth Congresses. House Appropriations included in the subsequent Congresses numbered 584 in the Eighty-ninth Congress, 705 in the Ninetieth, 709 in the Ninety-first, 854 in the Ninety-second, and 892 in the Ninety-third.

SOURCES: Arthur G. Stevens, "Indicators of Congressional Workload and Activity," Congressional Research Service, May 30, 1979. Updated for Ninety-sixth Congress: U.S. Congress, Congressional Record—Daily Digest, "Resume of Congressional Activity," vol. 126, no. 180, December 30, 1980. For 1981: U.S. Congress, Congressional Record—Daily Digest, "Resume of Congressional Activity," vol. 127, no. 188, pt. 3, December 16, 1981. Congressional Quarterly Almanac, annual volumes.

TABLE 6-2

SENATE WORKLOAD, EIGHTIETH TO NINETY-SEVENTH CONGRESSES, 1947–1981

Congress	Bills Introduced[a]	Average No. of Bills Introduced per Member	Bills Passed	Ratio of Bills Passed to Bills Introduced	Recorded Votes	Time in Session Days	Time in Session Hours	Hours per Day in Session	Committee, Subcommittee Meetings
80th (1947–48)	3,186	33.2	1,670	0.524	248	257	1,462	5.7	n.a.
81st (1949–50)	4,486	46.7	2,362	0.527	455	389	2,410	6.2	n.a.
82d (1951–52)	3,665	38.2	1,849	0.505	331	287	1,648	5.7	n.a.
83d (1953–54)	4,077	42.5	2,231	0.547	270	294	1,962	6.7	n.a.
84th (1955–56)	4,518	47.1	2,550	0.564	224	224	1,362	6.1	2,607
85th (1957–58)	4,532	47.2	2,202	0.486	313	271	1,876	6.9	2,748
86th (1959–60)	4,149	42.3	1,680	0.405	422	280	2,199	7.9	2,271

Congress									
87th (1961–62)	4,048	40.5	1,953	0.482	434	323	2,164	6.7	2,532
88th (1963–64)	3,457	34.6	1,341	0.388	541	375	2,395	6.4	2,493
89th (1965–66)	4,129	41.3	1,636	0.396	497	345	1,814	5.3	2,889
90th (1967–68)	4,400	44.0	1,376	0.313	595	358	1,961	5.5	2,892
91st (1969–70)	4,867	48.7	1,271	0.261	667	384	2,352	6.1	3,264
92d (1971–72)	4,408	44.1	1,035	0.235	955	348	2,294	6.6	3,559
93d (1973–74)	4,524	45.2	1,115	0.246	1,138	334	2,028	6.1	4,067
94th (1975–76)	4,114	41.1	1,038	0.252	1,290	320	2,210	6.9	4,265
95th (1977–78)	3,800	38.0	1,070	0.282	1,151	337	2,510	7.4	3,960
96th (1979–80)	3,480	34.8	977	0.281	1,028	333	2,324	7.0	3,790
97th, 1st session (1981)	2,142	21.4	274	0.128	483	165	1,080	6.5	1,893

NOTE: n.a. = not available.

a. All bills and joint resolutions introduced.

SOURCES: Stevens, "Indicators of Congressional Workload and Activity." Updated for Ninety-sixth Congress: Same as note in table 6-1. For 1981: Same as note in table 6-1. *Congressional Quarterly Almanac*, annual volumes.

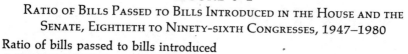
FIGURE 6–1

RATIO OF BILLS PASSED TO BILLS INTRODUCED IN THE HOUSE AND THE
SENATE, EIGHTIETH TO NINETY-SIXTH CONGRESSES, 1947–1980

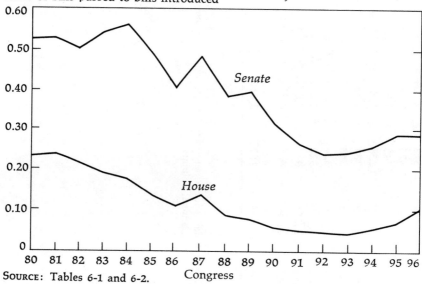

Ratio of bills passed to bills introduced

SOURCE: Tables 6-1 and 6-2.

134

TABLE 6–3
RECORDED VOTES IN THE HOUSE AND THE SENATE, 1947–1981

Year	House	Senate
1947	84	138
1948	75	110
1949	121	226
1950	154	229
1951	109	202
1952	72	129
1953	71	89
1954	76	181
1955	73	88
1956	74	136
1957	100	111
1958	93	202
1959	87	215
1960	93	207
1961	116	207
1962	124	227
1963	119	229
1964	113	312
1965	201	259
1966	193	238
1967	245	315
1968	233	280[a]
1969	177	245
1970	266	422
1971	320	423
1972	329	532
1973	541	594
1974	537	544
1975	612	602
1976	661	688
1977	706	635
1978	834	516
1979	672	497
1980	604	531
1981	353	483

a. This figure does not include one yea-and-nay vote that was ruled invalid for lack of a quorum.

SOURCE: *Congressional Quarterly Almanac*, annual volumes.

FIGURE 6–2
Recorded Votes in the House and the Senate, Eighthieth to Ninety-sixth Congresses, 1947–1980

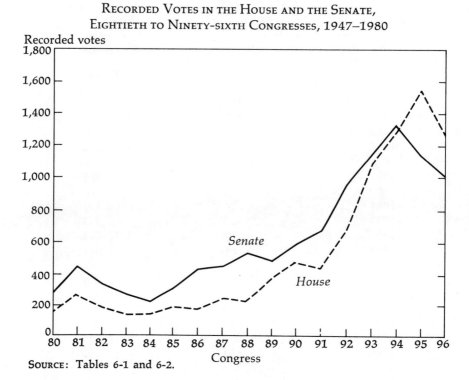

Recorded votes

Congress

Source: Tables 6-1 and 6-2.

TABLE 6-4

CONGRESSIONAL WORKLOAD, EIGHTIETH TO NINETY-SEVENTH CONGRESSES, 1947–1981

	Public Bills			Private Bills		
Congress	No. of bills enacted	Pages of bills enacted	Pages per statute	No. of bills enacted	Pages of bills enacted	Pages per statute
80th (1947–48)	906	2,236	2.5	458	182	0.40
81st (1949–50)	921	2,314	2.5	1,103	417	0.38
82d (1951–52)	594	1,585	2.7	1,023	360	0.35
83d (1953–54)	781	1,899	2.4	1,002	365	0.36
84th (1955–56)	1,028	1,848	1.8	893	364	0.41
85th (1957–58)	936	2,435	2.6	784	349	0.45
86th (1959–60)	800	1,774	2.2	492	201	0.41
87th (1961–62)	885	2,078	2.3	684	255	0.37
88th (1963–64)	666	1,975	3.0	360	144	0.40
89th (1965–66)	810	2,912	3.6	473	188	0.40
90th (1967–68)	640	2,304	3.6	362	128	0.35
91st (1969–70)	695	2,927	4.2	246	104	0.42
92d (1971–72)	607	2,330	3.8	161	67	0.42
93d (1973–74)	649	3,443	5.3	123	48	0.39
94th (1975–76)	588	4,117	7.0	141	75	0.53
95th (1977–78)	633	3,778	6.0	170	60	0.35
96th (1979–80)	613	3,582	5.8	123	63	0.51
97th (1981)	145	1,729	11.9	12	5	0.42

SOURCES: Stevens, "Indicators of Congressional Workload and Activity." Updated for 1981 with *U.S. Code Congressional and Administrative News*, February 1982 (St. Paul Minn.: West Publishing Co.).

FIGURE 6–3

PUBLIC BILLS IN THE CONGRESSIONAL WORKLOAD,
EIGHTIETH TO NINETY-SIXTH CONGRESSES, 1947–1980

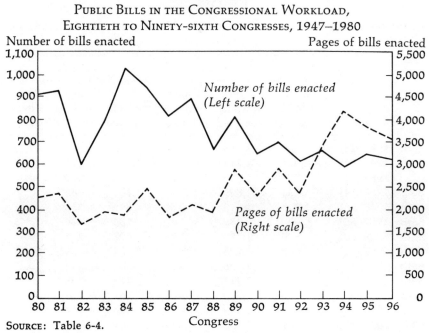

Number of bills enacted

Pages of bills enacted

SOURCE: Table 6-4.

138

TABLE 6–5
Pages in the Federal Register, 1936–1981

Year	Pages
1936	2,355
1946	14,736
1956	10,528
1966	16,850
1967	21,087
1968	20,068
1969	20,464
1970	20,032
1971	25,442
1972	28,920
1973	35,586
1974	45,422
1975	60,221
1976	57,072
1977	63,629
1978	61,261
1979	77,497
1980	87,012
1981	63,554

Source: Inspection of bound volumes of the *Federal Register* by Harvey Mansfield, January 17, 1980; updated by authors.

TABLE 6–6

Congressional Mailings, 1954–1981
(millions of pieces)

Fiscal Year	Franked Mail	
	Pieces	Percent of increase or decrease (−)
1954	43.5	—
1955	45.6	4.8
1956	58.2	27.6
1957	59.6	2.4
1958	65.4	9.7
1959	86.5	32.3
1960	108.0	24.9
1961	85.1	− 21.2
1962	110.1	29.4
1963	94.7	− 14.0
1964	110.5	16.7
1965	120.9	9.4
1966	197.5	63.4
1967	192.9	− 2.3
1968	178.2	− 7.6
1969	190.0	6.6
1970	201.0	5.8
1971	238.4	18.6
1972	308.9	29.6
1973	310.6	0.6
1974	321.0	3.3
1975	312.4	− 2.7
1976	401.4	28.5
Transition quarter	159.9	—
1977	293.3	− 26.9
1978	430.2	46.7
1979	409.9	− 4.7
1980	511.3	24.7
1981	395.6	− 22.6

Sources: U.S. House, Committee on Appropriations, *Hearings on Legislative Branch Appropriations, Fiscal Year 1980*. For 1978: U.S. Congress, House, Subcommittee on Legislative Branch Appropriations, *Hearings, Legislative Branch Appropriations for 1980*, 96th Congress, 1st session, pt. 2, p. 1593. For 1979: U.S. Congress, House, Subcommittee on Legislative Branch Appropriations, *Hearings, Legislative Branch Appropriations for 1981*, 96th Congress, 2d session, pt. 2, p. 189. For 1980-1981: Office of the Clerk of the House of Representatives.

TABLE 6–7

House and Senate Post Office Incoming Mail Volume, 1973–1981
(thousands)

	House		Senate	
	Incoming letters	Flats[a]	Incoming letters	Flats[a]
1973	20,600	11,344	—	—
1974	25,755	14,655	—	—
1975	25,106	14,546	—	—
1976	24,393	13,100	—	—
1977	26,842	12,351	—	—
1978	28,017	13,507	28,000	8,000
1979	27,508	13,535	24,500	8,400
1980	29,411	13,264	27,000	8,000
1981	40,075	17,837	29,000	5,600

NOTE: House figures have been calculated by the U.S. Postal Service. They do not include "Dear Colleague" letters, other internal correspondence, or mail from the Library of Congress, White House, State Department, Social Security Administration, or Government Printing Office. The Postal Service counts mail that is delivered in bulk, such as post cards from organizations that are delivered in cartons, as a single parcel unit. Hence a 1977 study by the Joint Committee on Congressional Operations estimated that the Postal Service's count reflects 40 to 50 percent of the House Post Office's total mail volume. Senate figures are estimates provided by the Senate Post Office. Senate mail volume includes internal and interagency deliveries.

a. Flats are large manila envelopes.

SOURCES: For House: for 1973-1974, House, Subcommittee on Legislative Branch Appropriations, *Hearings, Legislative Branch Appropriations for 1981*, pt. 2, pp. 108-10. For 1975-1981, U.S. Congress, House, Subcommittee on Legislative Branch Appropriations, *Hearings, Legislative Branch Appropriations for 1983*, 97th Congress, 2d session, pt. 2, pp. 79-80. For Senate: 1978-1981, U.S. Senate Post Office.

7

Budgeting

Allen Schick

The Constitution gives Congress the power to levy taxes and to appropriate money. The federal government is permitted to raise and spend money only if Congress enables it to do so. Although these are among the oldest and most basic powers of Congress, their exercise has been affected in recent years by two other processes: authorizations and budgeting. The rules of the House (and, to a lesser extent, those of the Senate) require that programs and agencies be authorized in law before funds are appropriated for them. Since 1975 Congress has used a budget process—centered on two budget resolutions each year—to coordinate its revenue, spending, and debt legislation.

Budget Resolutions

Since the inception of the congressional budget process, voting on budget resolutions has reflected party divisions in the House. Table 7–1 shows remarkable Republican cohesion, with only a few members breaking party ranks. During the 1976–1981 fiscal years, approximately 95 percent of the House Republicans voted against adoption of the budget resolutions. For the fiscal 1982 budget, however, the Republicans were able (despite their minority status in the House) to gain control of the budget process, and most of them voted in favor of budget resolutions supported by Republican President Ronald Reagan.

The Democrats have not been as united as the Republicans, and members from both the liberal and conservative wings of the party have voted against the position taken by most of their colleagues. Nevertheless, during the 1976–1981 fiscal years, House Democrats supplied sufficient votes to pass the budget resolutions, though on two occasions (the first resolution for fiscal 1978 and the second for fiscal 1980) only after an initial version was rejected. In voting on the 1982 budget resolutions, most House Democrats opposed the president's position, and, when their view was rejected, voted against adoption of the budget resolutions.

In the Senate, until the 1982 budget, the resolutions were supported by a bipartisan coalition of Republicans and Democrats, and most of the resolutions were passed by a wide margin (table 7–2). The two parties were polarized on the fiscal 1982 budget, and—for the first time since the budget process was introduced—a majority of Senate Democrats voted against approval of a budget resolution. Democratic opposition was mirrored by increased Republican support for the resolutions. The second budget resolution for fiscal year 1982 was approved by a one-vote margin, despite overwhelming Republican support for it.

In voting on the budget resolutions, Congress goes on record with respect to key budget aggregates (total revenues, budget authority, outlays, and deficit) and functional allocations. Table 7–3 compares congressional decisions on the aggregates with presidential budget recommendations and with the actual results for each fiscal year from 1976 through 1981. During the early years of the budget process, actual spending and the deficit tended to be below those set by Congress in its budget resolutions. Since 1980, however, the final results have shown higher spending and bigger deficits than those endorsed by Congress in its initial resolution for the fiscal year. This table also shows that Congress does not limit itself to the two budget resolutions required by the Congressional Budget Act. In most years Congress revised its budget in a "third" resolution, usually as part of the first resolution for the next fiscal year.

Congressional Control of the Budget

Although Congress holds the power of the purse, its ability to exercise this power effectively has been hampered by the rise of uncontrollable spending. During the sixteen years covered by table 7–4, "relatively uncontrollable" outlays soared from less than $100 billion to more than $500 billion and from less than 60 percent of total outlays to more than 75 percent.

Most uncontrollables are in the form of entitlements: provisions of law that mandate payments to eligible recipients. Most entitlements are open-ended and cannot be controlled through budgetary or appropriations actions. Moreover, many entitlements are "indexed" to the rate of inflation, so that payments are adjusted to increases in the cost of living without congressional action. Entitlements can be brought under control by changing the substantive laws mandating the payments. One of the main purposes of the reconciliation process used by Congress in 1980 and 1981 was to reduce certain entitlements so as to bring expenditures for them into line with congressional budget decisions.

The Authorizations Process

The rule that programs be authorized before appropriations are made for them does not mean that Congress considers authorizing legislation for all federal programs each year. Most programs have permanent authorizations; the law establishing them does not set either a dollar or a time limit. For these programs there is no need for authorizing legislation unless Congress wants to change the permanent law. Nevertheless, there has been a trend toward temporary authorizations; moreover, annual authorizations, as table 7–5 shows, now constitute almost 20 percent of the total budget authority (appropriations and other legislation enabling federal agencies to enter into obligations) acted on by Congress each year.

It should be noted, however, that almost half the total budget authority requires no annual legislative action. A major portion of the federal budget has permanent authorizations and permanent appropriations as well.

The Appropriations Process

Despite the increased emphasis on authorizing legislation and budget resolutions, the House and Senate Appropriations committees focus on the budget estimates submitted by the president. These committees take pride in their determination to appropriate less money than the president requests. Table 7–6, drawn from the official records of the Appropriations committees, shows that year after year the amount appropriated is below the president's budget. These figures do not include permanent appropriations (which are not reviewed by the Appropriations committees) or "backdoor" authority provided in other legislation.

Although the Appropriations committees provide less money than the president requests, they also enact sizable supplemental appropriations each year (table 7–7). Indeed, the number of supplemental bills and their amounts have been higher since the congressional budget process was introduced than they were before.

Supplemental appropriations are made for a number of reasons: to provide for agencies not funded in the regular appropriation bills, to pay for the salary increases of federal employees, to supplement the funds for agencies facing a deficiency, and to finance new or expanded programs.

Historically, the House Appropriations Committee has served as the "guardian of the Treasury," cutting budget requests, curtailing federal expenditures, and inhibiting the inclination of Congress to provide more money for various programs. This role depends on the committee's ability to protect appropriation bills against floor proposals to provide additional funds. But, as table 7–8 demonstrates, there has been a steady rise during the past two decades in the number of floor amendments and an even sharper increase in the number of amendments approved by the House. One important factor in this trend was the Legislative Reorganization Act of 1970, which provided for recorded votes in the committee of the whole, where most House action on appropriation bills (and other measures) takes place. Another factor has been the increase in efforts to attach "limitations" to appropriation bills. The House adopted three times as many limiting amendments in the 1970s as it did in the 1960s. These limits do not change the amounts appropriated, but restrict the uses to which the funds can be put.

The ability of the Appropriations committees to guard the Treasury also depends on the extent to which appropriations are considered by Congress. The trend displayed in table 7–9 suggests that appropriations control has been significantly weakened by the rise in permanent appropriations—funds that become available for expenditure without any new congressional action. Most of the permanent appropriations are in trust funds—such as the social security trust funds. The receipts of these funds are automatically appropriated and do not go through the appropriations process. A very small portion of the permanent appropriations are in the form of "advance appropriations," by which Congress provides funds for a future year.

Despite the rise in permanent appropriations that require no congressional action, Congress has had increasing difficulty in completing its work on regular appropriation bills by the start of the fiscal year. As a consequence, it has been compelled to provide stopgap funding through continuing appropriations, as table 7–10 shows. Except for fiscal year 1977, when the new congressional budget process and its timetable effectively prodded Congress to complete its appropriations work on schedule, it has been necessary to rely on continuing appropriations. In fiscal 1980, only three of the thirteen regular appropriation bills were enacted by the start of the fiscal year; for fiscal 1981, only one regular appropriation bill was enacted; none of these bills had been enacted into law when fiscal 1982 began.

Rescissions and Deferrals

One of the key purposes of the congressional budget process is to ensure that congressional spending priorities prevail when they are in conflict with those of the president. To achieve this end, the Impoundment Control Act established procedures for congressional review of presidential proposals to defer or rescind funds provided by Congress. When a president proposes rescission, Congress has a forty-five-day period during which it can pass a bill rescinding the funds; if Congress fails to act during this period, the president is required to make the funds available for expenditure. Table 7–11 shows that the use of the rescission process varies sharply from year to year. In 1975 and 1976 President Ford proposed billions of dollars in rescissions, but Congress actually rescinded less than 10 percent of the amount. During the Carter administration, rescissions dropped sharply. Reagan resorted to rescissions to implement his budget policy, however, and 90 percent of the amounts he proposed to rescind was approved by Congress.

When a president proposes deferrals, either the House or the Senate can approve an "impoundment resolution" compelling the release of the affected funds. Congress usually disapproves only a small portion of the deferrals submitted by the president.

TABLE 7–1

Republican and Democratic Votes on House Adoption of Budget Resolutions, Fiscal Years 1976–1982

Fiscal Year	Resolution	Total		Democrats		Republicans	
		Yes	No	Yes	No	Yes	No
1976	First resolution	200	196	197	68	3	128
	Second resolution	225	191	214	67	11	124
1977	First resolution	221	155	208	44	13	111
	Second resolution	227	151	215	38	12	113
	Third resolution	239	169	225	50	14	119
1978	First resolution (first round)	84	320	82	185	2	135
	First resolution (second round)	213	179	206	58	7	121
	Second resolution	199	188	195	59	4	129
1979	First resolution	201	197	198	61	3	136
	Second resolution	217	178	215	42	2	136
1980	First resolution	220	184	211	50	9	134
	Second resolution (first round)	192	213	188	67	4	146
	Second resolution (second round)	212	206	212	52	0	154
	Third resolution[a]	241	174	218	45	23	129
1981	First resolution	225	193	203	62	22	131
	Second resolution	203	191	201	45	2	146
1982	First resolution	270	154	84	153	186	1
	Second resolution	206	200	70	150	136	50

NOTE: These votes are on passage of the resolutions in the House, not on adoption of the conference report.

a. The third resolution for fiscal 1980 was part of the first resolution for the 1981 fiscal year, but it was voted on separately in the House.

SOURCES: *Congressional Record* and *Congressional Quarterly Almanac.*

TABLE 7–2

REPUBLICAN AND DEMOCRATIC VOTES ON SENATE ADOPTION OF BUDGET RESOLUTIONS, FISCAL YEARS 1976–1982

Fiscal Year	Resolution	Total Yes	Total No	Democrats Yes	Democrats No	Republicans Yes	Republicans No
1976	First resolution	69	22	50	4	19	18
	Second resolution	69	23	50	8	19	15
1977	First resolution	62	22	45	6	17	16
	Second resolution	55	23	41	5	14	18
	Third resolution	72	20	55	3	17	17
1978	First resolution	56	31	41	14	15	17
	Second resolution	63	21	46	8	17	13
1979	First resolution	64	27	48	8	16	19
	Second resolution	56	18	42	6	14	12
1980	First resolution	64	20	44	5	20	15
	Second resolution	62	36	45	14	17	22
1981	First resolution	68	28	49	6	19	22
	Second resolution	48	46	33	21	15	25
1982	First resolution	78	20	28	18	50	2
	Second resolution	49	48	2	44	47	4

NOTE: These votes are on passage of the resolutions in the Senate, not on adoption of the conference report.

SOURCES: *Congressional Record* and *Congressional Quarterly Almanac*.

148

TABLE 7–3

BUDGETED AND ACTUAL REVENUES, BUDGET AUTHORITY, OUTLAYS,
AND DEFICITS, FISCAL YEARS 1976–1981
(billions of dollars)

	Revenues	Budget Authority	Budget Outlays	Budget Deficit
1976				
President's budget	297.7	385.8	349.4	51.9
First budget resolution	298.2	395.8	367.0	68.8
Second budget resolution	300.8	408.0	374.9	74.1
Actual	300.0	415.3	366.4	66.4
1977				
President's budget	351.3	433.4	394.2	43.0
First budget resolution	362.5	454.2	413.3	50.8
Second budget resolution	362.5	451.6	413.1	50.6
Third budget resolution	347.7	472.9	417.5	69.8
Fourth budget resolution	356.6	470.2	409.2	52.6
Actual	357.8	464.4	402.7	44.9
1978				
Ford budget	393.0	480.4	440.0	47.0
Carter budget	401.6	507.3	459.4	57.8
First budget resolution	396.3	503.5	461.0	64.7
Second budget resolution	397.0	500.1	458.3	61.3
Actual	402.0	500.4	450.8	48.8
1979				
President's budget	439.6	568.2	500.2	60.6
First budget resolution	447.9	568.9	498.8	50.9
Second budget resolution	448.7	555.7	487.5	38.8
Third budget resolution	461.0	559.2	494.5	33.5
Actual	465.9	556.7	493.6	27.7
1980				
President's budget	502.6	615.5	531.6	29.0
First budget resolution	509.0	604.4	532.0	23.0
Second budget resolution	517.8	638.0	547.6	29.8
Third budget resolution	525.7	658.9	572.7	47.0
Actual	520.0	658.8	579.6	59.6
1981				
President's budget	600.0	696.1	615.8	15.8
Revised budget	628.0	691.3	611.5	−16.5
First budget resolution	613.8	697.2	613.6	−0.2
Second budget resolution	605.0	694.6	632.4	27.4
Third budget resolution	603.3	717.5	661.4	58.1
Actual	599.3	718.4	657.2	57.9

SOURCE: Congressional Budget Office.

TABLE 7-4

RELATIVELY UNCONTROLLABLE FEDERAL OUTLAYS UNDER PRESENT LAW, FISCAL YEARS 1967–1982

(billions of dollars)

Fiscal Year	Social Security and Other Retirement	Medical Care	Other Payments to Individuals	Net Interest	Outlays from Prior Obligations	Other Uncontrollables	Total Uncontrollables	Percent Budget Uncontrollable
1967	26.3	4.6	10.7	10.3	37.0	4.7	93.5	59.1
1968	29.1	7.2	11.4	11.1	42.3	6.2	107.3	60.0
1969	33.1	8.9	12.9	12.4	41.9	6.9	116.1	63.1
1970	36.9	9.9	15.4	14.4	41.5	7.6	125.7	64.0
1971	43.8	11.2	22.3	14.8	40.2	8.0	140.4	66.4
1972	49.2	13.4	25.8	15.5	39.2	10.4	153.5	66.2
1973	63.6	14.1	18.3	17.3	41.4	13.9	168.6	68.7
1974	72.5	17.2	21.4	21.4	46.0	11.9	190.4	70.8
1975	86.7	21.6	34.3	23.2	53.3	9.3	228.4	70.4
1976	97.2	26.3	43.5	26.7	53.7	10.1	257.5	70.7
1977	111.5	31.4	39.6	29.9	58.8	12.4	283.5	70.8
1978	122.8	35.9	36.9	35.4	76.9	15.8	323.7	72.2
1979	136.7	41.6	46.5	42.6	85.3	12.0	364.7	72.3
1980	156.5	49.0	47.0	52.5	103.2	16.2	424.4	73.6
1981	183.7	59.3	51.5	68.7	108.6	13.2	485.0	73.8
1982 (est.)	204.6	67.6	57.4	83.0	120.3	11.8	544.7	75.1

NOTE: This table excludes the transition quarter (July 1–September 30, 1976). Various uncontrollables for the 1973–1981 fiscal years were reclassified and recomputed retroactively in the 1983 budget.

SOURCES: For the 1967–1972 fiscal years: *The Budget of the United States Government Fiscal Year 1977*, table 16; for the 1973–1982 fiscal years, *The Budget of the United States Government Fiscal Year 1983*, table 17.

TABLE 7–5

Budget Authority Subject to Annual Authorization,
Fiscal Years 1976–1981
(billions of dollars)

Fiscal Year	Budget Authority Requested	Budget Authority Requiring Current Action by Congress	Budget Authority Subject to Annual Authorization	Percentage of Budget Authority Requiring Current Action Subject to Annual Authorization
1976	383.4	257.0	43.2	16.8
1977	431.4	263.2	51.2	19.5
1978	499.0	306.2	57.0	18.6
1979	566.2	348.6	61.9	17.8
1980	616.1	362.9	71.6	19.7
1981	696.1	395.2	78.3	19.8

Source: Congressional Budget Office scorekeeping reports.

TABLE 7–6

Comparison of Budget Estimates and Appropriations, 1968–1979
(thousands of dollars)

Year	Budget Estimates	Appropriations	Estimates Less Appropriations
1968	147,908,613	133,339,869	14,568,744
1969	142,701,346	134,431,463	8,269,883
1970	147,778,903	144,273,529	3,505,375
1971	167,969,354	165,300,662	2,668,692
1972	185,509,078	179,006,901	6,502,176
1973	178,014,404	174,902,319	3,112,085
1974	213,694,183	204,012,312	9,681,871
1975	268,312,351	262,194,920	6,117,432
1976	280,825,059	277,503,235	3,321,823
1977	366,590,877	354,014,031	12,576,846
1978	373,829,696	353,538,354	20,291,342
1979	402,054,743	386,991,810	15,062,933

Notes: The years are calendar, not fiscal, years. The budget estimates and appropriations are for budget authority provided in appropriation acts and do not include permanent appropriations or budget authority provided in legislative acts.

Source: U.S. Congress, *Appropriations, Budget Estimates, Etc.* (compiled by the Senate and House Appropriations committees and published annually as a Senate document).

TABLE 7-7

SUPPLEMENTAL APPROPRIATION BILLS, FISCAL YEARS 1964–1981

Fiscal Year	Number of Supplemental Bills[a]	Amount of Budget Authority[b] (millions of dollars)
1964	1	290
1965	4	5,645
1966	4	21,889
1967	3	19,420
1968	5	8,218
1969	4	5,835
1970	2	5,993
1971	4	9,870
1972	7	11,599
1973	5	11,371
1974	5	14,796
1975	7	27,587
1976	5	24,636
1977	5	49,835
1978	9	16,053
1979	1	13,845
1980	6	19,683
1981	1	20,943

a. The number of supplemental bills does not include regular and continuing appropriations in which supplemental budget authority was provided.

b. The amount of budget authority does include, for fiscal year 1976 and subsequent years, supplementals provided in regular or continuing appropriation bills.

SOURCES: For the 1964-1969 fiscal years, Louis Fisher, *Supplemental Appropriations History, Controls, Recent Record* (Congressional Research Service, April 12, 1979); for the 1970-1980 fiscal years, Congressional Budget Office, *Supplemental Appropriations in the 1970s*, Staff Working Paper, July 1981. For 1981 fiscal year, *Congressional Quarterly Almanac*, 1981.

TABLE 7–8

House Amendments to Appropriation Bills, 1963–1980

Year	Total Amendments	Amendments Adopted	Limitation Amendments[a]	Limitation Amendments Adopted
1963	47	15	17	7
1964	27	9	11	2
1965	26	9	11	1
1966	56	10	8	1
1967	70	15	16	4
1968	75	24	20	7
1969	89	27	20	10
1970	51	11	13	1
1971	83	34	23	7
1972	89	15	26	5
1973	99	31	31	12
1974	109	53	34	15
1975	106	52	34	12
1976	122	68	33	13
1977	107	54	44	24
1978	140	59	38	23
1979	156	96	43	26
1980	210	135	86	67

Note: The years are calendar, not fiscal, years.

a. Limitation amendments are amendments that bar the use of appropriated funds for specified purposes.

Sources: For 1963-1977, the Democratic Study Group, Special Report No. 95-12 (February 14, 1978); for 1978-1980, Daniel P. Strickland, "Limitation Amendments Offered on the Floor of the House of Representatives, 1978, 1979, and 1980" (Congressional Research Service, March 12, 1981).

TABLE 7-9

PERMANENT APPROPRIATIONS, FISCAL YEARS 1960–1981
(millions of dollars)

Fiscal Year	Federal Funds	Trust Funds	Total
1960	10,220	22,330	32,550
1961	9,651	24,915	34,566
1962	10,489	27,401	37,890
1963	11,366	29,472	40,838
1964	11,907	30,930	42,837
1965	12,272	33,747	46,019
1966	13,601	41,831	55,432
1967	15,045	48,206	63,251
1968	17,798	50,158	67,956
1969	21,819	53,053	74,872
1970	22,004	61,470	83,474
1971	23,369	61,890	85,259
1972	25,644	75,407	101,051
1973	37,187	94,458	131,645
1974	40,647	104,508	145,155
1975	48,851	126,261	175,112
1976	53,701	143,261	196,962
1977	53,996	158,586	212,582
1978	60,236	181,331	241,567
1979	70,749	199,126	269,875
1980	81,676	227,320	308,996
1981	125,326	247,984	373,310

SOURCE: U.S. Congress, *Appropriations, Budget Estimates, Etc.*

TABLE 7–10
Use of Continuing Appropriations, Fiscal Years 1972–1982

Fiscal Year	Regular Appropriation Bills Not Enacted by Start of Fiscal Year[a]	Continuing Resolutions Enacted for Fiscal Year
1972	5	5
1973	4	5
1974	10	2
1975	6	4
1976	11	3
1977[b]	0[c]	2
1978	4	3
1979	8	1
1980	10	2
1981	12	2
1982	13	4

a. In calendar year 1976, the start of the fiscal year was changed from July 1 to October 1.

b. Although all regular appropriation bills were enacted by the start of the fiscal year, continuing appropriations were needed for certain items not provided for in these bills.

c. The appropriation was signed into law on the first day of the fiscal year.

Sources: Robert A. Keith, "An Overview of the Use of Continuing Appropriations" (Congressional Research Service, September 26, 1980); Congressional Budget Office, "Consideration of Appropriation Bills" (unpublished memorandum, August 21, 1979); data for the 1980-1982 fiscal years are taken from the final House calendar.

TABLE 7-11
Rescissions and Deferrals, Fiscal Years 1975–1981

		Rescissions		
Fiscal Year	Number[a]	Amount proposed ($ thousand)	Amount approved ($ thousand)	Amount rescinded (percent)	Proposals approved (wholly or in part) (percent)
1975	91(4)	3,328,500	391,295	12	43
1976[b]	50(1)	3,608,363	138,331	4	14
1977	21(1)	1,835,602	1,271,040	69	48
1978	8(0)	644,055	55,255	9	38
1979	11(0)	908,692	723,609	80	80
1980	59(0)	1,618,061	778,127	48	58
1981	208(0)	16,204,936	14,509,878	90	67

(Table continues)

TABLE 7–11 (continued)

Deferrals

Fiscal Year	Number[a]	Amount proposed ($ thousand)	Amount disapproved ($ thousand)	Number of deferrals disapproved	Amount disapproved (percent)	Deferrals disapproved (percent)
1975	159	24,574,236	9,318,217	16	38	10
1976[b]	119(2)	9,209,780	393,081	24[c]	4	20
1977	68(4)	6,831,194	25,600	3	0.4	4
1978	66(0)	4,910,114	69,531	6	1	9
1979	70(1)	4,696,056	13,852	2	0.3	3
1980	73(0)	9,846,235	3,663,448	2	37	3
1981	119(0)	7,535,493	367,359	15	5	13

a. The numbers in parentheses are the number of unreported impoundments that Congress was notified of by the General Accounting Office.

b. Fiscal 1976 data include the transition quarter. A proposal to rescind or defer funds in both fiscal 1976 and the transition quarter is counted as a single proposal.

c. Two fiscal 1976 deferrals that were disapproved by both the House and the Senate are counted once here.

SOURCE: Tabulated from House Appropriations Committee data.

8
Roll Call Voting

Three important elements of voting on the floor of the House and the Senate are support for the president, the cohesion of the parties, and the strength of the ideological coalitions that cut across party lines. This chapter provides a description of the dynamics of these forces in congressional decision making since the 1950s, using the measures compiled annually by *Congressional Quarterly*.

Presidential Success and Support

Table 8–1 and figure 8–1 show the annual percentages of presidential victories on votes on which the president took clear-cut positions. *Congressional Quarterly* determines what the president wants in the way of legislative action by analyzing his messages to Congress, press conference remarks, and other public statements and documents. The measure combines the significant and the trivial, the controversial and the consensual; moreover, it reflects the position of the president at the time of a vote, even though that position may reflect a major concession from an earlier stand.

In spite of these problems, the measure does provide a rough indicator of the state of relations between the president and Congress. Table 8–1 provides an overall success score, as well as the president's success averages in the House and Senate. Presidential success is mainly a function of the number of seats in Congress held by the president's party. When one party controls both branches, success never drops below 75 percent; with divided government, presidents average well below that level of success (Ford, 58.3 percent; Nixon, 64.3 percent; Eisenhower after 1954, 66.5 percent). The anomaly is, of course, 1981, when the Republicans controlled the presidency and the Senate but not the House. Reagan's overall success score of 81.9 percent ranks with presidents whose party has controlled both houses; his score in the Senate places him alongside Eisenhower in 1953 and Johnson in 1964.

In addition, the scores sometimes reflect sharp partisan swings in the preceding elections. President Eisenhower's score dropped twenty-four percentage points after the Democratic victory in the 1958 elections. President Johnson achieved a modern high of 93 percent in the session following the 1964 elections. And, after his smashing victory in 1980, President Reagan enjoyed a level of support seven percentage points higher than that of his predecessor.

Success rates sometimes deteriorate over the course of a presidency (Johnson and Nixon); at other times they remain relatively stable (Carter); sometimes they increase (Kennedy).

The base for computing presidential scores varies widely, from a low of thirty-four House votes in 1953 and 1956 to 185 Senate votes in 1973. The average number of votes on which presidents have taken clear-cut positions has increased over time, but the percentage has declined. In 1979 President Carter made his position known on only 22 percent of all House recorded votes and 19 percent of Senate votes. The comparable figures for President Eisenhower's third year are 56 percent in the House and 59 percent in the Senate. While the congressional liaison workload of the White House has increased, so too has the relative independence of the Congress.

Table 8–2 presents presidential support scores (adjusted to remove the effects of absences) for all Democrats, Southern Democrats, and Republicans in the House and Senate. Senate Republicans have usually been more supportive of presidents, Republican and Democratic, than their House counterparts. No such consistent pattern is evident among Democrats. Whereas Democrats in the Senate were more supportive of Carter than their party colleagues in the House, the pattern was just the opposite under Presidents Kennedy and Johnson. The voting of Southern Democrats is at least partly responsible for this change. Among Southern Democratic members, President Kennedy fared better in the House than in the Senate. President Carter, on the other hand, received more support among these members in the Senate.

The figures in table 8–2 also make it clear that President Reagan's 1981 successes depended heavily on remarkable support among Republicans, especially in the Senate. While Southern Democrats provided the margin of victory on several important House votes, their overall support for Reagan was not particularly notable.

Party Unity

One important component of the structure of congressional voting is party-line voting. Table 8–3 presents for both the House and the Senate the percentage of all recorded votes on which a majority of voting Democrats opposed a majority of voting Republicans. In the

House that trend has been downward, beginning with Johnson's troubles with the war in Vietnam. Under Presidents Nixon and Ford, about 35 percent of all roll call votes produced a party split, down from an average of nearly 50 percent under President Eisenhower. The number rose to 40 percent during Carter's four years in office and then dropped back to 37 percent in Reagan's first year. There also appears to be an election year cycle in these figures, especially in recent years. The percentage of party votes increases in off years and declines in subsequent election years. This may reflect the efforts of congressional leaders during election years to avoid sharply partisan votes that may hurt members back home.

The Senate figures on party voting in table 8–3 are less patterned than the House figures. The percentage of party votes was higher under Presidents Carter and Reagan than under any recent president except Kennedy.

Table 8–4 presents the other information needed to gauge the level of party voting: the cohesion of the parties on those votes that elicit a party split. Party unity among Democrats has declined since the Kennedy and the early Johnson years, more so in the House (about ten percentage points) than in the Senate (about five percentage points). A decline in party unity was also registered among Republicans during this period, although in the House they appear to have turned the corner by the late 1970s and in the Senate they rebounded in 1981 to a very high 85 percent.

However important this recent decline in party voting or the 1981 resurgence, it pales in significance when compared with the long-term decline in party voting. During the years 1890–1910, two-thirds of all votes evoked a party split, and in several sessions more than half the roll calls found 90 percent of one party opposing 90 percent of the other. Since 1946 the percentage of votes showing such extreme partisan division has not gone above 10 percent.

Conservative Coalition

One reason for the decline in cohesion among the Democrats was the emergence in the late 1930s of a set of issues that brought together Southern Democrats and Republicans and pitted them against Northern Democrats. Since that time this "conservative coalition" has proved itself a formidable opponent to Democratic presidents.

Table 8–5 shows the percentage of all recorded votes in which the coalition has appeared (a majority of voting Southern Democrats and a majority of voting Republicans oppose the stand taken by a majority of voting Northern Democrats). It also shows the percentage of those votes won by the coalition.

Over the past several decades, the conservative coalition has appeared more often in the Senate than in the House, although its record of success is no greater in the Senate. Its percentage of success reached an all-time low in the House during the Eighty-ninth Congress, after the 1964 Democratic landslide, and a modern-day high in 1981, rivaling its record in the 1940s and 1950s.[1]

The coalition's success after the 1980 elections was due both to the increase in the number of Republicans in both chambers and to the increasingly conservative cast of Senate Republicans. Conservative coalition support scores (adjusted for absences) for Northern Democrats, Southern Democrats, and Republicans are presented in table 8–6. There has been a steady increase in the degree of support for the coalition among Northern Democrats, particularly in the House. (By definition, the conservative coalition support of Northern Democrats overall cannot exceed 50 percent.) Among Southern Democrats, however, support declined after the late 1960s and early 1970s, although again 1981 saw a modest reversal of that trend.

Conservative coalition support scores are perhaps most useful for gauging how ideologically representative smaller groups of members are of their party and of the entire chamber. Tables 8–7 and 8–8 present the mean conservative coalition support scores for House and Senate committees between 1959 and 1981. Figures 8–2 and 8–3 show the relative ideological makeup of each committee in 1959, 1977, and 1981. Scores are presented for all committee members and separately for Democratic and Republican members. Overall scores reflecting the average conservative coalition support among all members in the chamber and in each party caucus provide a view of the relative conservatism of each committee. The absolute scores are less reliable than the relative standing of the committees and their parent chamber over time.

The ideological makeup of some committees has changed dramatically. The House District of Columbia Committee, one of the most conservative committees in 1959, is now the least conservative. A similar though less drastic change has occurred in the committees on Rules and on Energy and Commerce. Other committees have not transformed their philosophical base but have moved further toward the ideological poles. Armed Services, always conservative, is now the most conservative major committee in the House; Judiciary, always more liberal than the House, has moved further to the left.

1. John F. Manley, "The Conservative Coalition in Congress," *American Behavioral Scientist*, vol. 17, no. 2 (1973).

Similar patterns can be discerned for Senate committees in table 8–8, at least before the 1980 elections. Between 1959 and 1979 the Finance and the Appropriations committees moved from right to center, Energy and Public Works from left to center. Armed Services and Agriculture remained more conservative than the Senate; Foreign Relations and Labor continued to be more liberal. In 1981, after the infusion of conservative Republicans from the 1980 elections, the Senate shifted distinctively to the right, upsetting many patterns of behavior, including those of its committees. Every committee shifted in a conservative direction.

There were still nine Senate committees in 1981 more liberal than the average, but two-thirds of these were more conservative than the average in the preceding Congress. Even the liberal Labor and Human Resources Committee had shifted by fifteen points in a more conservative direction and had an average score over fifty for the first time in at least three decades. The change, of course, came from the Republicans, with their great increase in numbers and the greater conservatism of the new members. The Democrats barely changed in ideology from the Ninety-sixth to the Ninety-seventh Congress, averaging in both cases forty-three or forty-four in conservative coalition support. Republican support, however, went up substantially, from an average of seventy-four to an average of eighty-four.

The partisan ideological gap on committees, of course, also grew. As table 8–8 shows, the change was greater on some committees than others, but was particularly significant among the committees of greatest prestige, such as Appropriations, Finance, Budget, and Foreign Relations. Some already polarized committees, like Labor and Banking, became even more polarized. Partisan conflict potentially increased also in the important Energy and Environment committees.

TABLE 8–1
PRESIDENTIAL VICTORIES ON VOTES IN CONGRESS, 1953–1981

Presidents and Years	House and Senate (%)	House (%)	No. of Votes	Senate (%)	No. of Votes
Eisenhower					
1953	89.2	91.2	34	87.8	49
1954	82.8	n.a.	n.a.	n.a.	n.a.
1955	75.3	63.4	41	84.6	52
1956	69.2	73.5	34	67.7	65
1957	68.4	58.3	60	78.9	57
1958	75.7	74.0	50	76.5	98
1959	52.0	55.5	54	50.4	121
1960	65.1	65.0	43	65.1	86
Kennedy					
1961	81.5	83.1	65	80.6	124
1962	85.4	85.0	60	85.6	125
1963	87.1	83.1	71	89.6	115
Johnson					
1964	87.9	88.5	52	87.6	97
1965	93.1	93.8	112	92.6	162
1966	78.9	91.3	103	68.8	125
1967	78.8	75.6	127	81.2	165
1968	74.5	83.5	103	68.9	164
Nixon					
1969	74.8	72.3	47	76.4	72
1970	76.9	84.6	65	71.4	91
1971	74.8	82.5	57	69.5	82
1972	66.3	81.1	37	54.3	46
1973	50.6	48.0	125	52.4	185
1974	59.6	67.9	53	54.2	83
Ford					
1974	58.2	59.3	54	57.4	68
1975	61.0	50.6	89	71.0	93
1976	53.8	43.1	51	64.2	53
Carter					
1977	75.4	74.7	79	76.1	88
1978	78.3	69.6	112	84.8	151
1979	76.8	71.7	145	81.4	161
1980	75.1	76.9	117	73.3	116
Reagan					
1981	81.9	72.4	76	87.5	128

NOTE: Percentages indicate number of congressional votes supporting the president divided by the total number of votes on which the president had taken a position. n.a. = not available.

SOURCES: *Congressional Quarterly Almanac*, various years; and *Congressional Quarterly Weekly Report*, vol. 40 (January 2, 1982). Some percentages recalculated.

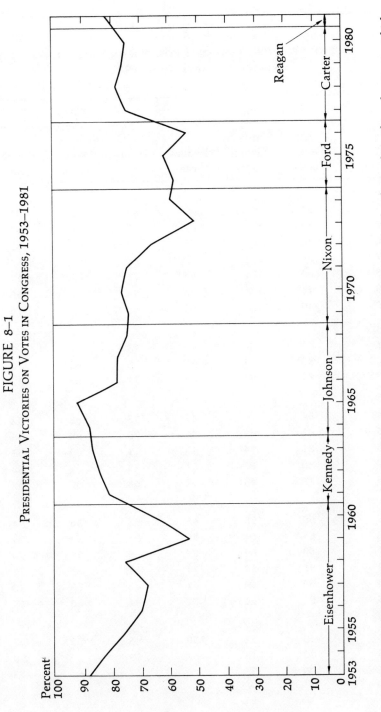

FIGURE 8-1

PRESIDENTIAL VICTORIES ON VOTES IN CONGRESS, 1953–1981

NOTE: Percentages indicate number of congressional votes supporting the president divided by the total number of votes on which the president has taken a position.

SOURCE: Table 8-1.

165

TABLE 8–2
SUPPORT FOR THE PRESIDENT'S POSITION ON VOTES IN
CONGRESS, BY PARTY, 1954–1981
(percent)

Presidents and Years	House			Senate		
	All Demo-crats	Southern Demo-crats	Repub-licans	All Demo-crats	Southern Demo-crats	Repub-licans
Eisenhower						
1954	54	n.a.	n.a.	45	n.a.	82
1955	58	n.a.	67	65	n.a.	85
1956	58	n.a.	79	44	n.a.	80
1957	54	n.a.	60	60	n.a.	80
1958	63	n.a.	65	51	n.a.	77
1959	44	n.a.	76	44	n.a.	80
1960	49	n.a.	63	52	n.a.	76
Kennedy						
1961	81	n.a.	41	73	n.a.	42
1962	83	71	47	76	63	48
1963	84	71	36	77	65	52
Johnson						
1964	84	70	42	73	63	52
1965	83	65	46	75	60	55
1966	81	64	45	71	59	53
1967	80	65	51	73	69	63
1968	77	63	59	64	50	57
Nixon						
1969	56	55	65	55	56	74
1970	64	64	79	56	62	74
1971	53	69	79	48	59	76
1972	56	59	74	52	71	77
1973	39	49	67	42	55	70
1974	52	64	71	44	60	65
Ford						
1974	48	52	59	45	55	67
1975	40	48	67	53	67	76
1976	36	52	70	47	61	73

Carter						
1977	69	58	46	77	71	58
1978	67	54	40	74	61	47
1979	70	58	37	75	66	51
1980	71	63	44	71	69	50
Reagan						
1981	46	60	72	52	63	84

NOTE: Percentages indicate number of congressional votes supporting the president divided by the total number of votes on which the president had taken a position. The percentages are normalized to eliminate the effects of absences, as follows: support = (support)/(support + opposition). n.a. = not available.

SOURCES: *Congressional Quarterly Almanac*, various years; and *Congressional Quarterly Weekly Report*, vol. 40 (January 2, 1982).

TABLE 8–3

Votes in Congress Showing Party Unity, 1953–1981
(percent of all votes)

Year	House	Senate
1953	52	n.a.
1954	38	47
1955	41	30
1956	44	53
1957	59	36
1958	40	44
1959	55	48
1960	53	37
1961	50	62
1962	46	41
1963	49	47
1964	55	36
1965	52	42
1966	41	50
1967	36	35
1968	35	32
1969	31	36
1970	27	35
1971	38	42
1972	27	36
1973	42	40
1974	29	44
1975	48	48
1976	36	37
1977	42	42
1978	33	45
1979	47	47
1980	38	46
1981	37	48

NOTE: Data indicate the percentage of all recorded votes on which a majority of voting Democrats opposed a majority of voting Republicans. n.a. = not available.

SOURCES: *Congressional Quarterly Almanac*, various years; and *Congressional Quarterly Weekly Report*, vol. 40 (January 9, 1982).

TABLE 8–4
Support for Party on Votes in Congress, 1954–1981
(percent)

Year	House			Senate		
	All Democrats	Southern Democrats	Republicans	All Democrats	Southern Democrats	Republicans
1954	80	n.a.	84	77	n.a.	89
1955	84	68	78	82	78	82
1956	80	79	78	80	75	80
1957	79	71	75	79	81	81
1958	77	67	73	82	76	74
1959	85	77	85	76	63	80
1960	75	62	77	73	60	74
1961	n.a.	n.a.	n.a.	n.a.	n.a.	n.a.
1962	81	n.a.	80	80	n.a.	81
1963	85	n.a.	84	79	n.a.	79
1964	82	n.a.	81	73	n.a.	75
1965	80	55	81	75	55	78
1966	78	55	82	73	52	78
1967	77	53	82	75	59	73
1968	73	48	76	71	57	74
1969	71	47	71	74	53	72
1970	71	52	72	71	49	71
1971	72	48	76	74	56	75
1972	70	44	76	72	43	73
1973	75	55	74	79	52	74
1974	72	51	71	72	41	68
1975	75	53	78	76	48	71
1976	75	52	75	74	46	72
1977	74	55	77	72	48	75
1978	71	53	77	75	54	66
1979	75	60	79	76	62	73
1980	78	64	79	76	64	74
1981	75	57	80	77	64	85

Note: Data represent percentage of members voting with a majority of their party on party unity votes. Party unity votes are those roll calls on which a majority of a party votes on one side of the issue and a majority of the other party votes on the other side. The percentages are normalized to eliminate the effects of absences, as follows: party unity = (unity)/(unity + opposition). n.a. = not available.

Sources: *Congressional Quarterly Almanac*, various years; and *Congressional Quarterly Weekly Report*, vol. 40 (January 9, 1982).

TABLE 8–5

CONSERVATIVE COALITION VOTES AND VICTORIES IN CONGRESS,
1957–1981
(percent)

Year	House		Senate	
	Votes	Victories	Votes	Victories
1957	16	81	11	100
1958	15	64	19	86
1959	13	91	19	65
1960	20	35	22	67
1961	30	74	32	48
1962	13	44	15	71
1963	13	67	19	44
1964	11	67	17	47
1965	25	25	24	39
1966	19	32	30	51
1967	22	73	18	54
1968	22	63	25	80
1969	25	71	28	67
1970	17	70	26	64
1971	31	79	28	86
1972	25	79	29	63
1973	25	67	21	54
1974	22	67	30	54
1975	28	52	28	48
1976	17	59	26	58
1977	22	60	29	74
1978	20	57	23	46
1979	21	73	18	65
1980	16	67	20	75
1981	21	88	21	95

NOTE: "Votes" is the percentage of all roll call votes on which a majority of voting Southern Democrats and a majority of voting Republicans—the conservative coalition—opposed the stand taken by a majority of voting Northern Democrats. "Victories" is the percentage of conservative coalition votes won by the coalition.

SOURCES: *Congressional Quarterly Almanac,* various years; and *Congressional Quarterly Weekly Report,* vol. 40 (January 9, 1982).

TABLE 8–6

SUPPORT FOR THE CONSERVATIVE COALITION ON VOTES IN CONGRESS,
1959–1981
(percent)

Year	House			Senate		
	Northern Demo-crats	Southern Demo-crats	Repub-licans	Northern Demo-crats	Southern Demo-crats	Repub-licans
1959	17	85	87	23	69	80
1960	8	66	77	21	77	74
1961	15	69	83	15	74	75
1962	14	65	75	29	77	79
1963	13	70	78	20	73	76
1964	13	72	76	20	78	72
1965	10	69	81	19	71	81
1966	13	69	82	17	75	80
1967	15	75	81	24	76	72
1968	16	77	75	31	77	74
1969	21	79	75	24	77	73
1970	19	79	78	21	74	72
1971	25	76	80	38	80	79
1972	24	75	79	20	78	74
1973	22	69	77	17	74	76
1974	24	72	69	19	79	69
1975	22	69	81	19	79	69
1976	25	72	80	21	73	76
1977	25	68	82	26	75	80
1978	26	68	79	24	70	69
1979	29	70	85	29	75	74
1980	27	69	81	26	72	74
1981	30	75	82	29	76	84

NOTE: Data indicate the percentage of conservative coalition votes on which members voted in agreement with the position of the conservative coalition. Conservative coalition votes are those on which a majority of Northern Democrats voted against a majority of Southern Democrats and Republicans—the conservative coalition. The percentages are normalized to eliminate the effects of not voting, as follows: conservative coalition support = (support)/(support + opposition).

SOURCES: *Congressional Quarterly Almanac*, various years; and *Congressional Quarterly Weekly Report*, vol. 40 (January 9, 1982).

TABLE 8–7

House Committee Support of the Conservative Coalition, 1959–1981
(percent)

Committee	1959	1969	1977	1979	1981
Chamber average					
All members	59	56	51	57	61
Democrats	44	42	38	41	45
Republicans	86	75	78	85	82
Agriculture					
All members	79	80	56	65	70
Democrats	69	72	44	42	58
Republicans	97	90	81	82	86
Appropriations					
All members	69	63	56	56	56
Democrats	55	54	42	42	42
Republicans	90	76	83	85	78
Armed Services					
All members	68	69	69	72	80
Democrats	55	63	59	65	71
Republicans	90	79	90	90	91
Banking, Finance, and Urban Affairs					
All members	44	50	45	51	52
Democrats	26	37	33	35	34
Republicans	75	68	68	80	77
Budget					
All members	—	—	43	46	63
Democrats	—	—	26	27	47
Republicans	—	—	79	87	87
District of Columbia					
All members	72	62	41	32	39
Democrats	65	54	37	13	17
Republicans	85	72	49	62	78
Education and Labor					
All members	39	40	42	47	44
Democrats	16	17	26	27	25
Republicans	86	72	73	82	70

TABLE 8–7 (continued)

Committee	1959	1969	1977	1979	1981
Energy and Commerce					
All members	65	60	48	53	58
Democrats	49	41	31	36	38
Republicans	92	84	81	84	85
Foreign Affairs					
All members	48	42	41	44	51
Democrats	32	20	25	30	38
Republicans	78	68	73	71	70
Government Operations					
All members	55	37	47	51	54
Democrats	37	25	32	34	37
Republicans	81	55	78	82	77
House Administration					
All members	61	55	49	52	58
Democrats	52	37	32	32	41
Republicans	78	79	87	90	83
Interior and Insular Affairs					
All members	56	57	51	54	57
Democrats	36	36	33	35	34
Republicans	86	85	88	90	91
Judiciary					
All members	58	43	45	50	51
Democrats	45	28	36	32	30
Republicans	83	63	62	84	79
Merchant Marine and Fisheries					
All members	54	52	49	58	63
Democrats	39	41	29	45	51
Republicans	82	67	71	81	79
Post Office and Civil Service					
All members	57	49	43	53	49
Democrats	40	28	24	36	23
Republicans	88	77	84	82	83

(Table continues)

TABLE 8–7 (continued)

Committee	1959	1969	1977	1979	1981
Public Works and Transportation					
All members	58	63	62	67	66
Democrats	45	45	53	52	51
Republicans	82	86	80	93	87
Rules					
All members	63	54	47	46	54
Democrats	44	39	26	27	36
Republicans	100	85	56	88	94
Science and Technology					
All members	52	58	56	60	58
Democrats	34	46	47	49	49
Republicans	85	73	73	82	70
Small Business					
All members	—	—	—	54	59
Democrats	—	—	—	41	44
Republicans	—	—	—	79	79
Standards of Official Conduct					
All members	—	—	70	69	63
Democrats	—	—	67	53	57
Republicans	—	—	74	85	82
Veterans' Affairs					
All members	53	63	62	73	73
Democrats	46	54	53	65	65
Republicans	65	74	80	88	83
Ways and Means					
All members	62	56	54	52	60
Democrats	42	38	39	33	45
Republicans	95	83	86	90	87

NOTE: Data indicate the percentage of conservative coalition votes on which members voted in agreement with the position of the conservative coalition. Conservative coalition votes are those on which a majority of Northern Democrats voted against a majority of Southern Democrats and Republicans—the conservative coalition. Dashes indicate data are not available.

SOURCE: *Congressional Directory*, various years; and *Congressional Quarterly Almanac*, various years.

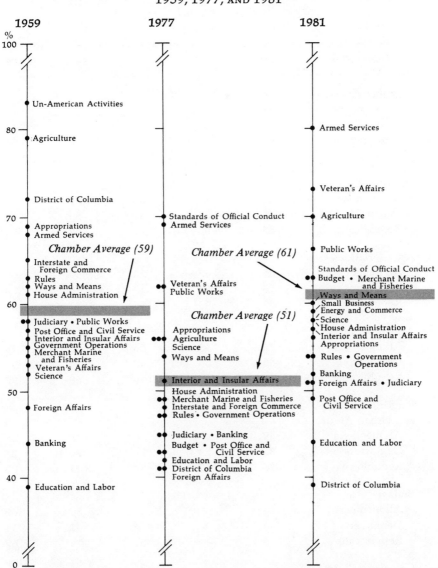

FIGURE 8–2
HOUSE COMMITTEE SUPPORT OF THE CONSERVATIVE COALITION, 1959, 1977, AND 1981

1959

%
100

● Un-American Activities

80
● Agriculture

● District of Columbia

70
● Appropriations
● Armed Services

Chamber Average (59)

● Interstate and
   Foreign Commerce
● Rules
● Ways and Means
● House Administration
60
●● Judiciary • Public Works
● Post Office and Civil Service
● Interior and Insular Affairs
● Government Operations
● Merchant Marine
   and Fisheries
● Veteran's Affairs
● Science

50
● Foreign Affairs

● Banking

40
● Education and Labor

0

1977

● Standards of Official Conduct
● Armed Services

Chamber Average (61)

●● Veteran's Affairs
    Public Works

Chamber Average (51)

● Appropriations
●●● Agriculture
    Science
    Ways and Means

● Interior and Insular Affairs
─ House Administration
●● Merchant Marine and Fisheries
    Interstate and Foreign Commerce
●● Rules • Government Operations

●● Judiciary • Banking
    Budget • Post Office and
               Civil Service
●● Education and Labor
    District of Columbia
    Foreign Affairs

0

1981

● Armed Services

● Veteran's Affairs

● Agriculture

● Public Works

  Standards of Official Conduct
●● Budget • Merchant Marine
               and Fisheries
  Ways and Means
● Small Business
● Energy and Commerce
● Science
  House Administration
  Interior and Insular Affairs
  Appropriations
●● Rules • Government
            Operations
● Banking
●● Foreign Affairs • Judiciary
● Post Office and
   Civil Service

● Education and Labor

● District of Columbia

0

NOTE: Percentage of conservative coalition votes on which members voted in agreement with the position of the conservative coalition. Conservative coalition votes are those on which a majority of Northern Democrats voted against a majority of Southern Democrats and Republicans—the conservative coalition.
SOURCE: Table 8-7.

175

TABLE 8–8

SENATE COMMITTEE SUPPORT OF THE CONSERVATIVE COALITION,
1959–1981

(percent)

Committee	1959	1969	1977	1979	1981
Chamber Average					
All members	54	55	51	56	65
Democrats	41	42	37	43	44
Republicans	80	73	73	74	84
Agriculture, Nutrition, and Forestry					
All members	63	81	67	71	77
Democrats	51	78	51	59	62
Republicans	85	83	91	87	90
Appropriations					
All members	65	67	50	59	68
Democrats	55	58	47	50	53
Republicans	85	79	55	72	83
Armed Services					
All members	70	65	66	69	76
Democrats	68	55	47	54	58
Republicans	84	77	96	89	92
Banking, Housing, and Urban Affairs					
All members	49	49	46	48	55
Democrats	35	29	27	26	23
Republicans	76	57	74	81	83
Budget					
All members	—	—	53	55	69
Democrats	—	—	36	42	44
Republicans	—	—	82	74	89
Commerce, Science, and Transportation					
All members	55	52	58	63	72
Democrats	40	38	45	55	58
Republicans	83	72	80	76	84

TABLE 8–8 (continued)

Committee	1959	1969	1977	1979	1981
Energy and Natural Resources					
All members	45	52	54	52	62
Democrats	23	29	34	40	37
Republicans	75	78	76	72	83
Environment and Public Works					
All members	40	53	51	47	63
Democrats	22	36	35	35	36
Republicans	75	78	76	63	85
Finance					
All members	67	63	51	52	67
Democrats	53	47	35	47	51
Republicans	94	90	74	60	80
Foreign Relations					
All members	44	45	36	48	55
Democrats	29	39	26	34	26
Republicans	71	55	51	69	78
Governmental Affairs					
All members	55	55	48	48	61
Democrats	39	43	41	45	47
Republicans	88	71	55	51	73
Judiciary					
All members	53	55	42	52	63
Democrats	43	36	35	35	36
Republicans	74	72	69	83	85
Labor and Human Resources					
All members	35	34	36	39	54
Democrats	12	14	18	19	14
Republicans	71	62	62	69	85
Rules and Administration					
All members	56	71	51	60	64
Democrats	43	65	39	49	38
Republicans	82	79	74	71	82

(Table continues)

TABLE 8–8 (continued)

Committee	1959	1969	1977	1979	1981
Veterans' Affairs					
All members	—	—	—	60	63
Democrats	—	—	—	47	34
Republicans	—	—	—	78	84

NOTE: Data indicate the percentage of conservative coalition votes on which members voted in agreement with the position of the conservative coalition. Conservative coalition votes are those on which a majority of Northern Democrats voted against a majority of Southern Democrats and Republicans—the conservative coalition. Dashes indicate data are not available.

SOURCES: *Congressional Directory*, various years; and *Congressional Quarterly Almanac*, various years.

FIGURE 8–3
Senate Committee Support of the Conservative Coalition, 1959, 1977, and 1981

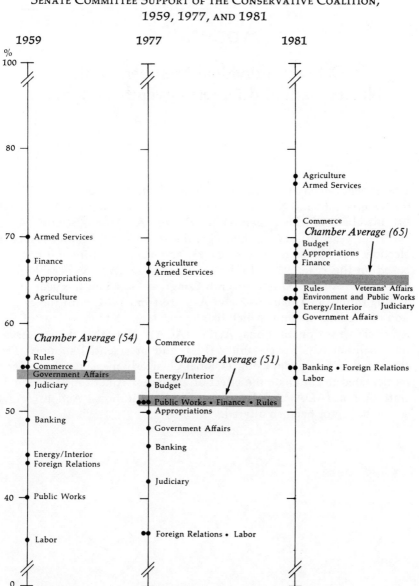

Note: Percentage of conservative coalition votes on which members voted in agreement with the position of the conservative coalition. Conservative coalition votes are those on which a majority of Northern Democrats voted against a majority of Southern Democrats and Republicans—the conservative coalition.

Source: Table 8-8.

Appendix

Data on Individual Members of the
Ninety-sixth and Ninety-seventh Congresses

The appendix contains data on individual members of Congress for the Ninety-sixth and Ninety-seventh Congresses. Tables A–1 and A–3 list members of the Ninety-sixth House (A–1) and Senate (A–3) and their years of service, their age, the returns for their most recent election (for House members, 1978), and various voting ratings, all based on the year 1980. Tables A–2 and A–4 give comparable data on members of the Ninety-seventh Congress, based on the year 1981. Voting ratings in Tables A–2 and A–4 are from 1981, with the exception of the final column, which lists career (cumulative) ratings of the Americans for Constitutional Action (ACA). Note that the conservative coalition (CC), party unity (PU), and presidential support (PS) scores, all derived from Congressional Quarterly measures, have been recalculated to eliminate the effect of absences. Americans for Democratic Action (ADA) and Americans for Constitutional Action (ACA) scores have not been so altered.

TABLE A–1
HOUSE OF REPRESENTATIVES, 1980

State, District	Representative	Party	Years of Service	Age	1978 % Vote in Primary	1978 % Vote in General	Voting Ratings[a] CC	PU	PS	ADA	ACA
Alabama											
1	J. Edwards	R	16	52	unopp.	64	89	73	49	17	83
2	W. Dickinson	R	16	55	unopp.	54	94	88	36	11	83
3	B. Nichols	D	14	62	unopp.	unopp.	95	39	53	17	59
4	T. Bevill	D	14	59	94	unopp.	86	62	62	22	35
5	R. Flippo	D	4	43	91	97	85	60	63	28	42
6	J. H. Buchanan	R	16	52	57	62	59	56	66	26	67
7	R. Shelby	D	2	46	59	96	95	49	49	11	67
Alaska											
AL	D. Young	R	7	47	unopp.	55	91	81	38	22	70
Arizona											
1	J. J. Rhodes	R	28	64	unopp.	71	75	71	52	0	86
2	M. K. Udall	D	18	58	unopp.	53	25	91	77	61	14
3	B. Stump	D	4	53	71	85	96	15	33	0	83
4	E. Rudd	R	4	60	84	63	99	95	29	6	95
Arkansas											
1	B. Alexander	D	12	47	unopp.	unopp.	45	88	80	44	33
2	E. Bethune	R	2	45	unopp.	51	96	87	44	11	74
3	J. P. Hammerschmidt	R	14	58	unopp.	78	94	79	37	6	77
4	B. Anthony, Jr.	D	2	49	52[b]	unopp.	71	70	64	22	36

(Table continues)

181

TABLE A–1 (continued)

State, District	Representative	Party	Years of Service	Age	1978 % Vote in		Voting Ratings[a]				
					Primary	General	CC	PU	PS	ADA	ACA
California											
1	H. T. Johnson	D	22	73	73	59	25	78	94	61	22
2	D. H. Clausen	R	18	57	unopp.	52	74	68	51	22	64
3	R. T. Matsui	D	2	39	36	53	6	96	83	94	13
4	V. Fazio	D	2	38	57	55	15	96	85	89	23
5	J. L. Burton	D	6	48	unopp.	67	14	80	56	94	33
6	P. Burton	D	16	54	unopp.	68	1	95	70	83	25
7	G. Miller	D	6	36	unopp.	63	8	86	67	94	27
8	R. V. Dellums	D	10	45	unopp.	57	9	89	67	100	23
9	F. H. Stark	D	8	48	78	65	4	89	67	94	17
10	D. Edwards	D	18	65	unopp.	67	2	96	76	100	17
11	L. Ryan	D	4	53	75	63	Died 11/78				
11	B. Royer	R	1	60	52	58	74	75	50	11	63
12	P. N. McCloskey, Jr.	R	13	52	76	73	29	32	73	78	35
13	N. Y. Mineta	D	6	49	unopp.	59	11	96	79	83	21
14	N. D. Shumway	R	2	46	37	53	95	93	36	0	95
15	T. Coelho	D	2	38	79	60	17	97	82	72	9
16	L. E. Panetta	D	4	42	unopp.	61	33	92	74	67	29
17	C. Pashayan, Jr.	R	2	39	65	54	85	81	48	11	77
18	W. M. Thomas	R	2	39	party nom.	59	92	85	38	0	91
19	R. J. Lagomarsino	R	6	54	unopp.	72	92	92	36	11	83
20	B. M. Goldwater, Jr.	R	11	43	unopp.	66	84	84	37	22	82

21	J. C. Corman	D	18	60	unopp.	62	14	96	87	78	9
22	C. J. Moorhead	R	8	58	81	65	92	91	38	11	96
23	A. C. Beilenson	D	4	48	80	66	7	91	84	94	21
24	H. A. Waxman	D	6	40	81	66	4	94	76	83	22
25	E. R. Roybal	D	18	64	unopp.	67	7	91	74	89	14
26	J. H. Rousselot	R	10	53	unopp.	unopp.	91	93	26	11	95
27	R. K. Dornan	R	4	47	unopp.	51	82	78	39	11	73
28	J. C. Dixon	D	2	46	50	unopp.	9	95	76	94	10
29	A. F. Hawkins	D	18	73	unopp.	85	2	94	72	89	6
30	G. E. Danielson	D	10	65	unopp.	71	21	97	87	67	18
31	C. H. Wilson	D	18	64	40	68	37	77	62	22	27
32	G. M. Anderson	D	12	61	unopp.	71	43	77	69	72	33
33	W. Grisham	R	2	57	24	56	90	88	39	6	90
34	D. Lungren	R	2	34	68	55	91	91	39	6	100
35	J. Lloyd	D	4	58	unopp.	54	43	85	80	56	38
36	G. E. Brown, Jr.	D	16	60	unopp.	63	9	94	82	94	10
37	J. Lewis	R	2	46	55	61	78	75	33	11	75
38	J. M. Patterson	D	6	46	unopp.	59	19	93	72	72	18
39	W. E. Dannemeyer	R	2	51	unopp.	64	93	92	33	6	100
40	R. E. Badham	R	4	51	unopp.	66	95	93	34	0	95
41	B. Wilson	R	28	64	unopp.	58	77	94	53	11	75
42	L. Van Deerlin	D	16	66	82	74	16	95	81	72	10
43	C. W. Burgener	R	8	59	76	69	90	82	43	6	86
Colorado											
1	P. Schroeder	D	8	40	unopp.	62	33	59	63	94	25
2	T. E. Wirth	D	6	41	unopp.	53	21	86	83	78	22

(Table continues)

183

TABLE A-1 (continued)

State, District	Representative	Party	Years of Service	Age	1978 % Vote in Primary	1978 % Vote in General	Voting Ratings[a] CC	PU	PS	ADA	ACA
3	R. Kogovsek	D	2	39	66	50	54	75	73	56	22
4	J. Johnson	R	6	50	64	61	66	63	46	28	58
5	K. Kramer	R	2	38	54	60	96	93	33	0	91
Connecticut											
1	W.R. Cotter	D	10	54	conv.	60	48	76	70	44	25
2	C. Dodd	D	6	36	conv.	70	8	93	77	72	24
3	R.N. Giaimo	D	20	61	conv.	59	29	81	86	28	33
4	S.B. McKinney	R	10	50	conv.	58	35	39	66	78	41
5	W.R. Ratchford	D	2	46	conv.	52	17	87	73	83	19
6	A.T. Moffett	D	6	36	conv.	64	5	86	73	94	15
Delaware											
AL	T.B. Evans, Jr.	R	4	49	conv.	59	63	70	63	56	65
Florida											
1	E. Hutto	D	2	54	62	63	85	59	59	22	48
2	D. Fuqua	D	18	47	86	82	77	69	76	33	29
3	C.E. Bennett	D	32	70	unopp.	unopp.	89	56	59	22	42
4	B. Chappell, Jr.	D	12	59	unopp.	73	91	48	50	6	63
5	R. Kelly	R	4	56	unopp.	51	95	91	30	6	95
6	C.W.B. Young	R	10	50	unopp.	79	96	87	42	11	88
7	S. Gibbons	D	18	61	71	unopp.	56	74	78	39	30

8	A. Ireland	D	4	50	unopp.	unopp.	91	50	64	6	46
9	B. Nelson	D	2	38	86	61	65	70	72	33	46
10	L. A. Bafalis	R	8	51	unopp.	unopp.	96	92	37	6	95
11	D. Mica	D	2	37	55	55	76	62	59	33	52
12	E. Stack	D	2	70	53	62	21	94	80	78	17
13	W. Lehman	D	8	67	unopp.	unopp.	19	94	87	83	17
14	C. Pepper	D	18	80	81	63	24	94	86	61	19
15	D. B. Fascell	D	26	63	unopp.	74	22	94	90	83	25
Georgia											
1	B. Ginn	D	8	46	unopp.	unopp.	75	68	62	33	30
2	D. Mathis	D	8	40	77	unopp.	79	47	50	11	56
3	J. Brinkley	D	14	50	unopp.	unopp.	89	53	51	11	59
4	E. H. Levitas	D	6	50	84	81	78	56	61	28	48
5	W. Fowler, Jr.	D	3	40	82	75	51	72	73	61	48
6	N. Gingrich	R	2	37	76	54	93	86	38	11	91
7	L. P. McDonald	D	6	45	51	67	96	5	27	6	100
8	B. L. Evans	D	4	39	unopp.	unopp.	74	48	54	6	70
9	E. Jenkins	D	4	48	64	77	86	45	54	6	60
10	D. Barnard, Jr.	D	4	58	72	unopp.	86	52	56	11	63
Hawaii											
1	C. Heftel	D	4	56	87	78	46	80	82	50	29
2	D. K. Akaka	D	4	56	unopp.	86	33	92	85	72	25
Idaho											
1	S. Symms	R	6	42	unopp.	60	98	96	36	0	83
2	G. Hansen	R	6	50	56	57	97	96	25	6	95

(Table continues)

TABLE A-1 (continued)

State, District	Representative	Party	Years of Service	Age	1978 % Vote in		Voting Ratings[a]				
					Primary	General	CC	PU	PS	ADA	ACA
Illinois											
1	B. M. Stewart	D	2	65	selected	59	8	96	83	63	16
2	M. A. Murphy	D	2	48	unopp.	88	32	93	95	22	17
3	M. Russo	D	6	36	unopp.	65	60	64	56	50	39
4	E. J. Derwinski	R	22	54	unopp.	67	73	76	48	11	74
5	J. G. Fary	D	5	69	unopp.	84	28	92	82	44	21
6	H. J. Hyde	R	6	56	unopp.	66	77	70	58	28	74
7	C. Collins	D	7	49	72	86	3	93	65	89	20
8	D. Rostenkowski	D	22	53	unopp.	86	28	92	87	50	17
9	S. R. Yates	D	30	71	87	75	2	93	72	100	17
10	J. E. Porter[c]	R	1	45	71	54	63	72	57	39	71
11	F. Annunzio	D	16	65	87	74	29	92	78	56	18
12	P. M. Crane	R	11	50	unopp.	80	94	97	25	6	95
13	R. McClory	R	18	73	59	61	68	68	48	17	67
14	J. N. Erlenborn	R	15	53	unopp.	75	75	74	58	11	85
15	T. Corcoran	R	4	41	unopp.	62	89	86	46	6	96
16	J. Anderson	R	20	59	58	65	7	26	57	22	0
17	G. M. O'Brien	R	8	63	unopp.	71	77	73	46	22	77
18	R. H. Michel	R	23	57	unopp.	66	87	91	42	6	82
19	T. Railsback	R	14	48	unopp.	unopp.	53	58	59	44	52
20	P. Findley	R	20	59	unopp.	70	74	67	57	28	70
21	E. R. Madigan	R	8	45	unopp.	78	85	84	44	11	76

22	D. B. Crane	R	2	45	46	54	91	97	23	11	96
23	M. Price	D	36	75	88	74	25	95	84	56	13
24	P. Simon	D	6	52	unopp.	66	14	92	75	78	24
Indiana											
1	A. Benjamin, Jr.	D	4	45	91	81	53	70	61	61	33
2	F. J. Fithian	D	6	52	unopp.	57	48	70	64	56	27
3	J. Brademas	D	22	53	unopp.	56	16	98	87	72	13
4	D. Quayle	R	4	33	unopp.	66	94	90	38	0	90
5	E. Hillis	R	10	54	unopp.	68	80	74	49	22	70
6	D. W. Evans	D	6	34	unopp.	52	79	36	57	28	63
7	J. T. Myers	R	14	53	79	56	93	88	38	11	75
8	H. J. Deckard	R	2	38	49	52	79	75	48	22	74
9	L. H. Hamilton, Jr.	D	15	49	unopp.	66	50	68	75	44	46
10	P. R. Sharp	D	6	38	89	57	54	63	71	50	29
11	A. Jacobs, Jr.	D	16	48	95	57	70	30	47	50	63
Iowa											
1	J. Leach	R	4	38	unopp.	64	50	64	53	61	58
2	T. Tauke	R	2	30	unopp.	53	75	80	55	33	61
3	C. Grassley	R	6	47	unopp.	75	75	90	39	17	74
4	N. Smith	D	22	61	unopp.	65	30	84	73	72	14
5	T. Harkin	D	6	41	unopp.	59	21	81	71	78	33
6	B. Bedell	D	6	59	unopp.	66	25	77	76	72	13
Kansas											
1	K. Sebelius	R	10	63	unopp.	unopp.	91	82	43	6	78
2	J. Jeffries	R	2	55	58	52	97	96	32	6	96
3	L. Winn, Jr.	R	14	61	unopp.	unopp.	84	81	48	11	79

(Table continues)

TABLE A–1 (continued)

State, District	Representative	Party	Years of Service	Age	1978 % Vote in		Voting Ratings[a]				
					Primary	General	CC	PU	PS	ADA	ACA
4	D. Glickman	D	4	36	unopp.	70	55	63	71	56	33
5	B. Whittaker	R	2	41	39	58	94	90	40	11	88
Kentucky											
1	C. Hubbard, Jr.	D	6	43	unopp.	unopp.	90	53	61	22	46
2	W. H. Natcher	D	27	71	unopp.	unopp.	75	65	60	50	29
3	R. L. Mazzoli	D	10	48	79	68	62	68	67	33	33
4	G. Snyder	R	16	53	unopp.	66	93	86	36	11	71
5	T. L. Carter	R	16	70	93	79	90	68	48	17	79
6	L. J. Hopkins	R	2	47	selected	52	93	87	42	6	87
7	C. D. Perkins	D	32	68	85	76	56	72	57	56	29
Louisiana[d]											
1	R. L. Livingston	R	3	37	86	—	92	83	45	11	83
2	L. Boggs	D	7	64	87	—	41	91	80	50	30
3	D. C. Treen	R	8	52	unopp.	unopp.	Resigned 3/10/80				
3	W. J. Tauzin	D	1	37	43	53	72	62	59	0	42
4	C. (Buddy) Leach	D	2	47	27	50	85	50	54	11	61
5	J. Huckaby	D	4	39	52	—	84	52	55	11	58
6	W. H. Moore	R	5	41	91	—	92	83	40	11	79
7	J. B. Breaux	D	8	36	60	—	77	62	64	11	48
8	G. W. Long	D	10	57	80	—	36	90	83	50	21

State / District		Party									
Maine											
1	D. F. Emery	R	6	31	unopp.	63	78	79	52	39	67
2	O. J. Snowe	R	2	34	unopp.	65	77	70	58	28	75
Maryland											
1	R. E. Bauman	R	6	43	unopp.	64	95	96	29	6	96
2	C. D. Long	D	18	72	86	66	29	83	76	83	25
3	B. A. Mikulski	D	4	44	90	unopp.	13	94	77	89	27
4	M. S. Holt	R	8	60	unopp.	62	87	88	42	6	86
5	G. N. Spellman	D	4	62	84	77	19	92	79	83	13
6	B. B. Byron	D	2	48	selected	90	86	44	57	22	65
7	P. J. Mitchell	D	10	58	78	89	2	95	71	89	9
8	M. D. Barnes	D	2	37	72	51	5	90	79	94	13
Massachusetts											
1	S. O. Conte	R	22	59	unopp.	unopp.	26	37	68	83	30
2	E. P. Boland	D	28	69	unopp.	73	26	88	77	78	21
3	J. D. Early	D	6	48	unopp.	75	33	66	60	67	20
4	R. F. Drinan	D	10	60	65	unopp.	0	96	76	100	17
5	J. M. Shannon	D	2	28	22	52	5	92	68	94	14
6	N. Mavroules	D	2	51	44	54	19	88	76	72	15
7	E. J. Markey	D	4	34	unopp.	85	7	91	75	83	22
8	T. P. O'Neill, Jr.[e]	D	28	68	unopp.	75	—	—	—	—	—
9	J. Moakley	D	8	53	unopp.	94	13	95	79	72	10
10	M. M. Heckler	R	14	49	unopp.	61	40	40	61	67	23
11	B. J. Donnelly	D	2	34	43	92	23	87	66	72	24
12	G. E. Studds	D	8	43	unopp.	unopp.	7	93	79	100	17

(Table continues)

TABLE A–1 (continued)

State, District	Representative	Party	Years of Service	Age	1978 % Vote in		Voting Ratings[a]				
					Primary	General	CC	PU	PS	ADA	ACA
Michigan											
1	J. Conyers, Jr.	D	16	51	unopp.	93	9	90	66	78	25
2	C. D. Pursell	R	4	48	unopp.	68	31	42	66	89	36
3	H. Wolpe	D	2	41	unopp.	51	17	85	73	94	30
4	D. Stockman	R	4	34	unopp.	71	83	79	37	17	92
5	H. S. Sawyer	R	4	60	unopp.	50	86	83	50	11	83
6	B. Carr	D	6	37	unopp.	57	20	84	73	94	25
7	D. E. Kildee	D	4	51	unopp.	78	12	89	74	89	21
8	B. Traxler	D	6	49	unopp.	67	36	82	67	56	17
9	G. Vander Jagt	R	14	49	unopp.	70	79	81	48	22	79
10	D. J. Albosta	D	2	55	59	51	60	81	66	28	42
11	R. W. Davis	R	2	48	58	55	66	67	59	39	55
12	D. E. Bonior	D	4	35	unopp.	55	8	93	76	83	18
13	C. Diggs, Jr.	D	26	58	62	79	10	89	64	73	0
14	L. N. Nedzi	D	19	55	78	67	13	94	84	61	11
15	W. D. Ford	D	16	53	unopp.	80	14	93	76	78	5
16	J. D. Dingell	D	25	54	unopp.	78	25	92	76	67	18
17	W. M. Brodhead	D	6	39	unopp.	95	6	95	79	94	4
18	J. J. Blanchard	D	6	38	unopp.	75	20	94	80	72	13
19	W. S. Broomfield	R	24	58	unopp.	71	79	84	48	11	75
Minnesota											
1	A. Erdahl	R	2	49	74	57	52	72	56	56	54

2	T. Hagedorn	R	6	37	unopp.	70	88	88	43	11	68
3	B. Frenzel	R	10	52	unopp.	66	73	76	45	22	70
4	B. F. Vento	D	4	40	unopp.	58	3	92	77	100	9
5	M. O. Sabo	D	2	42	81	62	7	96	85	94	9
6	R. Nolan	D	6	37	unopp.	55	0	94	63	94	19
7	A. Stangeland	R	3	50	97	54	84	88	38	0	79
8	J. L. Oberstar	D	6	46	unopp.	87	16	92	69	83	17
Mississippi										
1	J. L. Whitten	D	39	70	68	68	85	53	59	28	57
2	D. R. Bowen	D	8	48	75	62	69	68	76	28	43
3	G. V. Montgomery	D	14	60	91	92	96	31	46	0	58
4	J. Hinson	R	2	38	70	53	95	85	35	6	82
5	T. Lott	R	8	39	unopp.	unopp.	99	89	37	6	83
Missouri										
1	W. Clay	D	12	49	62	68	4	90	75	83	16
2	R. A. Young	D	4	57	85	56	42	82	73	50	33
3	R. A. Gephardt	D	4	39	91	82	35	82	82	56	33
4	I. Skelton	D	4	49	87	73	75	63	65	17	42
5	R. Bolling	D	32	64	77	73	15	96	91	72	23
6	E. T. Coleman	R	4	37	unopp.	56	98	89	42	6	87
7	G. Taylor	R	8	52	unopp.	61	97	91	30	11	88
8	R. H. Ichord	D	20	54	unopp.	60	96	21	35	0	76
9	H. L. Volkmer	D	4	49	unopp.	75	64	65	70	39	29
10	B. D. Burlison	D	12	45	64	65	47	80	80	44	22

(Table continues)

TABLE A–1 (continued)

State, District	Representative	Party	Years of Service	Age	1978 % Vote in Primary	General	Voting Ratings[a] CC	PU	PS	ADA	ACA
Montana											
1	P. Williams	D	2	43	41	57	35	76	67	72	18
2	R. Marlenee	R	4	45	unopp.	57	92	89	37	22	83
Nebraska											
1	D. K. Bereuter	R	2	41	52	58	73	77	55	33	74
2	J. J. Cavanaugh	D	4	35	88	52	20	84	78	83	27
3	V. Smith	R	6	69	unopp.	80	92	84	44	11	78
Nevada											
AL	J. Santini	D	6	43	88	70	81	42	50	17	58
New Hampshire											
1	N. E. D'Amours	D	6	43	unopp.	63	46	72	73	56	38
2	J. C. Cleveland	R	18	60	unopp.	68	82	79	43	22	68
New Jersey											
1	J. J. Florio	D	6	43	unopp.	80	21	89	76	72	13
2	W. J. Hughes	D	6	48	unopp.	66	58	64	68	61	42
3	J. J. Howard	D	16	53	unopp.	56	15	95	83	83	14
4	F. Thompson, Jr.	D	26	62	unopp.	62	0	95	77	89	15
5	M. Fenwick	R	6	70	unopp.	73	48	61	56	67	54
6	E. B. Forsythe	R	10	64	85	61	70	71	46	50	83
7	A. Maguire	D	6	41	unopp.	53	0	88	72	100	17

8	R. A. Roe	D	11	56	unopp.	74	35	87	74	67	17
9	H. C. Hollenbeck	R	4	42	82	49	25	31	66	89	32
10	P. W. Rodino, Jr.	D	32	71	unopp.	87	0	92	72	67	14
11	J. G. Minish	D	18	64	92	71	26	85	74	72	23
12	M. J. Rinaldo	R	8	49	unopp.	73	45	44	59	61	38
13	J. A. Courter	R	2	39	38	52	89	85	43	11	83
14	F. J. Guarini	D	2	56	82	65	37	81	70	67	39
15	E. J. Patten	D	18	75	59	51	25	94	85	67	14
New Mexico											
1	M. Lujan, Jr.	R	12	52	unopp.	63	81	80	47	28	58
2	H. Runnels (died 8/5/80)	D	10	56	unopp.	unopp.	83	18	41	15	73
New York											
1	W. Carney	R	2	38	31	57	88	84	38	11	83
2	T. J. Downey	D	6	31	unopp.	55	9	93	75	94	13
3	J. Ambro, Jr.	D	6	52	unopp.	51	52	73	63	50	42
4	N. F. Lent	R	10	49	unopp.	67	78	70	49	17	61
5	J. W. Wydler	R	18	56	unopp.	58	66	70	39	28	63
6	L. L. Wolff	D	16	61	unopp.	60	30	86	65	61	36
7	J. P. Addabbo	D	20	55	unopp.	95	13	96	72	72	5
8	B. S. Rosenthal	D	18	57	unopp.	83	1	97	71	78	10
9	G. A. Ferraro	D	2	45	53	55	22	93	80	72	17
10	M. Biaggi	D	8	63	unopp.	95	25	92	80	50	15
11	J. H. Scheuer	D	14	60	unopp.	78	14	95	81	89	13
12	S. Chisholm	D	12	56	unopp.	88	0	95	73	78	15

(Table continues)

TABLE A-1 (continued)

State, District	Representative	Party	Years of Service	Age	1978 % Vote in Primary	1978 % Vote in General	Voting Ratings[a] CC	PU	PS	ADA	ACA
13	S. J. Solarz	D	6	40	unopp.	81	9	95	83	78	20
14	F. W. Richmond	D	6	57	50	77	1	96	75	94	5
15	L. C. Zeferetti	D	6	53	74	68	32	88	69	44	14
16	E. Holtzman	D	8	39	unopp.	82	0	88	67	61	7
17	J. M. Murphy	D	18	54	47	54	35	87	74	39	28
18	S. W. Green	R	2	51	unopp.	53	16	31	71	94	29
19	C. B. Rangel	D	10	50	unopp.	96	2	96	76	78	14
20	T. S. Weiss	D	4	53	unopp.	85	4	90	72	100	22
21	R. Garcia	D	2	47	unopp.	98	1	95	77	72	14
22	J. B. Bingham	D	16	66	unopp.	84	3	95	74	94	22
23	P. A. Peyser	D	8	59	60	53	13	94	79	94	14
24	R. L. Ottinger	D	12	51	unopp.	57	6	93	73	94	13
25	H. Fish, Jr.	R	12	54	unopp.	79	56	54	55	61	52
26	B. A. Gilman	R	8	58	unopp.	62	47	44	53	61	46
27	M. F. McHugh	D	6	42	unopp.	56	12	92	79	83	21
28	S. S. Stratton	D	22	64	81	76	57	67	62	17	43
29	G. B. H. Solomon	R	2	50	unopp.	54	88	91	43	11	78
30	R. C. McEwen	R	16	60	unopp.	61	77	68	48	6	90
31	D. J. Mitchell	R	8	57	unopp.	unopp.	76	71	52	28	65
32	J. M. Hanley	D	16	60	unopp.	53	38	89	83	56	22
33	G. A. Lee	R	2	47	88	56	88	92	42	11	90
34	F. Horton	R	18	61	unopp.	87	52	44	56	78	43

35	B. B. Conable, Jr.	R	16	58	unopp.	69	69	76	53	28	79
36	J. J. LaFalce	D	6	41	unopp.	76	23	83	82	56	25
37	H. J. Nowak	D	6	45	unopp.	80	15	92	75	78	13
38	J. F. Kemp	R	10	45	unopp.	95	84	84	42	6	86
39	S. N. Lundine	D	4	41	unopp.	58	19	87	77	83	13
North Carolina											
1	W. B. Jones	D	14	67	82	80	73	70	62	22	38
2	L. H. Fountain	D	28	67	75	79	91	45	58	17	61
3	C. Whitley	D	4	53	84	71	85	63	62	28	39
4	I. F. Andrews	D	8	55	83	94	74	69	67	28	41
5	S. L. Neal	D	6	46	unopp.	54	71	70	71	44	50
6	R. Preyer	D	12	61	unopp.	68	56	80	83	44	35
7	C. Rose	D	8	41	unopp.	70	56	78	74	44	38
8	W. G. Hefner	D	6	50	unopp.	59	84	64	63	22	36
9	J. G. Martin	R	8	45	unopp.	69	93	87	40	11	88
10	J. T. Broyhill	R	18	53	unopp.	unopp.	96	84	40	11	87
11	L. Gudger	D	4	61	51	53	86	60	61	33	46
North Dakota											
AL	M. Andrews	R	17	54	unopp.	68	91	77	46	17	67
Ohio											
1	W. D. Gradison, Jr.	R	6	52	unopp.	66	79	73	58	22	67
2	T. A. Luken	D	4	55	unopp.	52	64	67	67	39	43
3	T. P. Hall	D	2	38	80	55	20	89	78	89	21
4	T. Guyer	R	8	67	unopp.	68	93	86	48	6	74
5	D. L. Latta	R	22	60	unopp.	63	91	91	36	17	88

(Table continues)

195

TABLE A–1 (continued)

State, District	Representative	Party	Years of Service	Age	1978 % Vote in		Voting Ratings[a]				
					Primary	General	CC	PU	PS	ADA	ACA
6	W. H. Harsha	R	20	59	90	65	82	77	41	11	63
7	C. J. Brown	R	15	53	unopp.	unopp.	87	86	43	11	67
8	T. N. Kindness	R	6	51	unopp.	71	90	88	35	6	96
9	T. L. Ashley	D	26	57	unopp.	68	25	90	87	78	21
10	C. E. Miller	R	14	63	unopp.	74	88	90	31	11	75
11	J. W. Stanton	R	16	56	unopp.	68	67	60	59	44	63
12	S. L. Devine	R	22	65	unopp.	57	98	95	34	6	96
13	D. J. Pease	D	4	49	78	65	18	84	80	83	17
14	J. F. Seiberling	D	10	62	unopp.	72	6	93	81	100	13
15	C. P. Wylie	R	14	60	unopp.	71	78	78	49	28	65
16	R. S. Regula	R	8	56	unopp.	78	86	77	50	28	63
17	J. M. Ashbrook	R	20	52	unopp.	67	95	92	28	6	91
18	D. Applegate	D	4	52	82	60	77	40	47	22	54
19	L. Williams	R	2	38	54	51	69	53	53	33	54
20	M. R. Oakar	D	4	40	81	unopp.	27	90	72	67	13
21	L. Stokes	D	12	55	unopp.	86	3	95	72	78	10
22	C. A. Vanik	D	26	67	unopp.	74	16	89	73	67	18
23	R. M. Mottl	D	6	46	84	75	69	39	41	33	46
Oklahoma											
1	J. R. Jones	D	8	41	unopp.	60	66	68	66	39	43
2	M. L. Synar	D	2	30	54	55	38	85	73	61	26

District	Name	Party									
3	W. Watkins	D	4	42	unopp.	unopp.	79	63	61	33	46
4	T. Steed	D	32	76	65	60	49	82	72	56	20
5	M. Edwards	R	4	43	unopp.	80	92	90	34	17	83
6	G. English	D	6	40	unopp.	74	95	46	47	6	63
Oregon											
1	L. AuCoin	D	6	38	unopp.	63	25	61	70	83	25
2	A. Ullman	D	24	66	unopp.	69	30	86	78	67	24
3	R. Duncan	D	6	60	unopp.	85	26	88	82	72	22
4	J. Weaver	D	6	53	60	56	27	66	57	83	35
Pennsylvania											
1	M. O. Myers	D	4	37	50	73	31	88	80	33	24
2	W. H. Gray III	D	2	38	58	82	6	94	76	72	19
3	R. F. Lederer	D	4	42	unopp.	71	24	89	78	44	21
4	C. F. Dougherty	R	2	43	unopp.	56	47	41	67	39	43
5	R. T. Schulze	R	6	51	93	75	94	92	38	0	86
6	G. Yatron	D	12	53	unopp.	74	62	47	54	39	50
7	R. W. Edgar	D	6	37	82	50	7	85	79	94	10
8	P. H. Kostmayer	D	4	34	85	61	16	84	77	89	21
9	B. Shuster	R	8	48	unopp.	75	98	96	45	6	91
10	J. M. McDade	R	18	49	unopp.	76	62	55	59	44	35
11	D. J. Flood	D	26	77	74	58	Resigned 1/31/80				
12	J. P. Murtha	D	6	48	unopp.	69	51	80	78	44	21
13	L. Coughlin	R	12	51	89	71	61	67	54	44	64
14	W. S. Moorhead	D	22	57	76	58	18	95	85	56	17
15	D. Ritter	R	2	40	47	53	83	80	47	22	74
16	R. S. Walker	R	4	38	76	77	85	92	39	17	92

(Table continues)

TABLE A-1 (continued)

State, District	Representative	Party	Years of Service	Age	1978 % Vote in		Voting Ratings[a]				
					Primary	General	CC	PU	PS	ADA	ACA
17	A. E. Ertel	D	4	44	unopp.	60	45	75	69	67	26
18	D. Walgren	D	4	40	77	58	31	80	79	78	8
19	W. F. Goodling	R	6	53	unopp.	79	77	85	49	28	73
20	J. M. Gaydos	D	12	54	82	72	62	60	60	33	48
21	D. Bailey	D	2	35	23	53	44	86	79	50	21
22	A. J. Murphy	D	4	53	69	72	52	67	61	44	42
23	W. F. Clinger, Jr.	R	2	51	63	54	77	69	57	22	71
24	M. L. Marks	R	4	53	83	64	69	61	61	44	59
25	E. V. Atkinson	D	2	53	25	48	71	51	54	28	42
Rhode Island											
1	F. J. St Germain	D	20	52	68	61	24	87	65	78	13
2	E. P. Beard	D	6	40	80	53	49	76	63	61	32
South Carolina											
1	M. J. Davis	D	9	38	86	61	55	73	65	39	31
2	F. Spence	R	10	52	unopp.	57	97	88	43	11	83
3	B. Derrick	D	6	44	unopp.	82	56	80	76	56	50
4	C. A. Campbell, Jr.	R	2	40	88	53	94	84	40	6	83
5	K. L. Holland	D	6	46	65	83	59	74	64	22	41
6	J. W. Jenrette	D	6	44	77	unopp.	69	48	62	17	57

South Dakota											
1	T. A. Daschle	D	2	33	59	50	48	67	64	72	35
2	J. Abdnor	R	8	57	unopp.	56	93	90	39	11	72
Tennessee											
1	J. H. Quillen	R	18	64	unopp.	65	94	73	42	17	57
2	J. J. Duncan	R	16	61	unopp.	82	98	78	47	17	67
3	M. L. Bouquard	D	6	51	unopp.	89	86	47	56	22	54
4	A. Gore, Jr.	D	4	32	unopp.	unopp.	46	85	78	50	29
5	W. H. Boner	D	2	35	53	51	77	65	63	39	38
6	R. L. Beard, Jr.	R	8	41	unopp.	75	95	90	36	11	91
7	E. Jones	D	11	68	unopp.	73	80	66	61	22	45
8	H. E. Ford	D	6	35	81	71	20	94	80	83	19
Texas											
1	S. B. Hall, Jr.	D	4	56	unopp.	78	97	34	48	0	73
2	C. Wilson	D	8	47	unopp.	70	79	66	65	17	43
3	J. M. Collins	R	12	64	unopp.	unopp.	95	95	30	11	96
4	R. Roberts	D	18	67	68	61	80	53	54	6	56
5	J. Mattox	D	4	37	unopp.	51	56	73	62	50	42
6	P. Gramm	D	2	38	53	65	96	25	40	0	71
7	B. Archer	R	10	52	unopp.	85	98	96	31	6	96
8	B. Eckhardt	D	14	67	54	62	16	93	79	89	21
9	J. Brooks	D	28	58	70	63	50	83	73	28	21
10	J. J. Pickle	D	17	67	unopp.	76	71	67	65	22	33
11	M. Leath	D	2	49	55 [f]	52	95	24	36	0	71

(Table continues)

199

TABLE A-1 (continued)

State, District	Representative	Party	Years of Service	Age	1978 % Vote in Primary	1978 % Vote in General	Voting Ratings[a] CC	PU	PS	ADA	ACA
12	J. Wright	D	26	58	unopp.	68	40	94	82	39	29
13	J. Hightower	D	6	54	unopp.	75	82	58	58	17	43
14	J. Wyatt	D	2	39	56	72	78	60	59	6	43
15	E. de la Garza	D	16	53	unopp.	66	73	62	63	22	52
16	R. C. White	D	16	57	80	70	83	56	57	11	55
17	C. W. Stenholm	D	2	42	67[g]	68	96	25	41	0	74
18	M. Leland	D	2	36	57[h]	97	5	93	75	83	5
19	K. Hance	D	2	38	64	53	79	58	63	11	43
20	H. B. Gonzalez	D	19	64	unopp.	unopp.	23	95	79	72	17
21	T. G. Loeffler	R	2	34	59	57	96	93	32	0	92
22	R. Paul	R	4	45	unopp.	51	87	96	20	22	92
23	A. Kazen, Jr.	D	14	61	80	90	64	68	60	22	30
24	M. Frost	D	2	38	55	54	51	82	74	50	23
Utah											
1	K. G. McKay	D	10	55	unopp.	52	75	64	64	17	40
2	D. Marriott	R	4	41	unopp.	62	84	82	40	17	74
Vermont											
AL	J. M. Jeffords	R	6	46	unopp.	75	38	54	64	67	30

Virginia											
1	P. S. Trible, Jr.	R	4	34	conv.	72	100	89	44	6	79
2	G. W. Whitehurst	R	12	55	conv.	unopp.	100	86	43	0	87
3	D. E. Satterfield III	D	16	60	conv.	88	96	19	35	6	91
4	R. W. Daniel, Jr.	R	8	44	conv.	unopp.	100	94	33	6	100
5	D. Daniel	D	12	66	conv.	unopp.	96	28	37	6	92
6	M. C. Butler	R	8	55	conv.	unopp.	92	87	46	17	91
7	J. K. Robinson	R	10	64	conv.	64	100	89	35	6	92
8	H. E. Harris II	D	6	54	conv.	52	19	88	81	89	21
9	W. C. Wampler	R	16	54	conv.	62	94	73	42	28	71
10	J. L. Fisher	D	6	66	conv.	53	22	87	79	83	31
Washington											
1	J. Pritchard	R	8	55	unopp.	65	43	48	69	72	42
2	A. Swift	D	2	45	44	51	15	94	83	94	17
3	D. Bonker	D	6	43	unopp.	59	16	90	75	83	30
4	M. McCormack	D	10	59	89	61	45	82	77	44	25
5	T. S. Foley	D	16	51	90	52	39	88	78	61	17
6	N. D. Dicks	D	4	40	84	62	45	84	78	67	26
7	M. E. Lowry	D	2	41	74	53	11	90	78	100	17
West Virginia											
1	R. H. Mollohan	D	16	71	unopp.	63	47	84	82	56	20
2	H. O. Staggers	D	32	73	unopp.	55	40	86	80	50	25
3	J. M. Slack	D	22	65	unopp.	59	58	61	52	33	—
4	N. J. Rahall II	D	4	31	56	unopp.	40	82	81	67	13

(*Table continues*)

TABLE A–1 (continued)

State, District	Representative	Party	Years of Service	Age	1978 % Vote in Primary	1978 % Vote in General	Voting Ratings[a] CC	PU	PS	ADA	ACA
Wisconsin											
1	L. Aspin	D	10	42	unopp.	54	21	90	86	67	25
2	R. W. Kastenmeier	D	22	56	unopp.	58	9	90	73	100	13
3	A. Baldus	D	6	53	unopp.	63	15	92	81	78	17
4	C. J. Zablocki	D	32	68	unopp.	66	26	92	90	61	13
5	H. S. Reuss	D	26	68	unopp.	74	4	96	75	89	22
6	T. E. Petri	R	1	40	35[i]	50	79	79	52	39	57
7	D. R. Obey	D	11	42	unopp.	63	8	93	85	94	21
8	T. Roth	R	2	42	69	59	86	93	38	22	75
9	F. J. Sensenbrenner, Jr.	R	2	37	43	61	87	95	32	22	79
Wyoming											
AL	R. B. Cheney	R	2	39	42	59	88	89	42	6	95

NOTE: AL = at large; D = Democratic; R = Republican; unopp. = unopposed; conv. = nominated by convention; dash = not available.

a. CC = conservative coalition; PU = party unity; PS = presidential support; ADA = Americans for Democratic Action; ACA = Americans for Constitutional Action. In compiling this table, the conservative coalition, party unity, and presidential support scores were calculated to eliminate the effects of absences, as follows: support = support/(support + opposition).

b. In the initial primary, Anthony finished with 26 percent of the vote, second to Winston Bryant (33 percent). Anthony defeated Bryant in a runoff primary with 52 percent.

c. Porter (Illinois 10th) elected in special election January 22, 1980, with 54 percent. Former Congressman Mikva was appointed to D.C. Circuit Court of Appeals in 1979.

d. If any candidate wins 50 percent or more of the vote in the primary, the election is won outright. If not, the top two candidates face each other in a runoff.

e. Speaker of the House does not usually vote.

f. In the initial primary, Leath won 30 percent, finishing second to Lane Denton (40 percent). Leath won the runoff primary with 55 percent.

g. Stenholm led in the initial primary with 36 percent, winning the runoff with 67 percent.

h. Leland led in the initial primary with 48 percent, winning the runoff with 57 percent.

i. Thomas E. Petri (Wisconsin 6th) elected in special election April 9, 1979, following the death of Congressman William A. Steiger.

SOURCES: *Congressional Quarterly Weekly Report* and *Congressional Quarterly Almanac*, various years; *Congressional Directory*, various years; Barone et al., *The Almanac of American Politics*, 1978, 1980, and 1982; and Alan Ehrenhalt, ed., *Politics in America 1982* (Washington, D.C.: Congressional Quarterly, 1981).

TABLE A–2

House of Representatives, 1981

State, District	Representative	Party	Years of Service	Age	1980 % Vote in		Voting Ratings[a]					
					Primary	General	CC	PU	PS	ADA	ACA	ACA (career)
Alabama												
1	J. Edwards	R	17	53	unopp.	95	70	65	76	20	63	85
2	W. Dickinson	R	17	56	unopp.	61	92	87	73	5	76	91
3	B. Nichols	D	15	63	85	unopp.	92	38	74	10	78	76
4	T. Bevill	D	15	60	unopp.	98	87	56	56	25	43	59
5	R. Flippo	D	5	44	unopp.	94	87	58	65	20	55	52
6	A. L. Smith, Jr.	R	1	50	55	51	99	92	82	0	87	87
7	R. Shelby	D	3	47	unopp.	73	96	26	78	0	83	72
Alaska												
AL	D. Young	R	8	48	unopp.	74	98	81	80	10	65	71
Arizona												
1	J. J. Rhodes	R	29	65	unopp.	74	85	81	85	0	72	80
2	M. K. Udall	D	20	59	unopp.	58	40	83	55	75	14	7
3	B. Stump	D	5	54	unopp.	64	100	21	80	0	91	94
4	E. Rudd	R	5	61	88	63	100	88	81	0	81	95
Arkansas												
1	B. Alexander	D	13	48	unopp.	unopp.	68	74	54	45	38	37
2	E. Bethune	R	3	46	unopp.	79	90	80	74	15	79	79

#	Name	Party										
3	J. P. Hammerschmidt	R	15	59	unopp.	unopp.	96	80	79	5	83	81
4	B. Anthony, Jr.	D	3	43	unopp.	unopp.	83	67	62	30	50	38

California

#	Name	Party										
1	G. Chappie	R	1	61	unopp.	54	95	94	80	0	90	90
2	D. H. Clausen	R	18	58	unopp.	54	95	83	73	0	71	77
3	R. T. Matsui	D	3	40	89	71	34	82	48	70	17	14
4	V. Fazio	D	3	39	80	65	34	83	42	80	5	12
5	J. L. Burton	D	7	49	unopp.	51	1	92	29	85	7	15
6	P. Burton	D	17	55	81	69	6	94	32	90	0	4
7	G. Miller	D	7	37	85	63	0	92	29	100	9	14
8	R. V. Dellums	D	11	46	unopp.	56	9	93	24	95	10	11
9	F. H. Stark	D	9	50	unopp.	55	13	91	31	95	8	7
10	D. Edwards	D	19	66	unopp.	62	3	95	31	95	9	5
11	T. Lantos	D	1	53	unopp.	46	42	83	48	70	29	29
12	P. N. McCloskey, Jr.	R	14	53	80	72	68	63	70	35	61	32
13	N. Y. Mineta	D	7	50	unopp.	59	35	87	51	80	4	7
14	N. D. Shumway	R	3	47	unopp.	61	96	93	84	5	92	96
15	T. Coelho	D	3	39	unopp.	72	47	83	50	55	22	14
16	L. E. Panetta	D	5	43	unopp.	71	45	78	50	90	21	32
17	C. Pashayan, Jr.	R	3	40	unopp.	71	94	85	84	5	77	78
18	W. M. Thomas	R	3	40	86	71	87	86	84	5	75	90
19	R. J. Lagomarsino	R	7	55	unopp.	78	96	95	82	5	92	88
20	B. M. Goldwater, Jr.	R	12	43	unopp.	79	87	90	70	0	71	91
21	B. Fiedler	R	1	44	74	49	82	84	80	10	83	83
22	C. J. Moorhead	R	9	59	unopp.	64	96	96	81	5	100	96
23	A. C. Beilenson	D	5	49	85	63	9	91	32	90	4	11

(Table continues)

205

TABLE A–2 (continued)

State, District	Representative	Party	Years of Service	Age	1980 % Vote in Primary	1980 % Vote in General	CC	PU	PS	ADA	ACA	ACA (career)
24	H. A. Waxman	D	7	41	unopp.	64	4	94	28	85	15	8
25	E. R. Roybal	D	19	65	unopp.	66	12	93	35	95	4	6
26	J. H. Rousselot	R	13	54	unopp.	71	94	92	85	10	95	96
27	R. K. Dornan	R	5	48	unopp.	51	88	88	69	10	84	87
28	J. C. Dixon	D	3	47	unopp.	79	13	94	41	80	9	6
29	A. F. Hawkins	D	19	74	unopp.	86	9	91	37	85	4	5
30	G. E. Danielson	D	11	66	unopp.	72	22	92	49	75	15	13
31	M. E. Dymally	D	1	55	49	64	14	94	40	55	10	10
32	G. M. Anderson	D	13	62	85	66	48	79	48	50	38	26
33	W. Grisham	R	3	58	76	71	94	91	83	5	91	91
34	D. Lungren	R	3	35	unopp.	72	92	92	80	20	87	96
35	D. Dreier	R	1	29	53	52	94	96	80	5	96	96
36	G. E. Brown, Jr.	D	17	61	73	53	26	88	40	85	5	8
37	J. Lewis	R	3	47	83	72	84	80	78	5	68	78
38	J. M. Patterson	D	7	47	unopp.	56	25	85	42	70	13	13
39	W. E. Dannemeyer	R	3	52	unopp.	76	88	95	75	10	100	100
40	R. E. Badham	R	5	52	76	70	95	90	83	0	79	94
41	B. Lowery	R	1	34	50	53	90	88	75	5	71	71
42	D. L. Hunter	R	1	33	52	53	95	89	75	10	75	75
43	C. W. Burgener	R	9	60	unopp.	87	83	85	79	5	82	90

Voting Ratings[a]

Colorado

District	Name	Party										
1	P. Schroeder	D	9	41	unopp.	60	12	78	29	95	26	26
2	T. E. Wirth	D	7	42	unopp.	56	24	85	43	85	10	16
3	R. Kogovsek	D	3	40	unopp.	55	27	88	41	80	9	13
4	H. Brown	R	1	41	unopp.	68	71	77	66	20	75	75
5	K. Kramer	R	3	39	unopp.	72	88	88	72	0	87	92

Connecticut

District	Name	Party										
1	W. R. Cotter	D	11	55	unopp.	63	Died 9/9/81					
2	S. Gejdenson	D	1	33	62	53	8	93	22	95	4	4
3	L. J. DeNardis	R	1	43	61	52	34	47	58	60	42	42
4	S. B. McKinney	R	11	50	unopp.	63	36	43	60	70	30	32
5	W. R. Ratchford	D	3	47	unopp.	50	9	93	33	90	9	13
6	A. T. Moffett	D	7	37	unopp.	59	5	93	25	85	10	11

Delaware

District	Name	Party										
AL	T. B. Evans, Jr.	R	5	50	unopp.	62	74	72	71	20	58	73

Florida

District	Name	Party										
1	E. Hutto	D	3	55	unopp.	61	95	46	75	10	63	49
2	D. Fuqua	D	19	48	unopp.	71	87	62	61	20	36	56
3	C. E. Bennett	D	33	71	unopp.	77	80	48	59	25	58	62
4	B. Chappell, Jr.	D	13	54	unopp.	66	88	41	75	5	67	77
5	B. McCollum	R	1	37	54	56	88	86	70	0	86	86
6	C. W. B. Young	R	11	51	unopp.	unopp.	93	87	75	5	83	90
7	S. Gibbons	D	19	62	unopp.	72	80	50	65	30	50	34
8	A. Ireland	D	5	51	unopp.	69	92	34	82	5	74	62

(Table continues)

207

TABLE A-2 (continued)

| State, District | Representative | Party | Years of Service | Age | 1980 % Vote in | | Voting Ratings[a] | | | | | |
					Primary	General	CC	PU	PS	ADA	ACA	ACA (career)
9	B. Nelson	D	3	39	unopp.	70	86	53	71	10	50	54
10	L. A. Bafalis	R	9	52	unopp.	79	97	93	82	5	86	91
11	D. Mica	D	3	37	unopp.	59	77	59	66	30	50	44
12	E. C. Shaw	R	1	42	unopp.	54	95	94	78	10	92	92
13	W. Lehman	D	9	68	unopp.	75	21	91	42	85	0	8
14	C. Pepper	D	19	81	79	75	36	89	41	55	19	9
15	D. B. Fascell	D	27	64	unopp.	65	21	89	43	80	5	11
Georgia												
1	B. Ginn	D	9	47	unopp.	unopp.	88	59	55	30	46	55
2	C. F. Hatcher	D	1	42	53	74	86	55	62	25	55	55
3	J. Brinkley	D	15	51	unopp.	unopp.	89	45	63	30	67	70
4	E. H. Levitas	D	7	51	unopp.	69	66	64	52	35	52	55
5	W. Fowler, Jr.	D	4	41	86	74	57	66	48	80	36	37
6	N. Gingrich	R	3	38	unopp.	59	83	81	73	10	74	86
7	L. P. McDonald	D	7	46	68	68	94	7	80	5	100	99
8	B. L. Evans	D	5	40	unopp.	75	84	42	65	10	71	59
9	E. Jenkins	D	5	49	unopp.	68	96	44	63	10	63	65
10	D. Barnard, Jr.	D	5	59	unopp.	80	99	30	79	0	73	70
Hawaii												
1	C. Heftel	D	5	57	72	80	54	76	46	50	26	20
2	D. K. Akaka	D	5	57	unopp.	90	52	83	46	65	30	15

Idaho												
1	L. E. Craig	R	1	36	53	54	96	95	75	0	88	88
2	G. Hansen	R	11	51	58	59	93	92	82	0	100	96
Illinois												
1	H. Washington	D	1	59	48	96	4	92	28	95	5	5
2	G. Savage	D	1	56	45	88	9	92	22	65	0	0
3	M. A. Russo	D	7	37	unopp.	69	41	72	41	55	26	32
4	E. J. Derwinski	R	23	55	83	68	70	83	74	15	78	86
5	J. G. Fary	D	6	70	72	80	58	77	60	50	32	19
6	H. J. Hyde	R	7	57	unopp.	67	83	80	80	10	74	73
7	C. Collins	D	8	50	78	85	4	92	29	85	5	7
8	D. Rostenkowski	D	23	53	89	85	46	81	50	55	22	10
9	S. R. Yates	D	31	72	87	73	5	91	27	100	4	9
10	J. E. Porter	R	2	46	unopp.	61	63	66	68	30	63	67
11	F. Annunzio	D	17	66	unopp.	70	59	77	55	45	25	14
12	P. M. Crane	R	12	51	unopp.	74	86	90	70	10	100	98
13	R. McClory	R	19	73	60	72	72	75	69	30	67	69
14	J. N. Erlenborn	R	17	54	81	77	71	74	76	20	68	75
15	T. Corcoran	R	5	42	unopp.	77	83	83	76	20	86	91
16	L. Martin	R	1	42	45	67	75	71	76	30	65	65
17	G. M. O'Brien	R	9	64	unopp.	66	78	71	58	20	65	69
18	R. H. Michel	R	25	58	unopp.	62	86	88	72	10	86	86
19	T. Railsback	R	15	49	unopp.	73	60	54	82	40	43	51
20	P. Findley	R	21	60	56	56	64	65	57	45	58	71
21	E. R. Madigan	R	9	45	unopp.	68	85	85	71	5	80	69
22	D. B. Crane	R	3	45	unopp.	69	84	90	77	10	96	97

(Table continues)

TABLE A–2 (continued)

State, District	Representative	Party	Years of Service	Age	1980 % Vote in		CC	PU	PS	ADA	ACA	ACA (career)
					Primary	General						
23	M. Price	D	37	76	86	64	56	85	58	50	27	10
24	P. Simon	D	7	53	73	49	30	87	38	75	0	7
Indiana												
1	A. Benjamin, Jr.	D	5	46	unopp.	72	40	88	42	60	17	23
2	F. J. Fithian	D	7	53	unopp.	54	49	68	39	55	29	35
3	J. P. Hiler	R	1	28	58	55	85	87	79	25	92	92
4	D. Coats	R	1	38	58	61	91	86	74	10	79	79
5	E. Hillis	R	11	55	unopp.	62	95	80	74	10	73	67
6	D. W. Evans	D	7	35	93	50	42	82	40	55	32	49
7	J. T. Myers	R	15	54	unopp.	66	91	79	75	0	88	87
8	H. J. Deckard	R	3	39	unopp.	55	65	66	59	40	74	79
9	L. H. Hamilton	D	16	50	90	64	56	72	48	65	33	22
10	P. R. Sharp	D	7	39	90	53	52	72	43	65	33	24
11	A. Jacobs, Jr.	D	15	49	unopp.	57	25	75	24	90	25	29
Iowa												
1	J. Leach	R	5	39	unopp.	64	48	55	58	55	54	58
2	T. Tauke	R	3	31	unopp.	54	70	68	62	45	57	65
3	C. Evans	R	1	57	45	51	82	76	67	30	71	71
4	N. Smith	D	23	61	unopp.	54	42	79	43	55	22	13
5	T. Harkin	D	7	42	unopp.	60	22	85	26	85	27	23
6	B. Bedell	D	7	60	unopp.	64	24	79	32	70	16	18

Voting Ratings[a]

Kansas													
1	P. Roberts	R	1	45	56	62	95	87	69	10	83	83
2	J. Jeffries	R	3	56	49	54	99	95	75	5	100	99
3	L. Winn, Jr.	R	15	62	unopp.	56	92	85	75	5	74	78
4	D. Glickman	D	5	37	unopp.	69	48	70	47	75	30	37
5	B. Whittaker	R	3	42	unopp.	74	91	86	70	15	70	85
Kentucky													
1	C. Hubbard, Jr.	D	7	44	83	unopp.	87	49	59	25	61	58
2	W. H. Natcher	D	28	72	unopp.	66	75	69	54	35	33	33
3	R. L. Mazzoli	D	11	49	79	64	58	68	52	60	29	26
4	G. Snyder	R	17	53	unopp.	67	77	77	66	20	79	86
5	H. Rogers	R	1	44	23	67	91	82	72	10	79	79
6	L. J. Hopkins	R	3	48	unopp.	59	83	80	70	20	79	84
7	C. D. Perkins	D	33	69	86	unopp.	58	77	42	60	33	16
Louisiana[b]													
1	R. L. Livingston	R	4	38	88	—	82	78	78	20	62	81
2	L. Boggs	D	8	65	61	—	60	72	54	45	29	23
3	W. J. Tauzin	D	1	38	85	—	93	37	70	0	64	56
4	B. Roemer	D	1	38	27	64	85	34	69	5	67	67
5	J. Huckaby	D	5	40	89	—	83	35	73	10	78	75
6	W. H. Moore	R	6	42	91	—	83	80	70	10	75	85
7	J. B. Breaux	D	9	37	unopp.	—	90	45	72	0	55	58
8	G. W. Long	D	9	58	69	—	62	76	56	40	29	25
Maine													
1	D. F. Emery	R	7	32	unopp.	68	84	76	64	25	74	61
2	O. J. Snowe	R	3	35	unopp.	79	69	68	67	45	57	68

(Table continues)

TABLE A–2 (continued)

State, District	Representative	Party	Years of Service	Age	1980 % Vote in		Voting Ratings[a]					
					Primary	General	CC	PU	PS	ADA	ACA	ACA (career)
Maryland												
1	R. Dyson	D	1	33	69	52	92	52	61	30	58	58
2	C. D. Long	D	19	73	57	57	34	78	47	75	4	23
3	B. A. Mikulski	D	5	45	75	76	11	90	32	100	17	14
4	M. S. Holt	R	9	61	unopp.	72	96	84	78	10	82	87
5	S. Hoyer	D	1	42	30	55	32	87	42	72	11	11
6	B. B. Byron	D	3	49	71	70	96	40	65	15	62	61
7	P. J. Mitchell	D	9	59	81	88	3	94	31	95	5	5
8	M. D. Barnes	D	3	38	unopp.	59	13	87	33	95	4	8
Massachusetts												
1	S. O. Conte	R	23	60	unopp.	75	45	45	57	55	35	33
2	E. P. Boland	D	29	70	71	67	30	84	35	80	17	11
3	J. D. Early	D	7	49	unopp.	72	27	85	29	85	27	20
4	B. Frank	D	1	41	52	52	9	88	31	100	4	4
5	J. M. Shannon	D	3	29	54	66	12	90	33	90	8	8
6	N. Mavroules	D	3	52	69	51	28	86	36	80	17	13
7	E. J. Markey	D	5	35	85	unopp.	8	92	34	90	21	13
8	T. P. O'Neill, Jr.[c]	D	29	69	unopp.	78	—	—	—	—	—	—
9	J. Moakley	D	9	54	unopp.	unopp.	24	91	43	55	16	8
10	M. M. Heckler	R	15	50	unopp.	61	45	46	56	50	38	30

11	B. J. Donnelly	D	3	35	unopp.	unopp.	28	89	37	65	15	23
12	G. E. Studds	D	9	44	unopp.	73	7	92	33	100	8	8

Michigan

1	J. Conyers, Jr.	D	17	52	unopp.	95	10	90	35	90	5	12
2	C. D. Pursell	R	5	49	90	57	34	46	52	65	42	41
3	H. Wolpe	D	3	42	unopp.	52	8	92	27	95	8	15
4	M. Siljander	R	1	30	40	74	87	88	71	10	90	90
5	H. S. Sawyer	R	5	61	81	53	74	65	63	15	67	76
6	J. Dunn	R	1	38	81	51	57	62	59	50	61	61
7	D. E. Kildee	D	5	52	unopp.	93	15	90	26	90	17	13
8	B. Traxler	D	7	50	unopp.	61	40	85	41	65	18	18
9	G. Vander Jagt	R	15	50	unopp.	97	86	84	75	10	86	73
10	D. J. Albosta	D	3	56	unopp.	52	75	66	48	40	33	29
11	R. W. Davis	R	3	49	unopp.	66	88	73	62	15	74	69
12	D. E. Bonior	D	5	36	82	55	10	91	25	90	17	12
13	G. W. Crockett, Jr.	D	1	72	42	92	10	94	32	70	5	5
14	D. M. Hertel	D	1	33	62	53	27	87	28	80	29	29
15	W. D. Ford	D	17	54	unopp.	68	15	96	31	70	13	9
16	J. D. Dingell	D	26	55	88	70	33	87	40	70	17	12
17	W. M. Brodhead	D	7	40	unopp.	73	11	89	24	90	13	7
18	J. J. Blanchard	D	7	39	unopp.	65	21	92	36	80	23	13
19	W. S. Broomfield	R	25	59	91	73	75	80	71	20	70	67

Minnesota

1	A. Erdahl	R	3	50	unopp.	72	53	59	54	55	48	60
2	T. Hagedorn	R	7	38	unopp.	61	89	86	68	0	78	86
3	B. Frenzel	R	11	53	91	76	73	81	72	30	71	57

(Table continues)

213

TABLE A-2 (continued)

State, District	Representative	Party	Years of Service	Age	1980 % Vote in Primary	General	CC	PU	PS	ADA	ACA	ACA (career)
4	B. F. Vento	D	5	41	unopp.	59	10	90	33	90	4	5
5	M. O. Sabo	D	3	43	unopp.	70	7	92	30	90	4	7
6	V. Weber	R	1	29	87	53	76	80	57	30	71	71
7	A. Stangeland	R	4	51	unopp.	52	93	86	72	0	78	85
8	J. L. Oberstar	D	7	47	56	70	16	92	33	85	4	5
Mississippi												
1	J. L. Whitten	D	40	71	unopp.	63	68	64	51	30	35	68
2	D. R. Bowen	D	9	49	unopp.	70	87	63	63	20	48	64
3	G. V. Montgomery	D	15	61	unopp.	unopp.	97	28	79	0	79	85
4	W. Dowdy[d]	D	1	39	25	50	89	53	66	21	57	57
5	T. Lott	R	9	40	unopp.	74	97	94	84	0	86	86
Missouri												
1	W. Clay	D	13	50	72	70	4	98	24	95	9	6
2	R. A. Young	D	5	58	86	64	84	62	56	40	32	32
3	R. A. Gephardt	D	5	40	unopp.	78	72	66	56	45	39	33
4	I. Skelton	D	5	50	89	68	95	50	60	25	48	48
5	R. Bolling	D	33	65	82	70	20	88	34	55	8	6
6	E. T. Coleman	R	5	38	unopp.	71	88	80	71	0	73	86
7	G. Taylor	R	9	53	unopp.	68	96	87	74	0	83	90
8	W. Bailey	R	1	41	34	57	91	88	77	10	87	87

214

District	Name	Party									
9	H. L. Volkmer	D	5	50	86	56	70	67	46	30	38	42
10	B. Emerson	R	1	43	77	55	99	90	78	0	88	88
Montana												
1	P. Williams	D	3	44	75	61	22	90	35	95	8	17
2	R. Marlenee	R	5	46	unopp.	59	87	77	73	20	81	83
Nebraska												
1	D. K. Bereuter	R	3	42	unopp.	79	81	76	69	20	75	74
2	H. Daub	R	1	41	61	53	91	87	73	15	87	87
3	V. Smith	R	7	70	unopp.	84	89	85	70	10	79	85
Nevada												
AL	J. Santini	D	7	44	79	68	83	40	61	20	72	56
New Hampshire												
1	N. E. D'Amours	D	7	44	unopp.	61	39	80	37	70	27	31
2	J. Gregg	R	1	34	34	64	74	82	70	25	86	86
New Jersey												
1	J. J. Florio	D	7	44	unopp.	77	28	84	35	40	24	18
2	W. J. Hughes	D	7	49	unopp.	57	41	67	41	65	21	35
3	J. J. Howard	D	17	54	unopp.	50	21	92	41	70	10	6
4	C. H. Smith	R	1	28	83	57	67	65	64	40	63	63
5	M. Fenwick	R	7	71	70	78	47	59	63	55	46	41
6	E. B. Forsythe	R	11	65	90	56	63	70	72	35	50	53
7	M. Roukema	R	1	52	unopp.	51	58	71	67	35	63	63
8	R. A. Roe	D	12	57	unopp.	67	41	81	50	60	24	21
9	H. C. Hollenbeck	R	5	43	unopp.	59	37	42	55	75	35	37

(Table continues)

215

TABLE A-2 (continued)

State, District	Representative	Party	Years of Service	Age	1980 % Vote in		Voting Ratings[a]					
					Primary	General	CC	PU	PS	ADA	ACA	ACA (career)
10	P. W. Rodino, Jr.	D	33	72	62	85	5	94	31	100	9	6
11	J. G. Minish	D	19	65	unopp.	63	27	88	37	80	24	13
12	M. J. Rinaldo	R	9	50	unopp.	77	72	60˙	66	20	52	39
13	J. A. Courter	R	3	40	unopp.	72	86	80	66	15	76	80
14	F. J. Guarini	D	3	57	unopp.	64	17	94	36	85	10	19
15	B. J. Dwyer	D	1	60	32	53	16	95	42	75	13	13
New Mexico												
1	M. Lujan, Jr.	R	13	53	unopp.	51	84	72	74	10	71	75
2	J. Skeen[e]	R	1	54	none	38	96	85	76	0	75	75
New York												
1	W. Carney	R	3	39	58	56	82	79	78	5	82	83
2	T. J. Downey	D	7	32	unopp.	56	13	92	31	80	9	10
3	G. W. Carman	R	1	44	unopp.	50	87	85	71	10	83	83
4	N. F. Lent	R	11	50	unopp.	67	82	76	69	10	70	66
5	R. J. McGrath	R	1	39	unopp.	58	77	80	65	15	79	79
6	J. LeBoutillier	R	1	28	unopp.	53	84	82	78	10	83	83
7	J. P. Addabbo	D	21	56	unopp.	95	14	93	33	75	9	11
8	B. S. Rosenthal	D	19	58	unopp.	76	1	99	22	80	0	6
9	G. A. Ferraro	D	3	46	unopp.	58	17	96	32	85	17	15
10	M. Biaggi	D	13	64	unopp.	95	38	84	44	45	24	27

11	J. H. Scheuer	D	15	51	unopp.	74	14	95	34	90	4	9
12	S. Chisholm	D	13	57	62	87	4	97	34	60	0	9
13	S. J. Solarz	D	7	41	unopp.	80	14	93	38	90	15	7
14	F. W. Richmond	D	7	58	74	76	1	85	24	90	11	5
15	L. C. Zeferetti	D	7	54	71	50	62	77	46	50	35	24
16	C. E. Schumer	D	1	31	59	77	13	85	31	100	4	4
17	G. V. Molinari	R	1	53	unopp.	48	75	77	69	25	65	65
18	S. W. Green	R	3	52	unopp.	57	36	40	58	70	25	28
19	C. B. Rangel	D	11	51	unopp.	96	4	93	34	95	5	6
20	T. Weiss	D	5	54	unopp.	82	4	90	36	100	8	10
21	R. Garcia	D	3	48	unopp.	98	4	96	33	70	5	7
22	J. B. Bingham	D	17	67	unopp.	84	9	92	33	100	4	5
23	P. A. Peyser	D	9	60	unopp.	56	19	89	44	80	24	16
24	R. L. Ottinger	D	13	52	unopp.	59	3	93	24	100	13	12
25	H. Fish, Jr.	R	13	55	unopp.	81	42	51	60	50	42	49
26	B. A. Gilman	R	9	59	unopp.	74	48	42	64	45	50	43
27	M. F. McHugh	D	7	43	unopp.	55	19	90	32	95	8	10
28	S. S. Stratton	D	23	65	unopp.	78	77	61	53	30	26	31
29	G. B. H. Solomon	R	3	51	unopp.	67	96	95	74	5	88	86
30	D. Martin	R	1	37	70	64	91	91	72	5	81	81
31	D. J. Mitchell	R	9	58	unopp.	77	76	67	63	20	68	63
32	G. Wortley	R	1	55	40	60	84	77	69	10	65	65
33	G. A. Lee	R	3	48	unopp.	77	86	86	65	0	68	81
34	F. Horton	R	19	62	unopp.	73	46	55	59	35	37	39
35	B. B. Conable, Jr.	R	17	59	unopp.	72	78	86	79	25	81	70
36	J. J. LaFalce	D	7	42	unopp.	72	28	84	37	70	14	18
37	H. J. Nowak	D	7	46	unopp.	83	18	90	38	75	13	10

(Table continues)

217

TABLE A-2 (continued)

State, District	Representative	Party	Years of Service	Age	1980 % Vote in		Voting Ratings[a]					
					Primary	General	CC	PU	PS	ADA	ACA	ACA (career)
38	J. F. Kemp	R	11	46	unopp.	82	87	87	81	10	82	86
39	S. N. Lundine	D	5	42	unopp.	55	26	84	33	85	24	17
North Carolina												
1	W. B. Jones	D	15	68	79	unopp.	73	70	55	25	24	67
2	L. H. Fountain	D	29	68	unopp.	73	87	47	62	25	65	71
3	C. Whitley	D	5	54	80	68	90	55	63	30	45	56
4	I. F. Andrews	D	9	56	77	53	83	64	56	15	37	48
5	S. L. Neal	D	7	47	unopp.	51	69	71	43	55	33	50
6	E. Johnston	R	1	45	unopp.	51	89	90	74	10	95	95
7	C. Rose	D	9	42	80	69	72	71	53	50	33	38
8	W. G. Hefner	D	7	51	74	59	77	63	56	35	48	49
9	J. G. Martin	R	9	46	unopp.	59	86	85	78	15	87	88
10	J. T. Broyhill	R	19	54	unopp.	70	87	88	76	10	96	88
11	W. M. Hendon	R	1	37	unopp.	54	91	87	76	5	92	92
North Dakota												
AL	B. L. Dorgan	D	1	39	unopp.	57	41	82	40	65	13	13
Ohio												
1	W. D. Gradison, Jr.	R	7	53	unopp.	75	66	71	70	35	60	73
2	T. A. Luken	D	5	56	unopp.	59	69	64	57	40	39	38

218

3	T. P. Hall	D	3	39	unopp.	57	54	74	50	45	43	22
4	M. Oxley	R	1	37	50	51	88	87	70	0	85	85
5	D. L. Latta	R	23	61	unopp.	70	95	91	80	0	91	88
6	B. McEwen	R	1	31	45	55	93	92	76	0	83	83
7	C. J. Brown	R	16	54	unopp.	76	89	82	77	5	80	76
8	T. N. Kindness	R	7	52	unopp.	76	89	84	74	10	78	91
9	E. Weber	R	1	50	76	56	78	75	71	20	70	70
10	C. E. Miller	R	15	64	unopp.	74	91	86	72	5	92	86
11	J. W. Stanton	R	17	57	unopp.	69	79	76	72	25	65	60
12	B. Shamansky	D	1	54	unopp.	53	37	84	43	70	22	22
13	D. J. Pease	D	5	50	69	64	17	90	33	95	14	14
14	J. F. Seiberling	D	11	63	unopp.	65	5	95	30	100	4	5
15	C. P. Wylie	R	15	61	unopp.	73	80	75	69	20	71	77
16	R. Regula	R	9	57	unopp.	79	79	75	72	15	75	65
17	J. M. Ashbrook	R	21	53	unopp.	73	90	92	76	0	91	96
18	D. Applegate	D	5	53	unopp.	76	74	47	46	35	54	50
19	L. Williams	R	3	39	unopp.	58	84	69	69	15	68	60
20	M. R. Oakar	D	5	41	unopp.	unopp.	26	88	37	55	22	20
21	L. Stokes	D	13	56	unopp.	88	5	96	30	90	0	6
22	D. E. Eckart	D	1	31	41	55	27	83	34	80	33	33
23	R. M. Mottl	D	7	47	unopp.	unopp.	52	43	44	20	70	52
Oklahoma												
1	J. R. Jones	D	9	42	unopp.	58	74	65	59	35	38	60
2	M. Synar	D	3	31	unopp.	54	27	90	38	80	17	26
3	W. Watkins	D	5	43	91	unopp.	89	57	57	30	50	65
4	D. McCurdy	D	1	31	51	51	88	56	58	35	57	57

(Table continues)

219

TABLE A-2 (continued)

State, District	Representative	Party	Years of Service	Age	1980 % Vote in		Voting Ratings[a]					
					Primary	General	CC	PU	PS	ADA	ACA	ACA (career)
5	M. Edwards	R	5	44	unopp.	68	89	85	76	5	88	90
6	G. English	D	7	41	unopp.	65	80	54	56	25	58	76
Oregon												
1	L. AuCoin	D	7	39	unopp.	66	18	86	34	70	14	26
2	D. Smith	R	1	43	77	49	96	93	74	10	96	96
3	R. Wyden	D	1	32	60	72	12	89	28	100	21	21
4	J. Weaver	D	7	54	75	55	12	82	26	90	23	19
Pennsylvania												
1	T. M. Foglietta	D	1	53	unopp.	38	15	91	30	90	21	21
2	W. H. Gray III	D	3	40	unopp.	96	4	98	33	90	0	6
3	J. F. Smith	D[f]	1	61	—	53	56	86	57	50	36	36
4	C. F. Dougherty	R	3	44	51	63	81	72	64	25	67	50
5	R. T. Schulze	R	7	52	unopp.	75	96	93	83	10	92	88
6	G. Yatron	D	13	54	unopp.	67	74	60	49	40	58	35
7	R. W. Edgar	D	7	38	unopp.	53	1	89	23	100	14	9
8	J. K. Coyne	R	1	35	unopp.	51	69	75	70	25	75	75
9	B. Shuster	R	9	49	unopp.	unopp.	99	89	77	0	88	91
10	J. M. McDade	R	19	50	unopp.	77	72	62	67	25	55	41
11	J. L. Nelligan	R	1	52	54	52	91	80	66	15	74	74
12	J. P. Murtha	D	7	49	unopp.	59	66	72	47	45	29	28

13	L. Coughlin	R	13	52	85	70	60	65	67	35	61	53
14	W. J. Coyne	D	1	45	57	69	16	90	38	95	13	13
15	D. Ritter	R	3	41	unopp.	59	80	83	75	10	83	80
16	R. S. Walker	R	5	39	unopp.	77	84	87	80	10	91	94
17	A. E. Ertel	D	5	45	unopp.	61	52	73	39	55	22	35
18	D. Walgren	D	5	41	unopp.	68	28	79	42	80	35	19
19	W. F. Gooding	R	7	54	unopp.	76	76	81	62	30	83	79
20	J. M. Gaydos	D	13	55	unopp.	73	68	72	49	40	39	31
21	D. Bailey	D	3	36	60	68	68	72	53	40	38	27
22	A. J. Murphy	D	5	54	unopp.	70	57	66	42	55	41	38
23	W. F. Clinger, Jr.	R	3	52	unopp.	74	72	69	63	30	63	67
24	M. L. Marks	R	5	54	unopp.	50	65	53	68	40	54	45
25	E. V. Atkinson	D	3	54	75	67	68	74	66	30	70	70
Rhode Island												
1	F. J. St Germain	D	21	53	79	68	41	84	36	70	10	10
2	C. Schneider	R	1	34	unopp.	55	33	45	48	70	29	29
South Carolina												
1	T. F. Hartnett	R	1	40	75	52	96	90	82	5	91	91
2	F. Spence	R	11	53	unopp.	56	96	92	74	0	92	90
3	B. Derrick	D	7	45	unopp.	60	61	67	53	60	43	45
4	C. A. Campbell, Jr.	R	3	41	unopp.	93	96	88	87	0	87	88
5	K. Holland	D	7	47	unopp.	88	87	52	72	25	47	43
6	J. L. Napier	R	1	34	60	52	97	82	80	0	78	78
South Dakota												
1	T. A. Daschle	D	3	34	unopp.	66	38	82	42	70	29	27
2	C. Roberts	R	1	46	65	58	92	89	70	0	87	87

(Table continues)

TABLE A–2 (continued)

State, District	Representative	Party	Years of Service	Age	1980 % Vote in Primary	1980 % Vote in General	CC	PU	PS	ADA	ACA	ACA (career)
Tennessee												
1	J. H. Quillen	R	19	65	77	86	96	83	79	5	85	84
2	J. J. Duncan	R	17	62	unopp.	76	99	77	72	5	64	82
3	M. L. Bouquard	D	7	52	unopp.	61	87	57	62	30	50	48
4	A. Gore, Jr.	D	5	33	92	79	47	82	40	70	14	20
5	W. H. Boner	D	3	36	unopp.	65	82	63	60	35	39	35
6	R. L. Beard, Jr.	R	9	42	unopp.	unopp.	95	88	80	0	80	88
7	E. Jones	D	12	69	unopp.	77	88	61	59	25	45	51
8	H. E. Ford	D	7	36	73	unopp.	10	96	37	85	0	12
Texas												
1	S. B. Hall, Jr.	D	5	57	unopp.	unopp.	85	39	67	15	87	83
2	C. Wilson	D	9	48	78	69	74	60	63	20	62	41
3	J. M. Collins	R	13	65	unopp.	79	89	90	75	10	96	95
4	R. M. Hall	D	1	58	57	52	84	42	64	5	67	67
5	J. Mattox	D	5	38	unopp.	51	25	92	36	55	28	39
6	P. Gramm	D	3	39	unopp.	71	100	21	77	0	88	78
7	B. Archer	R	11	53	unopp.	82	93	95	69	5	88	97
8	J. Fields	R	1	29	unopp.	52	99	92	81	0	91	91
9	J. Brooks	D	29	59	50	unopp.	62	70	56	45	38	21
10	J. J. Pickle	D	18	68	75	59	76	60	63	40	33	43
11	M. Leath	D	3	50	unopp.	unopp.	93	31	71	0	82	79

12	J. Wright	D	27	59	unopp.	60	69	72	53	30	28	23
13	J. Hightower	D	7	55	unopp.	55	84	49	69	15	61	60
14	B. Patman	D	1	54	52	57	78	53	54	20	61	61
15	E. de la Garza	D	17	54	unopp.	70	72	66	59	45	50	48
16	R. C. White	D	17	58	unopp.	85	92	48	76	10	65	56
17	C. W. Stenholm	D	3	43	unopp.	unopp.	95	29	76	0	82	80
18	M. Leland	D	3	37	unopp.	80	9	94	36	95	10	5
19	K. Hance	D	3	39	unopp.	94	86	42	73	15	65	64
20	H. B. Gonzalez	D	20	65	unopp.	82	33	84	35	70	17	17
21	T. Loeffler	R	3	35	unopp.	76	93	86	79	0	83	92
22	R. Paul	R	4	46	unopp.	51	62	76	62	25	79	88
23	A. Kazen, Jr.	D	15	62	76	70	85	60	60	35	54	43
24	M. Frost	D	3	39	unopp.	61	56	80	33	50	40	31
Utah												
1	J. V. Hansen	R	1	49	unopp.	52	95	95	82	0	100	100
2	D. Marriott	R	5	42	unopp.	67	93	84	79	5	83	90
Vermont												
AL	J. M. Jeffords	R	7	47	unopp.	79	26	38	43	60	24	35
Virginia												
1	P. S. Trible, Jr.	R	5	35	conv.	91	94	92	81	10	78	85
2	G. W. Whitehurst	R	13	56	conv.	90	93	88	74	10	82	82
3	T. J. Bliley, Jr.	R	1	49	conv.	52	91	89	75	0	79	79
4	R. W. Daniel, Jr.	R	9	45	conv.	61	99	96	82	10	96	94
5	D. Daniel	D	13	67	conv.	unopp.	96	16	80	0	83	92
6	M. C. Butler	R	9	56	conv.	unopp.	88	90	82	10	83	87

(Table continues)

223

TABLE A-2 (continued)

| State, District | Representative | Party | Years of Service | Age | 1980 % Vote in | | Voting Ratings[a] | | | | | |
					Primary	General	CC	PU	PS	ADA	ACA	ACA (career)
7	J. K. Robinson	R	11	65	conv.	unopp.	96	90	82	5	78	93
8	S. Parris	R	3	52	60	49	86	86	77	5	83	83
9	W. C. Wampler	R	17	55	conv.	69	93	76	70	5	67	79
10	F. R. Wolf	R	1	42	75	51	88	83	76	10	79	79
Washington												
1	J. Pritchard	R	9	56	unopp.	78	58	56	68	25	48	42
2	A. Swift	D	3	46	92	64	31	86	44	85	8	12
3	D. Bonker	D	7	44	91	63	39	81	39	75	19	14
4	S. Morrison	R	1	48	59	57	92	83	74	5	79	79
5	T. S. Foley	D	17	52	unopp.	52	53	82	55	55	18	15
6	N. D. Dicks	D	5	41	91	54	63	74	54	50	26	16
7	M. Lowry	D	3	42	94	57	11	89	34	100	9	14
West Virginia												
1	R. H. Mollohan	D	17	72	unopp.	64	66	68	57	40	45	30
2	C. Benedict	R	1	46	62	56	91	80	75	10	68	68
3	D. M. Staton	R	1	41	74	53	95	90	79	5	91	91
4	N. J. Rahall II	D	5	32	unopp.	77	41	82	41	75	30	23

Wisconsin

	Member	Party										
1	L. Aspin	D	11	43	unopp.	56	27	88	28	75	17	12
2	R. W. Kastenmeier	D	23	57	unopp.	54	5	89	23	95	13	10
3	S. Gunderson	R	1	30	69	51	75	75	70	30	75	75
4	C. J. Zablocki	D	33	69	89	70	61	72	52	50	30	18
5	H. S. Reuss	D	27	69	88	77	15	90	35	70	9	6
6	T. E. Petri	R	2	41	unopp.	59	68	75	58	40	68	65
7	D. R. Obey	D	12	43	unopp.	65	15	88	29	85	21	16
8	T. Roth	R	3	43	unopp.	68	87	85	66	10	96	89
9	F. J. Sensenbrenner, Jr.	R	3	38	unopp.	78	76	78	59	20	92	91

Wyoming

	Member	Party										
AL	R. B. Cheney	R	3	40	unopp.	69	88	86	86	5	79	92

NOTE: AL = at large; D = Democratic; R = Republican; unopp. = unopposed; conv. = nominated by convention; dash = not available.

a. CC = conservative coalition; PU = party unity; PS = presidential support; ADA = Americans for Democratic Action; ACA = Americans for Constitutional Action. In compiling this table, the conservative coalition, party unity, and presidential support scores were calculated to eliminate the effects of absences, as follows: support = support/(support + opposition).

b. See note d, table A-1.

c. Speaker of the House does not usually vote.

d. In the initial nonpartisan special election, Dowdy finished with 25 percent second to Liles Williams (45 percent). In the runoff, Dowdy defeated Williams.

e. Skeen (New Mexico 2d) won the general election as a write-in candidate.

f. Smith ran as a Republican-Independent in a special election and decided to caucus with Democrats.

SOURCES: *Congressional Quarterly Weekly Report* and *Congressional Quarterly Almanac*, various years; *Congressional Directory*, various years; Barone et al., *Almanac of American Politics*, 1978, 1980, and 1982; and Ehrenhalt, *Politics in America 1982*.

TABLE A-3
SENATE, 1980

| | | | | Previous Senate Election | | | Voting Ratings[a] | | | | |
	Party	Years of Service	Age	Year	Primary	General	CC	PU	PS	ADA	ACA
						(percent)					
Alabama											
Howell Heflin	D	2	59	1978	65	94	70	60	55	39	50
Donald Stewart	D	2	40	1978	57	56	58	75	66	61	39
Alaska											
Ted Stevens	R	12	57	1978	unopp.	76	76	76	45	39	71
Mike Gravel	D	12	50	1974	54	58	13	96	85	39	33
Arizona											
Barry Goldwater	R	24	71	1974	unopp.	58	94	80	44	0	100
Dennis DeConcini	D	4	43	1976	53	54	57	68	67	67	39
Arkansas											
Dale Bumpers	D	6	55	1974	65	85	47	77	78	56	35
David Pryor	D	2	46	1978	55[b]	77	61	70	73	44	46
California											
Alan Cranston	D	12	66	1974	86	61	6	93	86	83	5
S. I. Hayakawa	R	4	74	1976	38	50	92	82	50	22	92
Colorado											
Gary Hart	D	6	43	1974	40	57	28	78	74	61	36
William Armstrong	R	2	43	1978	73	59	97	98	31	17	92

State / Senator	Party			Year							
Connecticut											
Abraham Ribicoff	D	18	70	1974	conv.	68	17	90	87	56	15
Lowell Weicker, Jr.	R	10	49	1976	conv.	58	18	34	73	72	43
Delaware											
William Roth, Jr.	R	10	59	1976	conv.	56	90	88	43	22	73
Joseph Biden, Jr.	D	8	38	1978	conv.	58	26	82	89	67	18
Florida											
Lawton Chiles	D	10	50	1976	unopp.	63	74	68	77	50	38
Richard Stone	D	6	52	1974	51	43	56	65	64	33	35
Georgia											
Herman Talmadge	D	24	67	1974	81	72	84	52	58	33	43
Sam Nunn	D	8	42	1978	80	83	92	54	78	56	54
Hawaii											
Daniel Inouye	D	18	56	1974	unopp.	83	34	90	80	67	23
Spark Matsunaga	D	4	64	1976	52	54	12	92	78	78	13
Idaho											
Frank Church	D	24	56	1974	86	57	30	80	75	50	18
James McClure	R	8	56	1978	unopp.	68	91	91	34	17	92
Illinois											
Charles Percy	R	14	61	1978	84	53	52	56	70	39	64
Adlai Stevenson III	D	10	50	1974	83	63	19	86	87	61	29
Indiana											
Birch Bayh	D	18	52	1974	conv.	52	27	80	71	61	18
Richard Lugar	R	4	48	1976	65	59	89	87	45	17	83

(Table continues)

227

TABLE A–3 (continued)

	Party	Years of Service	Age	Previous Senate Election Year	Primary	General	CC	PU	PS	ADA	ACA
					(percent)						
Iowa											
John Culver	D	6	48	1974	unopp.	52	5	90	69	78	0
Roger Jepsen	R	2	52	1978	57	51	96	95	36	22	77
Kansas											
Robert Dole	R	12	57	1974	unopp.	51	79	75	49	22	77
Nancy Kassebaum	R	2	48	1978	31	54	68	71	56	44	70
Kentucky											
Walter Huddleston	D	8	54	1978	76	61	49	85	84	44	26
Wendell Ford	D	6	56	1974	85	55	63	75	75	78	27
Louisiana											
Russell Long	D	32	62	1974	75	unopp.	87	56	62	28	29
Bennett Johnston	D	8	48	1978	59	—[c]	85	65	75	33	29
Maine											
William Cohen	R	2	40	1978	unopp.	57	66	74	51	33	68
George Mitchell	D	1	47	[d]	appointed		21	86	76	67	18
Maryland											
Charles Mathias, Jr.	R	12	58	1974	76	57	14	23	74	72	8
Paul Sarbanes	D	4	47	1976	55	57	4	89	74	83	0

Voting Ratings[a]

Massachusetts										
Edward Kennedy	D	18	48	1976	75	69	0	88	63	33	20
Paul Tsongas	D	2	39	1978	36	55	9	89	77	89	12
Michigan										
Donald Riegle	D	4	42	1976	44	52	13	84	72	83	4
Carl Levin	D	2	47	1978	39	52	11	82	72	94	12
Minnesota										
David Durenberger	R	2	46	1978	67	61	46	59	56	44	72
Rudy Boschwitz	R	2	50	1978	87	57	67	76	54	28	96
Mississippi										
John Stennis	D	33	79	1976	85	unopp.	86	63	75	17	43
Thad Cochran	R	2	43	1978	69	45	85	79	42	22	88
Missouri										
Thomas Eagleton	D	12	51	1974	87	60	32	83	67	78	8
John Danforth	R	4	44	1976	93	57	69	72	58	50	48
Montana										
John Melcher	D	4	56	1976	89	64	37	69	49	50	13
Max Baucus	D	2	39	1978	65	56	14	87	82	72	16
Nebraska										
Edward Zorinsky	D	4	52	1976	49	53	90	36	55	22	62
J. James Exon	D	2	59	1978	unopp.	68	90	52	67	39	44
Nevada										
Howard Cannon	D	22	68	1976	86	63	68	67	73	33	39
Paul Laxalt	R	6	58	1974	81	47	92	90	30	11	100

(Table continues)

229

TABLE A-3 (Continued)

	Party	Years of Service	Age	Previous Senate Election			Voting Ratings[a]				
				Year	Primary	General	CC	PU	PS	ADA	ACA
						(percent)					
New Hampshire											
John Durkin	D	5	44	1975	50	55[e]	25	75	57	50	7
Gordon Humphrey	R	2	40	1978	50	51	99	95	32	6	96
New Jersey											
Harrison Williams, Jr.	D	22	61	1976	85	61	4	90	74	72	13
Bill Bradley	D	2	37	1978	59	56	7	86	74	72	0
New Mexico											
Pete Domenici	R	8	48	1978	unopp.	53	91	80	59	17	71
Harrison Schmitt	R	4	45	1976	72	57	89	86	40	17	86
New York											
Jacob Javits	R	24	66	1974	unopp.	46	18	29	67	61	13
Daniel Moynihan	D	4	53	1976	36	54	13	85	82	72	8
North Carolina											
Jesse Helms	R	8	59	1978	unopp.	55	98	93	34	11	100
Robert Morgan	D	6	55	1974	50	63	79	57	67	22	52
North Dakota											
Milton Young	R	35	83	1974	unopp.	50	90	71	46	11	60
Quentin Burdick	D	20	72	1976	unopp.	62	27	89	66	78	19

State / Senator	Party			Year								
Ohio												
John Glenn	D	6	59	1974	54	65	33	83	77	67	17
Howard Metzenbaum	D	5	63	1976	54	50	12	87	76	83	12
Oklahoma												
Henry Bellmon	R	12	59	1974	87	50	77	67	63	28	71
David Boren	D	2	39	1978	60^f	66	81	48	54	28	52
Oregon												
Mark Hatfield	R	14	58	1978	66	62	45	45	57	50	65
Robert Packwood	R	12	48	1974	unopp.	55	39	48	77	56	43
Pennsylvania												
Richard Schweiker	R	12	54	1974	unopp.	54	85	76	46	17	71
John Heinz	R	4	42	1976	38	52	54	60	58	50	44
Rhode Island												
Claiborne Pell	D	20	62	1978	87	75	23	88	81	78	10
John Chafee	R	4	58	1976	unopp.	58	35	40	83	72	29
South Carolina												
Strom Thurmond	R	25	78	1978	unopp.	56	96	87	46	17	88
Ernest Hollings	D	14	58	1974	unopp.	71	74	63	69	39	43
South Dakota												
George McGovern	D	18	58	1974	unopp.	53	14	86	75	56	21
Larry Pressler	R	2	38	1978	74	67	71	77	47	17	65
Tennessee												
Howard Baker	R	14	55	1978	83	56	86	83	46	17	81
James Sasser	D	4	44	1976	44	53	55	75	72	67	23

(Table continues)

231

TABLE A–3 (continued)

			Previous Senate Election			Voting Ratings[a]				
Party	Years of Service	Age	Year	Primary	General	CC	PU	PS	ADA	ACA
				(percent)						
Texas										
John Tower	R	19	55	1978	unopp.	50	97	85	44	6	91
Lloyd Bentsen	D	10	59	1976	64	57	67	69	79	39	43
Utah										
Jake Garn	R	6	48	1974	unopp.	50	95	90	33	17	96
Orrin Hatch	R	4	46	1976	65	54	85	84	32	17	96
Vermont										
Robert Stafford	R	9	67	1976	69	50	40	39	75	61	38
Patrick Leahy	D	6	40	1974	84	50	15	82	74	83	16
Virginia										
Harry Byrd	I	15	66	1976	no primary	57	98	30	47	22	69
John Warner	R	2	53	1978	party nom.g	50	94	81	46	22	77
Washington										
Warren Magnuson	D	36	75	1974	91	63	24	86	70	72	22
Henry Jackson	D	28	68	1976	87	72	19	90	75	72	19

West Virginia											
Jennings Randolph	D	22	78	1978	80	50	35	85	65	72	12
Robert Byrd	D	22	63	1976	unopp.	unopp.	42	88	74	56	15
Wisconsin											
William Proxmire	D	23	65	1976	unopp.	72	39	63	54	56	54
Gaylord Nelson	D	18	64	1974	unopp.	63	8	90	72	89	16
Wyoming											
Malcolm Wallop	R	4	47	1976	77	55	84	86	43	22	92
Alan Simpson	R	2	49	1978	55	62	88	91	52	17	91

NOTE: D = Democratic; R = Republican; I = independent; unopp. = unopposed; conv. = nominated by convention; party nom. = nominated by party.

a. CC = conservative coalition; PU = party unity; PS = presidential support; ADA = Americans for Democratic Action; ACA = Americans for Constitutional Action. In compiling this table, the conservative coalition, party unity, and presidential support scores were calculated to eliminate the effects of absences, as follows: support = support/(support + opposition).

b. In the initial primary, Pryor led with 34 percent of the vote, winning the runoff primary with 55 percent.

c. See note d, table A-1.

d. Appointed in 1980 to fill the unexpired term of Edmund S. Muskie. The seat is up in 1982.

e. J. Durkin (Dem., N.H.) after a ten-vote victory in the 1974 general election, won a special election in 1975 with 55 percent of the vote.

f. In the initial primary, Boren led with 46 percent, winning the runoff primary with 60 percent.

g. After convention nominee Richard Obenshain died, Warner was selected by the Republican party leadership to replace him.

SOURCES: Congressional Quarterly Weekly Report and Congressional Quarterly Almanac, various years; Congressional Directory, various years; Barone et al., Almanac of American Politics, 1978, 1980, and 1982; and Ehrenhalt, Politics in America 1982.

TABLE A–4
SENATE, 1981

| | | Years of Service | Age | Previous Senate Election | | | Voting Ratings[a] | | | | | |
	Party			Year	Primary	General	CC	PU	PS	ADA	ACA	ACA (career)
					(percent)							
Alabama												
Howell Heflin	D	3	60	1978	65	94	84	65	68	35	57	51
Jeremiah Denton	R	1	57	1980	64	50	97	95	90	0	80	80
Alaska												
Ted Stevens	R	13	58	1978	unopp.	76	86	89	84	15	61	45
Frank Murkowski	R	1	48	1980	59	54	90	88	87	15	65	65
Arizona												
Barry Goldwater	R	25	72	1980	unopp.	50	96	92	85	0	86	96
Dennis DeConcini	D	5	44	1976	53	54	72	71	57	45	61	47
Arkansas												
Dale Bumpers	D	7	56	1980	unopp.	59	22	91	43	95	15	25
David Pryor	D	3	47	1978	55[b]	77	56	84	50	75	48	45
California												
Alan Cranston	D	13	67	1980	80	57	12	88	44	85	6	4
S. I. Hayakawa	R	5	75	1976	38	50	93	96	94	5	79	80

Colorado												
Gary Hart	D	7	44	1980	unopp.	50	13	89	39	95	17	15
William Armstrong	R	3	44	1978	73	59	93	92	86	5	90	95
Connecticut												
Lowell Weicker	R	11	50	1978	conv.	58	45	56	66	55	17	37
Christopher Dodd	D	1	37	1980	conv.	56	3	91	36	90	0	0
Delaware												
William Roth	R	11	60	1976	conv.	56	76	73	75	20	70	75
Joseph Biden	D	9	39	1978	conv.	58	24	87	46	80	33	17
Florida												
Lawton Chiles	D	11	51	1976	unopp.	63	78	74	59	45	55	41
Paula Hawkins	R	1	54	1980	48	52	94	83	88	15	62	62
Georgia												
Sam Nunn	D	9	43	1978	80	83	85	60	64	35	71	63
Mack Mattingly	R	1	50	1980	60	51	98	93	87	5	86	86
Hawaii												
Daniel Inouye	D	19	57	1980	88	78	22	85	53	70	26	7
Spark Matsunaga	D	5	65	1976	52	54	18	86	50	80	21	9
Idaho												
James McClure	R	9	57	1978	unopp.	68	95	92	83	10	74	91
Steven Symms	R	1	43	1980	unopp.	50	96	93	85	0	81	81

(Table continues)

TABLE A-4 (continued)

		Years of Service	Age	Previous Senate Election			Voting Ratings[a]					
Party				Year	Primary	General	CC	PU	PS	ADA	ACA	ACA (career)
					(percent)							
Illinois												
Charles Percy	R	15	62	1978	84	53	74	83	90	35	43	29
Alan Dixon	D	1	54	1980	67	56	60	74	58	65	48	48
Indiana												
Richard Lugar	R	5	49	1976	65	59	90	93	90	5	76	84
Dan Quayle	R	1	34	1980	77	54	92	94	86	10	81	81
Iowa												
Roger Jepsen	R	3	53	1978	57	51	96	93	87	5	81	83
Charles Grassley	R	1	48	1980	66	54	93	85	82	5	90	90
Kansas												
Robert Dole	R	13	58	1980	82	64	95	95	91	5	70	74
Nancy Kassebaum	R	3	49	1978	31	54	82	79	82	35	67	66
Kentucky												
Walter Huddleston	D	9	55	1978	76	61	56	80	56	65	33	23
Wendell Ford	D	7	57	1980	87	65	59	86	57	70	40	33
Louisiana[c]												
Russell Long	D	33	63	1980	58	—	93	39	72	15	61	40
Bennett Johnston	D	9	49	1978	59	—	97	52	71	25	48	50

Maine												
William Cohen	R	3	41	1978	unopp.	57	62	73	79	35	61	64
George Mitchell	D	2	48	[d]	appointed	57	25	90	51	90	19	18
Maryland												
Charles Mathias, Jr.	R	13	59	1980	55	66	35	56	67	50	26	14
Paul Sarbanes	D	5	48	1976	55	57	7	94	40	95	10	8
Massachusetts												
Edward Kennedy	D	19	49	1976	75	69	4	90	35	100	17	4
Paul Tsongas	D	3	40	1978	36	55	9	83	44	95	16	13
Michigan												
Donald Riegle	D	5	43	1976	44	53	7	96	36	90	15	8
Carl Levin	D	3	47	1978	39	52	7	95	37	100	10	11
Minnesota												
David Durenberger	R	3	47	1978	67	61	64	72	75	40	52	54
Rudy Boschwitz	R	3	51	1978	87	57	71	79	81	25	47	71
Mississippi												
John Stennis	D	34	80	1976	85	unopp.	94	45	71	15	67	70
Thad Cochran	R	3	44	1978	69	45	93	89	89	10	62	74
Missouri												
Thomas Eagleton	D	13	52	1980	86	52	10	90	35	90	14	12
John Danforth	R	5	45	1976	93	57	84	85	86	25	62	51
Montana												
John Melcher	D	5	57	1976	89	64	63	74	52	55	53	26
Max Baucus	D	3	40	1978	65	56	30	86	48	85	38	21

(Table continues)

TABLE A-4 (continued)

| | | Years of | | Previous Senate Election | | | Voting Ratings[a] | | | | | |
	Party	Service	Age	Year	Primary	General	CC	PU	PS	ADA	ACA	ACA (career)
					(percent)							
Nebraska												
Edward Zorinsky	D	5	53	1976	49	52	83	53	65	20	80	69
J. James Exon	D	3	60	1978	unopp.	68	68	72	58	45	48	43
Nevada												
Howard Cannon	D	23	69	1976	86	63	63	70	66	30	38	36
Paul Laxalt	R	7	59	1980	90	59	99	99	89	5	80	90
New Hampshire												
Gordon Humphrey	R	3	41	1978	50	51	85	87	83	10	86	92
Warren Rudman	R	1	51	1980	20	52	74	84	84	15	60	60
New Jersey												
Harrison Williams[e]	D	23	62	1976	85	61	14	87	49	75	12	5
Bill Bradley	D	3	38	1978	59	56	12	88	49	90	20	7
New Mexico												
Pete Domenici	R	9	49	1978	unopp.	53	96	91	86	15	70	72
Harrison Schmitt	R	5	46	1976	72	57	94	91	90	10	80	81
New York												
Daniel Moynihan	D	5	54	1976	36	54	8	83	48	75	28	14
Alfonse D'Amato	R	1	44	1980	56	45	82	87	87	10	47	47

State / Senator	Party			Year	Election %								
North Carolina													
Jesse Helms	R	9	59	1978	unopp.	55	94	89	83		0	95	98
John East	R	1	50	1980	unopp.	50	98	96	86		0	94	94
North Dakota													
Quentin Burdick	D	21	73	1976	unopp.	62	42	83	54		75	29	19
Mark Andrews	R	1	55	1980	unopp.	70	86	77	79		30	52	52
Ohio													
John Glenn	D	7	60	1980	86	69	34	78	57		80	25	17
Howard Metzenbaum	D	5	64	1976	54	50	8	94	35		85	22	13
Oklahoma													
David Boren	D	3	40	1978	60[f]	65	90	57	62		30	76	66
Don Nickles	R	1	33	1980	35	54	90	89	86		5	86	86
Oregon													
Mark Hatfield	R	15	59	1978	66	62	60	73	79		55	38	33
Robert Packwood	R	13	49	1980	62	52	74	83	87		35	50	42
Pennsylvania													
John Heinz	R	5	43	1976	38	52	55	63	78		35	32	34
Arlen Specter	R	1	51	1980	36	51	52	65	77		50	38	38
Rhode Island													
Claiborne Pell	D	21	63	1978	87	75	11	87	45		95	24	7
John Chafee	R	5	59	1976	unopp.	58	51	70	77		45	38	28
South Carolina													
Strom Thurmond	R	26	79	1978	unopp.	56	100	94	92		0	90	93
Ernest Hollings	D	15	59	1980	81	70	69	62	58		55	29	45

(Table continues)

TABLE A–4 (continued)

	Years of Party Service	Age	Previous Senate Election			Voting Ratings[a]					
			Year	Primary	General	CC	PU	PS	ADA	ACA	ACA (career)
					(percent)						
South Dakota											
Larry Pressler	R	3	39	1978	74	67	70	64	71	30	55	59
James Abdnor	R	1	58	1980	73	58	95	83	80	5	67	67
Tennessee											
Howard Baker	R	15	56	1978	83	56	94	94	88	20	67	68
James Sasser	D	5	45	1976	44	53	66	81	58	45	40	30
Texas											
John Tower	R	20	56	1978	unopp.	50	99	95	89	10	72	91
Lloyd Bentsen	D	11	60	1976	64	57	88	57	74	25	57	44
Utah											
Jake Garn	R	7	49	1980	unopp.	74	94	96	90	0	90	95
Orrin Hatch	R	5	47	1976	65	54	93	92	88	0	85	93
Vermont											
Robert Stafford	R	10	68	1976	69	50	68	77	80	35	47	25
Patrick Leahy	D	7	41	1980	unopp.	50	4	90	37	95	5	12
Virginia											
Harry Byrd, Jr.	I	16	67	1976	no primary	57	91	27	78	10	95	87
John Warner	R	3	54	1978	party nom.[g]	50	98	92	87	5	80	81

Washington												
Henry Jackson	D	29	69	1976	87	72	41	82	57	60	24	13
Slade Gorton	R	1	53	1980	57	54	79	87	87	10	67	67
West Virginia												
Jennings Randolph	D	23	79	1978	80	50	43	84	49	60	44	20
Robert Byrd	D	23	64	1976	unopp.	unopp.	45	85	50	70	29	34
Wisconsin												
William Proxmire	D	24	66	1976	unopp.	72	60	53	52	55	71	31
Robert Kasten, Jr.	R	1	39	1980	37	50	89	85	80	10	70	70
Wyoming												
Malcolm Wallop	R	5	48	1976	77	55	99	97	90	10	70	86
Alan Simpson	R	3	50	1978	55	62	92	93	88	5	86	86

NOTE: D = Democratic; R = Republican; I = independent; unopp. = unopposed; conv. = nominated by convention.

a. CC = conservative coalition; PU = party unity; PS = presidential support; ADA = Americans for Democratic Action; ACA = Americans for Constitutional Action. In compiling this table, the conservative coalition, party unity, and presidential support scores were calculated to eliminate the effects of absences, as follows: support = support/(support + opposition).

b. See note b, table A-3.

c. See note d, table A-1.

d. See note d, table A-3.

e. Resigned from Senate in 1982. Replaced for remainder of term by Nicholas F. Brady (R).

f. See note f, table A-3.

g. See note g, table A-3.

SOURCES: *Congressional Quarterly Weekly Report* and *Congressional Quarterly Almanac*, various years; *Congressional Directory*, various years; Barone et al., *Almanac of American Politics*, 1978, 1980, and 1982; and Ehrenhalt, *Politics in America 1982*.

Selected AEI Publications

Public Opinion, published bimonthly (one year, $18; two years, $34; single copy, $3.50)

President and Congress: Assessing Reagan's First Year, Norman J. Ornstein, ed. (107 pp. $6.95)

How Capitalistic Is the Constitution? Robert A. Goldwin and William A. Schambra, eds. (171 pp., paper $6.25, cloth $14.25)

The Dream of Christian Socialism: An Essay on Its European Origins, Bernarch Murchland (74 pp., $4.25)

Canada at the Polls, 1979 and 1980: A Study of the General Elections, Howard R. Penniman, ed. (426 pp., paper $9.25, cloth $17.25)

The Role of the Legislature in Western Democracies, Norman J. Ornstein, ed. (192 pp., paper $7.25, cloth $15.25)

Liberation South, Liberation North, Michael Novak, ed. (99 pp., $4.25)

British Political Finance, 1830-1980, Michael Pinto-Duschinsky (339 pp., paper $10.50, cloth $17.95)

A Conversation with Michael Novak and Richard Schifter: Human Rights and the United Nations (25 pp., $2.25)

Reconciliation and the Congressional Budget Process, Allen Schick (47 pp., $4.25)

Whom Do Judges Represent? John Charles Daly, mod. (31 pp., $3.75)

Prices subject to change without notice.

AEI Associates Program

The American Enterprise Institute invites your participation in the competition of ideas through its AEI Associates Program. This program has two objectives:

The first is to broaden the distribution of AEI studies, conferences, forums, and reviews, and thereby to extend public familiarity with the issues. AEI Associates receive regular information on AEI research and programs, and they can order publications and cassettes at a savings.

The second objective is to increase the research activity of the American Enterprise Institute and the dissemination of its published materials to policy makers, the academic community, journalists, and others who help shape public attitudes. Your contribution, which in most cases is partly tax deductible, will help ensure that decision makers have the benefit of scholarly research on the practical options to be considered before programs are formulated. The issues studied by AEI include:

- Defense Policy
- Economic Policy
- Energy Policy
- Foreign Policy
- Government Regulation
- Health Policy
- Legal Policy
- Political and Social Processes
- Social Security and Retirement Policy
- Tax Policy

For more information, write to:

AMERICAN ENTERPRISE INSTITUTE
1150 Seventeenth Street, N.W.
Washington, D.C. 20036

A NOTE ON THE BOOK

This book was edited by
Gertrude Kaplan and Margaret Seawell of the
Publications Staff of the American Enterprise Institute.
The staff also designed the cover and format, with Pat Taylor.
The figures were drawn by Hördur Karlsson.
The text was set in Palatino, a typeface designed by Hermann Zapf.
Hendricks-Miller Typographic Company, of Washington, D.C.,
set the type, and R. R. Donnelley & Sons Company,
of Harrisonburg, Virginia, printed and bound the book,
using paper made by the S. D. Warren Company.